The Invisible War

The Invisible War

The Untold Secret Story of
Number One Canadian Special
Wireless Group,
Royal Canadian Signal Corps,
1944-1946

Gil Murray

THE DUNDURN GROUP
TORONTO · OXFORD

Publisher: Anthony Hawke
Editor: Lloyd Davis
Design: Jennifer Scott
Printer: Transcontinental

Canadian Cataloguing in Publication Data

Murray, Gil, 1925–
    The invisible war: the untold secret story of Number One Canadian Special Wireless Group, Royal Signal Corps, 1944–1946

ISBN 1-55002-371-3

1. Canada. Canadian Army. Royal Canadian Corps of Signals — Canadian Special Wireless Group, 1 — History — World War, 1939–1945. 2. World War, 1939–1945. — Communications. 3. Canada. Canadian Army — Communication systems. 4. World War, 1939–1945 — Regimental histories — Canada. I. Title.

D768.15.M87 2001   940.54'8671   C2001-902249-2

1   2   3   4   5   05   04   03   02   01

THE CANADA COUNCIL | LE CONSEIL DES ARTS
FOR THE ARTS | DU CANADA
SINCE 1957 | DEPUIS 1957

Canadä

ONTARIO ARTS COUNCIL
CONSEIL DES ARTS DE L'ONTARIO

We acknowledge the support of the **Canada Council for the Arts** and the **Ontario Arts Council** for our publishing program. We also acknowledge the financial support of the **Government of Canada** through the **Book Publishing Industry Development Program** and **The Association for the Export of Canadian Books**, and the **Government of Ontario** through the **Ontario Book Publishers Tax Credit** program.

Care has been taken to trace the ownership of copyright material used in this book. The author and the publisher welcome any information enabling them to rectify any references or credit in subsequent editions.

J. Kirk Howard, President

Printed and bound in Canada.
Printed on recycled paper.
www.dundurn.com

Dundurn Press
8 Market Street
Suite 200
Toronto, Ontario, Canada
M5E 1M6

Dundurn Press
73 Lime Walk
Headington, Oxford,
England
OX3 7AD

Dundurn Press
2250 Military Road
Tonawanda NY
U.S.A. 14150

Contents

Prologue

The true story told in the following pages is neither one of daring Second World War valour nor of gory hand-to-hand combat. For those we refer readers to the many books on the spectacular campaigns in which thousands of heroic Canadians died in bloody land, sea, and air battles. What will be described here is how a group of young Canadians fought secretly and helped to win the war in the Pacific on an invisible battlefield: the airwaves that carried vital facts about Imperial Japanese troop strengths, supply states, and targets of their next assaults. Without the continuous secret interception and deciphering of Japanese military signals by Allied Special Wireless units, of which Number One Canadian Special Wireless Group (1CSWG) was an important part, the Allied forces would not have had the vital advance information about Japanese battle plans that enabled them to win time after time.

Long after the war's end, the very existence of 1CSWG and its part in the Pacific victory has remained unknown to Canadians. Canada's contribution to the top-secret Allied operations known in the Pacific as "Magic" and in Europe as "Ultra" could not be told under the Official Secrets Act. After the war, top Allied leaders would quietly praise Magic and Ultra as being among the overwhelming factors that led to victory on both the Pacific and European fronts. With the help of these inspired operations, the Allied land and sea forces were able to inflict heavy damage upon the enemy. Many more lives would have been lost had the Allies been forced to fight "blind."

While Canadian military strength was necessarily focused on the war in Europe, the 336 officers and Other Ranks of Number One Canadian Special Wireless Group represented Canada's principal contribution to the war against an enemy that once threatened to invade its west coast. *The Invisible War* is the story of their part in the unseen and unsung "War of the Airwaves" over the Pacific, told by a member of 1CSWG.

Note: In some cases, names have been changed to protect those who either did not wish to be identified or who could not be consulted.

Publisher's Foreword

In the spring of 1944, Gilbert S. "Gil" Murray, the author of this account, was six months past his eighteenth birthday, at which point he had to make the grand decision so many others of his countrymen had made before him: whether to volunteer for active wartime service in the Canadian armed forces, or let himself be called up into the non-combatant militia. When the frail-looking youngster who saw himself as a "155-pound weakling" chose to volunteer for active service anywhere in the world, he fully expected to be rejected as physically unfit. Instead, he was classified A-1 and, two months before D-Day, he found himself in the Canadian Infantry Corps.

By the time they'd completed both the basic and the rigorous advanced infantry training, Murray and his fellow riflemen were poised to be sent into action in France or Italy, where the battle for Europe was at its height. But before that could happen, Murray was asked to volunteer for active service a second time, for an unexplainably secret assignment "in the Far East." He and three others in his battalion accepted the challenge, not knowing what it might involve. From that moment on, he was part of a top-secret group of more than three hundred Canadian volunteers for the war in the Pacific. Number One Canadian Special Wireless Group (1CSWG) of the Royal Canadian Signal Corps was the first and only Canadian Army unit sent to the Pacific since 1941, when two thousand ill-trained recruits had been killed or captured at Hong Kong.

Born under the tightest military secrecy, 1CSWG was meant to take Canada's already well-established success at intercepting Japanese military signals closer to the theatre of war. So sensitive were the unit's activities that, under Canada's Official Secrets Act, its members were strictly forbidden for thirty years afterward to reveal what kind of work they had done in the Pacific theatre. Contrary to the general belief that the war in the Pacific involved only the United States and Japan, the Allied cause received extensive co-operation from Britain, Australia, Canada, New Zealand, the Netherlands, and India. Indeed, Canada and other Allied countries had been monitoring Japanese military signals since before the outbreak of war in the Pacific in 1941.

To this day, long after the thirty-year embargo was lifted, the story of Number One Canadian Special Wireless Group has been waiting to be told. All clues to the existence of 1CSWG — as with Camp X, the secret Ontario training base for Allied spies and saboteurs — have been buried in government files. Gil Murray wonders why.

Book One:

Canada's Key Role in the War in the Pacific

Chapter 1

Canada Joins the Pacific War

A blinding flash, a single thunderclap, and a crash signalled the violent end of the clandestine wartime operations of some homesick Canadian radio spies perched on the northern coast of Australia, across the narrow Timor Sea from the Dutch East Indies and a now-defeated enemy. It was October 1945, and the war in the Pacific was over.

The lightning bolt might have been one last supreme effort by the *kamikaze*, the divine wind of Shinto, to send an avenging blast from the heavens, albeit two months too late to save Nippon, over the vast scene of Imperial Japan's defeat. Whatever it was, it knocked down the 100-foot-high radio antenna tower of Number One Canadian Special Wireless Group, Royal Canadian Signal Corps (1CSWG — or the even more concise SWIG — for short) early on that morning of the new peace.

It was the very day that we 336 expatriates were to abandon the top-secret eavesdropping station we'd built outside Darwin, in the wilderness of Australia's Northern Territory, to intercept military message traffic emanating from Japanese forces deep in the jungles of New Guinea, scattered among the islands off the northern coast of Australia, and reaching all the way to Tokyo. Our mission was over and it was time to head back home, having played a significant, if unsung, part in the war.

To most Canadians of the time — and ever since — "the war" meant the dust-up that had taken place in Europe and North Africa and which ended in May 1945. But to us misplaced Canadian Army volunteers who had stepped forward twice over for active service, "the war" was the one that raged on half a world away from Canada. That war had officially ended in August 1945, aboard the United States Navy battleship *Missouri*, anchored in Tokyo Bay. But in 1CSWG's assigned area, the Japanese troops continued to hold out for two more months.

The Pacific war was one that few outside military circles — and even many on the inside — knew Canada was actively involved in. In India and Burma, Royal Canadian Air Force (RCAF) units were actively attacking Japanese strongholds. Throughout Asia — in Malaya, parts of China, and many of the Pacific islands — there were also a few hundred Canadians attached to British, Australian, and American special forces, carrying out top-secret activities of many kinds. There were other Canadians based elsewhere in Australia, such as RCAF members providing radar training to Australian forces. And the Royal Canadian Navy cruiser *Uganda* and smaller Canadian warships were also active in the Pacific theatre. But no Canadian Army unit had been risked in the Pacific since the government of Mackenzie King sent an ill-trained force of two thousand to Hong Kong just before the outbreak of the Pacific war in December 1941. All of those men were killed or captured in the Japanese attack that ensued.

Number One Canadian Special Wireless Group would be the first and only complete Canadian Army unit to be active in the South West Pacific theatre. It had started out as a secret, belated, token commitment by Ottawa to put the country somewhat in line with its allies and to satisfy a request from the Australian High Command for help in monitoring Japanese military signals. It would become the last complete Canadian Army unit active in a theatre of war after May 1945, and the last to return intact from overseas.

Simply put, 1CSWG's job was to help intercept Imperial Japanese military messages to produce up-to-the-minute information on shipping movements, troop strengths, military supplies, and anything else upon which

Allied army, navy, and air forces could take action. And successful action the Allied forces did take, time and again — no doubt to the mystification of Japanese commanders who had no idea their wireless codes had long since been cracked by Allied cryptanalysts.

Close co-operation among Australian, British, Dutch, and American eavesdropping units had made possible the invisible branch of the Allied military effort known as signals intelligence. Its reach covered every place that the Japanese forces had penetrated in 1942. By the 1990s, electronic technology had changed the face of warfare so that only minimal forces — themselves heavily aided by technology — would be required for ground attack. In the Pacific war it was still necessary to commit manned military units to do battle, but signals intelligence, with its advance knowledge of the enemy's plans, greatly reduced Allied casualties and made strike actions more effective.

The main task assigned to 1CSWG was to monitor Japanese signals throughout the 2,000-mile chain of islands known as the Dutch East Indies — later Indonesia — where nearly a million Japanese troops were lodged in the jungles and along coastlines. The Canadians were to concentrate on naval and supply-shipping signals. They would relay the information they obtained to the Central Bureau (CB) in Brisbane, the great signals clearinghouse for the entire South West Pacific Area (SWPA). Equipped with two banks of IBM computers — arguably the earliest military use of that new invention in history — CB's cryptanalysts crunched Japanese codes to extract vital intelligence from the thousands of messages it received each day from Allied monitoring stations scattered throughout the SWPA.

In the 1980s, Major Stan Clark, a veteran traffic analyst of Australian Special Wireless and one of the founders of CB, told me: "Along with the other intercept groups, the Canadian Special Wireless Group kept the volume of intercepted traffic at a tremendously high level, which was essential if the cryptanalysts were to succeed. Depth in volume in any code or cipher was essential to their study."

Major Clark, who was second-in-command at CB under Lieutenant-Colonel A.W. Sandford — another key figure in signals intelligence — echoes the sentiments of U.S. Navy Lieutenant-Commander R.J. Fabian, the man who smuggled the Allies' only Japanese "Purple" coding machine out of the Philippine fortress of Corregidor in 1942. Commander Fabian had regarded the analysis of radio traffic activity as a much more important source of intelligence than the actual deciphering of the messages' content. By studying tremendous volumes of message traffic, analysts could spot repetitions of names, call signs, and technical jargon that offered valuable clues to the meaning of a newly introduced enemy code. And locations that were responsible for a heavy flow of communications could be identified as having strategic military importance.

The crash of our radio tower in the early hours of our last day at Darwin, which jolted us out of our iron cots in the pre-dawn dark, was a deafening "Vic Eddy," or end of message, into the electronic ear of 1CSWG. We didn't know whether to laugh at the coincidence or marvel at the power of the unknown.

For more than two months after the official Japanese surrender, 1CSWG's assignment was revised from the pirating of Japanese messages to the sending of orders of surrender from Australian high command to those scattered Japanese forces still holding out among the Pacific islands. Only after the final capitulation by these hard-core Japanese units did the necessity for 1CSWG cease to exist, and only then was the station shut down.

A Canadian Army unit in the South West Pacific? Whoever heard of such a thing? The answer: very few. And deliberately so. The fact that such a unit existed was given no public exposure anywhere, during or after the war, although many books published in the decades that followed would unveil the secret wartime work of the Magic and Ultra programs. Canada's part was buried along with the failed Japanese war effort.

Special Wireless, as our temporary profession was called in the Royal Canadian Signal Corps, was top secret. In February 1946, when our unit arrived at Camp Chilliwack in British Columbia to be officially disbanded, commanding officer Lieutenant-Colonel Harry D.W. Wethey made a final speech to the gathered Swiggers. In it, he gave his final order: that we were not to utter a word about the reason for 1CSWG's presence in Australia, even after we'd been fully discharged from the army. Otherwise, the Royal Canadian Mounted Police would follow through accordingly.

Under the Official Secrets Act, no mention of the unit was to be made for the next thirty years. Even in civilian life we would not be beyond the reach of the long arm of military — or civilian — law. And it would seem that we Swiggers did keep a tight lip: until the 1990s, no public mention was ever made of 1CSWG, or of the kind of work it did. Even then, only one reference surfaced, in the official history of the Royal Canadian Signal Corps, where it was noted that a Canadian unit served in Australia during World War II. Information about specific battles made possible by 1CSWG's close monitoring of Japanese military signals has long since vanished, along with wartime daily operational records. But unqualified appreciation of the Canadian unit's role in countering Japanese manoeuvres has been expressed by top-ranking generals and other Allied officials in more confidential records.

In 1980, when I went to the National Archives in Ottawa and the Directorate of Military History in search of the unit's war diary, I was promised a copy. First of all, my request would have to be cleared by the minister of Defence, even though it had been thirty-four years since the unit was phased out. When that was done, I was told over the next year that the war diary existed but that it had been lost somewhere in the archives because a clerk couldn't remember where he'd put it. Although the diary had been examined and declassified, it was beginning to seem as if my mission to get at the record of 1CSWG's accomplishments would be hopeless.

In time I would be sent the wrong diary, then finally an innocuous document that told me next to nothing about the battle effects of 1CSWG's daily operations. But all wasn't lost: in the meantime I'd already borrowed Lieutenant-Colonel Wethey's personal diary, and I also had my own illicit, detailed diaries. Other sources would later come through with valuable information, and even more has appeared in recent years due to the Signal Corps's interest in 1CSWG.

Given the strange lack of information volunteered by authorities through the 1980s and 1990s, I can't help but draw a parallel between the vanishing of 1CSWG and the case of the wartime Camp X, which had been situated east of Toronto along the shore of Lake Ontario. There, most of the Allies' secret agents and saboteurs were trained in what was then largely bush country. As recounted in William Stevenson's 1976 book *A Man Called Intrepid*, every trace of Camp X was erased after the war, and the fact that it had ever existed faded from all nearby residents' memories. Similarly, 1CSWG's training camp on Mills Road, deep in the forest north of Victoria and a few miles west of Sidney, British Columbia, has completely disappeared, forest and all.

In 1944, the northern part of Vancouver Island's Saanich Peninsula was heavily forested with old-growth trees, effectively hiding what had originally been an abandoned prewar army camp. It was an ideal location for our top-secret training. When I returned to the area in 1992, I expected to see, perhaps, recent residential housing nestled in a thinned-out forest. Not only did I find no housing and no trace of a camp, but there was hardly a single tree still standing from the old, dense forest. There were one or two aged farmhouses in distant fields and a paved road running through the site of the vanished woodland.

When I asked a man in Sidney where our camp had been located, he shook his head and said he'd never heard of an army camp anywhere nearby. We even consulted an old map, with no luck. Whether deliberately or through the march of time, 1CSWG's birthplace had been absolutely obliterated. One could perhaps draw the conclusion that someone in the Canadian government wanted to make sure no trace was left in Canada of the means of training Allied forces in unorthodox, top-secret methods of defeating the enemies who threatened the nation. In any event, until 2001, no effort was made to commemorate the unique work of the people who dedicated themselves to defeating the Imperial Japanese enemy in the Pacific and the Nazis in Europe.

A case in point was the "discovery" in October 1999 of the grave of one of 1CSWG's officers, Lieutenant J.D. Miller, by members of a newly formed Canadian Army task force sent to Darwin to help deal with unrest on the island of Timor, three hundred miles off the northern coast of Australia. At first the Canadian soldiers were understandably mystified as to why a Canadian army officer would be buried in 1945 in such a remote and far-off place. Obscure records revealed part of the story, but nothing about Miller's reason for being there.

To those of us who formed Miller's burial party in 1945, there was no mystery. The lieutenant had died of acute encephalitis during 1CSWG's stay in Darwin, and we were obliged to bury him in an Australian military cemetery. Oddly, when the Canadian U.N. peacekeepers came across the headstone fifty-four years later, it was in a military cemetery at Adelaide River, seventy-five miles south of Darwin. The Canadian U.N. detachment held a memorial ceremony at the grave site. A full account of Lieutenant Miller's burial will be given later.

After the hostilities in Europe ended in May 1945, the Canadian government displayed a short-lived burst of enthusiasm for the Pacific war. There was a great to-do about forming a Pacific Force, made up of veterans of the European conflict, to bring Canada into line alongside its allies. By that time, 1CSWG had already been in the Pacific theatre for seven months, and was still to remain there for a further six. Our unit had been formed more than a year before for the express purpose of going to the Pacific, but of course this fact never came to light publicly thanks to 1CSWG's top-secret status.

When we in Darwin heard about the new Pacific Force, which promised higher pay and a Pacific Star medal to all volunteers, we naturally assumed that we would form the nucleus of the new force and get a boost in pay — not to mention the medal. No such luck. To reveal that a Canadian unit was already well ensconced in the Pacific would have prompted newspaper inquiries into what we were doing there. By the time Canada managed to attract enough recruits for the new Pacific Force, the atomic bomb had put an official end to the war. We heard nothing further about the Pacific Force, and we got no pay raise. Even in the year 2001, some veterans of 1CSWG were still trying, without success, to pry the higher Pacific pay out of the government. On the other hand, the Pacific Star medal *was* distributed to all 1CSWG survivors, thanks to the efforts of my son, Alan, in 1976, on my behalf and later of SWIG member Ronald O'Reilly in 1998. That would seem to be an official recognition that the members of 1CSWG had actually served in the Pacific theatre; it would also make a case for us to receive the long-denied pay raise, which Pacific Force volunteers were already drawing in 1945 without even going there.

Chapter 2

How Special Wireless Began

In 1929, long before the attack on Pearl Harbor, U.S. Secretary of State Henry Stimson said, "Gentlemen don't read other people's mail," and put a temporary stop to American cryptanalysts' work on decoding Japanese military messages disguised as diplomatic despatches. Given Canadians' long-standing reputation for being mild-mannered and polite, the idea that a group of them were eavesdropping on anyone — even during mankind's most vicious war — would have been hard to swallow. After all, Canadians hadn't been considered sophisticated enough to be part of the greatest weapons system of World War II, Magic and Ultra.

In fact, the Royal Canadian Corps of Signals, the Royal Canadian Air Force, and the Royal Canadian Navy had been secretly monitoring Imperial Japan's radio communications since the outbreak of World War II. Australian units were doing the same. The British Special Operations Executive had been busy since before the war monitoring German signals through the Ultra system, and they quickly established Special Liaison

Units in India, Burma, and other points in Asia. For whatever reason, the Americans may have not wanted it known that allies such as Canada and Australia were deeply involved in eavesdropping and might have insisted on permanent top-secret classification for these "minor" groups. There may also be something to the suggestion that Prime Minister William Lyon Mackenzie King, given his obsessive opposition to British colonialism, didn't want to advertise the fact that Canadians had been sent to the Pacific during the war, making him party to helping Britain regain such colonies as Hong Kong and the Malay Peninsula.

Royal Canadian Signal Corps intercept stations were located early at Gordon Head on Vancouver Island, Grande Prairie, Alberta, and Leitrim, near Ottawa. Canadian army, navy, and air force eavesdroppers began monitoring in 1940. Two years earlier, British and U.S. signals units had begun scrutinizing Japanese communications after the Japanese "Blue Code" was deciphered and the "Purple" encoding machine was duplicated by an American team.

The Canadians at Gordon Head, and later at Mills Road camp on Vancouver Island's Saanich Peninsula, also were experienced at monitoring signals coming from the midst of the Japanese-Canadian fishing fleet innocently going about its business in Canadian waters. Hidden amongst those vessels, Imperial Japanese naval officers in fishermen's clothing were mingling with the Canadian fleet in boats equipped with powerful radios. According to RCMP sources and 1CSWG veteran eavesdroppers, these spies were observing Canadian and U.S. naval movements up and down the west coast, from California to Alaska and the Aleutian Islands. Canadian operators monitored the floating spies' Japan-bound signals but, even though their radio direction finders (RDF) could pinpoint the sources, there was never enough time for the Mounties to move in before the spies escaped or ditched their radio equipment.

The problem was solved only when the Japanese-Canadians in British Columbia, innocent of any wrongdoing, were arbitrarily moved wholesale to eastern Canada, leaving the Imperial Japanese waterborne spies exposed. They instantly disappeared. The authorities could not publicly explain the removal of the Canadian Nisei for fear of revealing that secret Canadian monitoring of Japanese signals was actually going on. This, many decades later, caused as great a problem again for the Canadian government, as millions of dollars in reparations had to be made to the former B.C. Nisei to compensate them for their wartime relocation. By the

1990s, with facts of the actual situation forgotten, it was difficult to show how the mass move was seen as the only workable solution at the time.

By necessity, almost all of Canada's massive war effort was concentrated upon the European war. Army, navy, and air force personnel recruited from the western provinces were sent far across the Atlantic alongside their eastern counterparts. But immediately after Pearl Harbor, the Japanese began offensive action against North America's poorly guarded west coast. In June 1942, the Japanese submarine *I.26* fired seventeen shells into the naval wireless station at Point Estevan on Vancouver Island. Royal Canadian Navy personnel put out the lamps in the lighthouse there — a dangerous move for nearby shipping — and sent out an SOS to the naval base at Esquimalt. The shelling caused only slight damage, while the *I.26* escaped unscathed.

At about the same time, the Japanese sub *I.25* bombarded the U.S. Navy submarine base at Astoria, Oregon, 200 miles from Estevan, killing two people. The *I.25* surfaced off the coast in the middle of a fishing fleet and dived again. The next night, the moon was full and the night clear. The *I.25* surfaced with no vessels nearby and heaved twenty shells at shore targets. Again, there was little damage, and this time no one was killed.

In November 1944, as 1CSWG was training at Pat Bay camp, the Japanese launched the first of nine thousand balloons loaded with incendiary bombs from Japan into the jet stream, which carried them into the U.S. and Canada as far east as northern Ontario. One of these drifting bombs killed six people upon landing at Lakeview, Oregon. Some started forest fires, as the Japanese intended. News of the continuous, high-altitude killer flotilla was kept quiet in North America for fear of causing panic.

Long-held apprehensions among British Columbians of an ultimate Asian invasion revived. The rapid successes of the Japanese in sweeping down through the Pacific and, more threateningly, occupying two Aleutian Islands, Kiska and Attu, in May 1942, seemed to provide clear proof that North America's west coast would be next. It appeared inevitable that Canada would be actively involved in the Pacific war. The small Royal Canadian Navy group at Esquimalt was little comfort against the presence of Japanese naval units loose in the North Pacific. Militia reservists — most of them, like the Rocky Mountain Rangers, overage veterans of World War I — made preparations to stave off an invasion that might occur if the U.S. Navy suffered further decisive defeats in the South

Pacific. They improvised rudimentary and inadequate defences, such as earth-and-log dugouts and logs simulating cannon placed in earthwork bunkers. Later, a few units of inexperienced militia artillery were posted here and there along the coast.

Early in 1944, the Canadian government agreed to take a limited role in the Pacific conflict. The decision was apparently made after requests came, first from India and then from Australia, for Canada to help monitor Japanese military signals in Burma and the South West Pacific islands. At first it was thought a mobile group able to move close to enemy lines would be needed, but the Americans had already found that the jungles made it impractical for heavy radio trucks to move about in the gumbo-like mud during the rainy season. Instead it was decided to locate a Canadian monitoring station, powerful enough to sweep the entire Pacific for enemy signals as far north as Tokyo, on the northern coast of Australia. Ultimately, 1CSWG was assigned to concentrate on the islands of the Dutch East Indies — now Indonesia. On these islands, as the U.S. Navy and General Douglas MacArthur's armies moved farther north, about a million dedicated Japanese veteran troops were trying to extend their conquests; meanwhile, Allied land, sea, and air forces fought to dislodge them. While most of the action took place on the large islands of New Guinea, New Britain, New Ireland, and smaller islands and seas, the Japanese were in complete control of Borneo, Java, and Timor. It was left mainly to the Australians and some American units to root them out.

Australian forces had been actively at war with the Germans in North Africa and the Middle East since 1940. At the outbreak of war in the Pacific they returned to their homeland to fight the Japanese. After three years of this, many of their units were close to exhaustion, among them their Special Wireless groups. This prompted the request to Ottawa for Canadian signals intelligence help.

One question that still haunts those who worry about such things is whether U.S. President Franklin Roosevelt and his military staff had advance knowledge of Japanese Admiral Chuichi Nagumo's fleet as it approached Pearl Harbor on December 7, 1941. It may remain forever unanswered — no concrete evidence of such knowledge has appeared, despite postwar U.S. Congressional hearings into the Pearl Harbor attack. But there lingers a suggestion that British and Canadian monitoring in the days before the attack picked up a great deal of information about the Japanese fleet's progress across the Pacific in the early part of December 1941. Lord Cavendish-Bentinck, chairman of the British Joint Intelligence Committee, is reported to have said that the British knew when the Japanese fleet changed course toward Hawaii the day before the attack, and that they warned the Americans.

Although U.S. cryptanalysts were said to have broken the Japanese diplomatic ciphers and naval codes long before the war, it was the British who had in 1940 supplied the Americans with the key to the important JN25 code, making possible the monitoring of later Japanese naval moves into the South China Sea. A recent book claims that it was really British and Australian cryptographers who broke JN25, but that the Americans were able to claim credit "because of the British obsession with secrecy." That will no doubt be a subject for future debate.

When a "Purple" machine for deciphering Japanese signals was given to the British Government Code and Cipher School at Bletchley Park, England, by the U.S. Army Signal Intelligence Services early in 1941, the sharing of wireless interception information between the U.S. and U.K. began in earnest. The British intercept and cryptanalysis station at Singapore and an American counterpart at Corregidor — under U.S. Navy Commander R.J. Fabian — were the two most important listening posts in the Pacific when war came.

Meanwhile, in Canada, monitoring stations were also picking up Japanese signals — particularly at Halifax, where a British intercept station was operating with Royal Canadian Navy co-operation. Besides collecting information radioed to U-boats in the North Atlantic from Germany, the station also gathered Japanese military and diplomatic radio traffic. At the 1946 Congressional hearings, U.S. Navy Commander L.F. Safford testified that he thought the Japanese signals that would have given the alert to the U.S. Navy might have been picked up by the Royal Air Force monitoring station at Cheltenham, England, "or Halifax. They would be in a receiving condition and the Canadians were guarding those Japanese stations the way we were.... Halifax could have got it if they were capable of copying the Japanese Morse code.... I do not know what the qualifications of the operators at Halifax were or at other stations outside of those the United States Navy controlled..."

General Sherman Miles, head of U.S. military intelligence, testified that the United States had given "the British" (Canadians!) the means for intercepting Japanese messages via Magic. He'd had talks in 1941 with the Canadian military attaché in Washington "because certain messages were being intercepted by Canada but not by any other part of the British Empire. The Canadians did not have the means of breaking them nor did they know anything about the technical details of decoding. We were very anxious, however, to get from them any messages that they could pick up out of the air which for any reason we could not or the British could not…" From that point on, armed with the key to cracking Japanese codes, Canadian military branches began to train intelligence personnel in deciphering the information contained in the accumulating masses of messages.

Within months, Canada's three armed services were operating Special Wireless stations at five points across the country: at Leitrim, Halifax, Grande Prairie, Vancouver, and Gordon Head. There may have been other stations as well. The Canadian eavesdroppers became an integral part of the worldwide Allied signals intelligence system. Still, in his landmark book *The Ultra Secret*, F.W. Winterbotham makes no mention of Canada's part, and even Canadian writer William Stevenson, in *A Man Called Intrepid*, makes only cursory reference to Canadian activities in gathering "large quantities of coded Japanese transmissions." But there was no doubt among several hundred Canadian signals servicemen of their contribution to the defeat of Japan, not to mention Germany.

Turning eighteen in October 1943 brought with it a certain air of mixed expectations and fatalism that only selected generations of youth are allowed to experience. Not every eighteen-year-old has a war waiting for him to join, and even fewer would have the bemusing choice of *two* major wars being waged simultaneously — both of them just about to reach their peaks of intensity. On the one hand, prospects for excitement could be great, yet the odds of surviving beyond the age of nineteen were at their lowest. The youth of the day had only to read the newspaper on any given evening to see the names of former schoolmates killed in action. Still, most viewed it all as just another stage of being young, much like moving on to the next grade of high school.

You had until six months past your eighteenth birthday to make up your mind which branch of the armed forces you might join before you simply were conscripted into the militia. If you were willing to play the role of the pariah and not fight for your country, you waited to be conscripted under the National Registration Mobilization Act (NRMA) and be posted anywhere in Canada. The nobler choice was to take the bull by the horns and join up for active service anywhere in the world.

For me the choice seemed quite simple at the time. To wield a bayonet and march for hours required, I believed, a reasonably husky and healthy volunteer who could hold up his part of the battle and even thrive on it. At eighteen, I weighed about 155 pounds, was light of bone and generally a weakling, and looked so unhealthy that, while on a train trip, I was once offered a seat by an elderly lady who feared for my survival if I continued to stand.

With this apparent fragility on my side, about one week before I turned eighteen and a half I travelled from St. Catharines, Ontario, where I was working for radio station CKTB, to Toronto to go through the motions of volunteering for active duty. I felt secure in the belief that the medical officer would laugh uproariously at the sight of this skinny stripling, call over his colleagues to ridicule the medical marvel before him, and then, probably still chuckling, tell me to put my clothes back on and go home to wait out the few months I probably had left anyway.

That wasn't the way it went. They classed me A-1, gave me a haircut similar to the skinhead style that would be popular more than fifty years later, brutally stuck several needles into me, and told me to come back in a week for a uniform. Somewhere along the recruiting line I'd filled out a form that asked what branch of the army I'd like to be in. Since I'd been working as a radio announcer and operator, I wrote down that — if worse came to worst — I favoured the signal corps. The worst came. Despite my image of myself as a 155-pound weakling, they took me. My dog tag said I was now Rifleman Murray, G.S., of the Canadian Infantry Corps (CIC). None of us knew it, but D-Day was less than two months away, and cannon fodder would be desperately needed.

D-Day came and went in June 1944, but my mates and I were still in Canada and only just completing our basic infantry training at Simcoe, Ontario. On the famous day, I was hut cleanup man — or "hut-slut," as the rank was called. That was why I was one of the first in camp to know that the Normandy landings had happened. The news came over the radio in the barracks hut, interrupting the program of Glenn Miller music that was accompanying my cleanup duties. I spread the word, and we all knew immediately that we were really in trouble. Up until that point, we had been lulled by the thought that we'd be shipped over to England when our training was done, and probably sit out a war that didn't seem to be happening, at least on the ground.

By late July, well into advanced infantry training at Camp Ipperwash on Lake Huron in southwestern Ontario, this skinny stripling was on the ropes from the unbelievably tough daily grind of the obstacle course, the live ammunition fired above us as we crawled, the frequent fifteen-mile, full-pack route marches in 95-degree (Fahrenheit) heat, and the execrable food. All this was routine army training, but it seemed better suited to professional football players and wrestlers. We, on the other hand, were being prepared like raw steak for a barbecue as replacements for casualties in Normandy and Italy. So, one day when advanced training was almost over and a sergeant gave me the word to hop over to the camp's orderly office on the double, I was only too happy, because it got me off the obstacle course for a moment.

Three other riflemen were waiting in the orderly office when I got there. I knew only one of them: Don Laut, from Bracebridge, Ontario. Don and I had joined up the same day in Toronto and had shared the privilege of living for two weeks in a stall in the Horse Palace barracks at the Canadian National Exhibition grounds before being shipped off to Simcoe and ultimately to Ipperwash. What had we done to be called on the carpet? None of us knew. We were all extremely nervous. Then we were marched into the office of a major, who sat in official splendour behind a regulation oak desk. He didn't seem that unfriendly, an observation that made us all the more apprehensive, because we hadn't yet met an officer who *wasn't* hostile. He even dismissed the accompanying sergeant and let us stand at ease in his presence.

We four had been singled out, he said, from the other two thousand or so riflemen at Ipperwash because of our previous records. That struck me as mysterious, and ominous. I thought that he must have the wrong man — I hadn't dared step out of line since the first time a sergeant-major blasted me for having an untied bootlace. Then the major said we must make up our own minds about the next item of business. He asked us if we'd like to volunteer for active service — in the Far East!

When a major asked a rifleman to volunteer, he didn't usually expect the rifleman to decline. But this major was genuinely asking us to make up our own minds. We could refuse, if we wished to go back to the obstacle course. He couldn't tell us what we were volunteering to do, or even what part of the Far East was involved. It could mean anywhere in Asia, from the

Kamchatka Peninsula to Tasmania. But he did divulge that the assignment would be with the Royal Canadian Signal Corps. Lo and behold, here was the chance to join what I'd originally volunteered for! I instantly volunteered for active service a second time. So did the other three.

The major's face turned grim as he leaned forward and said we must not breathe a word about where we were going, even to our fellow riflemen in the barracks. If any of us did, it would mean a long stretch in the digger — the army jail. Thus, we four who had originally volunteered for active service anywhere in the world were volunteering a second time for more active service, but in some unknown place in the mysterious East. No matter. It would get us out of Ipperwash.

Back at the barracks, the boys did their mightiest to pry out of us the reason why we'd been called over to the orderly office. Were we charged with something? If so, what? We didn't tell them a thing beyond saying we were being shipped out. Understandably, we quickly became unpopular. The very next day, allowed just one phone call home to say we were going somewhere — but were prohibited from saying where or what for — we were taken by truck to the railway station in nearby Forest to catch a train to Toronto, where we switched to one bound for Vancouver.

In those days, a trip from Toronto to Vancouver by rail took four and a half days. We'd been ticketed for the Pullman car, where porters converted the seats into curtained upper and lower bunks, ensuring that we would travel in relative comfort. After our brutal diet in camp, the meals in the dining car were treats.

For four young soldiers who hadn't been farther west than Camp Ipperwash, this trip was a dazzler. Prairie, mountain, and west coast scenery, all packed into four and a half days of almost constant motion, were dizzying after three months of steady, mind-numbing infantry "toughening up." It was a lark that we had never imagined we would ever have.

The journey provided an opportunity to live it up, and two of our foursome did just that. In the double seats around us were three loud ground crew corporals from the air force, also on their way to Vancouver, and a comely young lady travelling alone, who gave her name as Elsie. She sat next to a window, and at first glance seemed to be shy and quiet, perhaps somebody's pretty young daughter returning from school in the east. She watched the noisy RCAFers with a kind of wary amusement. They, of course, performed all the more as she watched. In a short while, she was laughing and even joining in some of the barracks ballads we held forth with, though she didn't know the words, which was just as well. We made for quite a party, especially when Tim Jones — the leader of our group, a lance-corporal who was carrying our essential order papers — produced a bottle of Scotch and began pouring. Even our new young lady friend had her share.

There was a hint of guardedness in the air between the air force men and the army grunts, with Elsie acting as a sort of moderating influence. Her presence kept the language and side references clean. The more we all joked and carried on, the more she loosened up. Here she was, a young woman surrounded by seven young servicemen and a bottle of Scotch. It might have been the highlight of her school year, so delightedly did she take part. At dinner we all went together to the dining car. As there could only be four to a table, there was a slight scramble to be at the same one as Elsie. Laut and I and one of the RCAFers ended up as the odd men out. Tim and the other two air force men crowded in close to Elsie.

By the time we headed back to our coach, there was a noticeable absence of Elsie and one of the RCAFers. The porters made up the curtained double bunks. Still, there was no sign of Elsie and our seventh man. Then, as we passed through the stretch where our daytime seats were located, we detected a giggle from behind the curtains. Mystery solved. Next morning, with the bunks made down into seats again, Elsie was demure but polite. The three RCAFers were playing cards in their own double seats. Tim Jones was sitting next to Elsie, talking earnestly to her about something.

We other three Ipperwash exiles really knew only one thing about Lance-Corporal Jones: he had gotten married the day before we left Simcoe for Ipperwash. As far as the rest of us were concerned, that made him the father figure, the moral compass, of our small contingent. Being a one-woman man, I found the next episode depressing. That evening, Elsie and Tim were missing. Again, giggles came from behind the black curtained upper bunk. This time, though, we three Ipperwashers broke into "Friggin' in the Riggin'," a Newfoundland ballad with obvious implications. The giggling stopped.

Next morning, Corporal Jones was visibly fuming when he met us. But he said nothing. What *could* he say? Would we tell Elsie he was married? Would we write to his new wife about the upper bunk? No, we let the matter drop, but Corporal Jones never again had even a polite glance for any of us. As far as I was concerned, it wouldn't have been welcome anyway. That night, Elsie's upper bunk again emanated giggles, as yet a different air force man was missing. Elsie was a busy girl on that trip. The demure look had been a wonderful cover for what probably was a pro performance. I don't think either of them even noticed the Rocky Mountains when we passed through them.

As a postscript, when we disembarked at the Vancouver train station, the three RCAFers — whose names we never learned — rushed past us on the platform, obviously in a great hurry. I could hear Elsie's first partner mutter to his pals, "Let's get the hell out of here before she spots us," and they vanished into the street and anonymity. As we waited nearby in full pack and rifles for our ferry tickets to Victoria, we picked a distracted Elsie, carrying her own suitcases, out of the crowd. She noticed us and asked in a small, whining voice, "Have you see where Bob went?" No, we hadn't, and we doubted if Bob would ever be found. In fact, we had a pretty good idea he wouldn't. Elsie went on her way, plainly mourning the loss of at least two prospective catches.

And so the four riflemen of the apocalypse boarded the ferry for Victoria and our mysterious destination on Vancouver Island. But even as "tough" riflemen, nothing could have prepared us for what we were to encounter at the end of our journey: the camp on Mills Road on the Saanich Peninsula.

Hours later, the Ipperwash four, loaded down in full battledress, web packs, steel helmets tucked into the straps, black boots sparkling, overseas wedge caps tipped down on our foreheads in regulation style, and hefting heavy Lee-Enfield .303 rifles, got off the ferry. In those days, the boats went to Victoria's own harbour, lorded over by the Empress Hotel and the British Columbia Legislature. Standing confused on the dock, wondering where to go next, we were hailed by a lance-jack at the wheel of a snub-nosed, 15-cwt. army truck parked a little way off.

Despite our gear, we managed to climb in the back of the truck — a form of travel we were accustomed to by this time — and were hauled out of Victoria in the roaring vehicle along a long, dusty country road through rolling, forested hills to Mills Road, about 17 miles north of the city. Here the disinterested driver, badged as Royal Canadian Army Service Corps, turned off Mills Road and onto a crude track that led into a forest so dense it seemed as if dusk had fallen. For another ten minutes the truck bumped and jolted us about as the track wound and dipped its way deeper into the woods. At last our destination appeared: a collection of broken-down pre-war barracks huts scattered among the lofty Douglas firs. We climbed down from the truck and it immediately took off, the driver not bestirring himself to tell us where to report.

There was no sign of an orderly hut. We stood for a while, rifle butts down on the ground, looking around, inadvertently making the very picture of smartly drilled, gung-ho soldiers. Our old company sergeant-major's heart, made of stone as it was, would have thumped with pride if he could have seen us. We were glad, if only for his sake, that he wasn't around. Some loosely uniformed servicemen loped sloppily across the open space in front of us, all going in different directions, and all ignoring us. It was apparent that just the four of us could have easily, with only our rifles, captured the whole place. It was just as clear that there was nothing worth capturing here.

After months of spit-and-polish army training, during which the initiative had been pounded out of us, we were at a loss for what action to take. Even though we'd all hated every moment of our military career to date, something repelled us about the absolute sloth that permeated this mouldering ruin of an old prewar Permanent Force camp and the men we saw in it. It was all very unmilitary.

And it was in the middle of nowhere. There was a distant noise of engines, after which a P-40 Kittyhawk fighter plane, visible for only an instant through an opening in the tree canopy, made a fast, low-level pass. It seemed we must be somewhere near airplanes. As we would find out later, we were: just across Patricia Bay from an RCAF base, which later became Victoria International Airport. Its presence reassured us that we hadn't been completely abandoned in the wilderness.

"Jeez, b'y, where yiz been? We come near winnin' te war wit'out yiz!"

The singsongy voice belonged to an improperly dressed, militarily speaking, soldier who happened to be skulking past when we asked him where we were supposed to report. He was hatless, his tunic hung open, he was bleary-eyed, and he sported a days-old growth of beard. There were no short puttees around the ankles of his baggy battledress pants as there should have been, and his boots were so covered in dust that you couldn't tell if they were black or green. Still, he was one of the few moving bodies we could spot among the long shacks that made up the camp. We later learned that this apparent vagrant was known as "the Gunner," and he was a Torontonian with a Newfie accent — acquired during a four-year stint with an artillery regiment defending the coast of Newfoundland — and an enormous capacity for beer. We got no more out of him than a wave of the arm in the general direction of the huts, before he went off to the wet canteen to take something for his hangover.

Next, a tall, loosely-put-together individual with sergeant's stripes on his sleeve and an artillery shoulder flash on his open tunic loped by, ignoring us thoroughly. A sergeant! we thought. Well, there was some officialdom here after all! Trained to the hilt to put unquestioning faith in the infallibility of sergeants, we were stunned when he just looked us up and down as he continued on his way, his lip a little curled and with no pause in his step. He turned and came back, and only then could we see that, on his other sleeve where the matching set of sergeant's stripes should have been, there were only three light-beige V-shaped marks on the battledress cloth and a hanging thread or two. Ex-sergeant John Ferguson, we were to learn, was a master artillery instructor who, like the Gunner and the rest of us, had volunteered to join this strange group and get posted overseas — anywhere. He'd had to give up his coveted sergeant's rank — and pay — and come down among the lowest, like us. Now his sergeant's sense of duty returned momentarily, and he steered us to a long, empty barracks hut where we could dump our gear and wait for orders, like everyone else. There was indeed, he confirmed, no orderly hut to report to.

Having dumped our gear, we got back outside as soon as we could — two of us hoping to find a wet canteen — and marvelled at the swelling parade of oddly assorted service personnel who were coming alive. Besides Artillery Corps and Service Corps badges, and our own Infantry flashes, there were the insignia of the Armoured Corps, the Electrical and Mechanical Engineers, the Ordnance Corps, and, of all things, the Royal Canadian Signals. On left lower sleeves the red initials GS — not for G.S. Murray, but "General Service" — were darkened with age and wear. Some also had, on the same sleeve, three, four, and even five hash marks — small red upside-down Vs, one for each year of active service. There was the odd fellow here and there who had neither a G.S. badge nor any hash marks, but seemed to be experienced in the service. These would be, we reasoned, reformed zombies.

For variety, there were a few blue Royal Canadian Air Force uniforms and even a sailor suit or two. Among the army tunics I noticed still more evidence of stripes having been removed from sleeves, and even an occasional sign of the ghostly shadows of second-lieutenants' pips on shoulder straps. All in all, our group made up a broad cross-section of the Canadian armed forces.

But what struck me odd was that there wasn't a genuine officer's uniform to be seen. This camp was a ship without a skipper — adrift, rudderless.

We found the mess hall, diligently manned by cooks who, fortunately, felt some measure of duty to provide food, and we got something to eat. Night fell, and with nothing better to do we flopped into bunks in the otherwise empty barracks hut and fell asleep. Back at Ipperwash we'd been wakened every morning at 0530 hours by the pibroch of bagpipes. At Simcoe it had been an off-key bugle. On our first morning at the Mills Road camp, there was nobody — and nothing — to awaken us. We all, incredibly, slept in until nearly 0900 hours, or 9:00 a.m. Feeling guilty and panicky, we shaved and scrambled into our uniforms. We still had the long barn of a barracks hut all to ourselves, except for one lone body — in full, but filthy, uniform — sprawled on a cot at a far end, snoring off the bender of the night before.

In true Ipperwash form — boots polished, freshly shaven, ties and bootlaces done up tight and straight — and braced for the worst blast some raging sergeant-major might give us, we ran out on the double to look for the parade ground and morning inspection. Look as we might, we found no parade ground, no sergeant-major, and no inspection. There were only a few dozen ill-dressed soldiers ambling toward the mess hall for what was either breakfast or early lunch. Even we four of the CIC, innately rebellious but obedient toward the rigid discipline that had been drilled into us by parade-ground terrorists, were put off by the debauchery of this raggle-taggle assortment of military delinquents.

It turned out that most of them had come to this camp from far-off points across Canada — and, thanks to careless clerking at innumerable camp orderly offices across the country, far ahead of schedule. They'd taken advantage of the absence of disciplinarians in the form of officers or non-coms, as well as the presence of a mess hall and a wet canteen well stocked with all the necessities, and were enjoying the freedom while it lasted. The artful old hands with all the hash marks on their sleeves knew that any pretense of discipline was a fool's game. They also knew there'd be a day of reckoning when the officers finally arrived, but, like all good old soldiers, they'd worry about that another day.

For the next two weeks or so the tottery old camp was more like a seedy holiday resort than a military establishment. We Ipperwashers had tossed our gear, including rifles, into a corner of our dusty, empty barracks hut, where it was gathering its own coating of new dust. Lights in all the barracks, required under normal army regulations to be put out by 2230 hours (10:30 p.m.) burned most of the night. We took to getting up in the morning whenever it pleased us, and usually didn't bother to shave. While the food wasn't gourmet quality, it was plentiful, and so was the beer. For me, as for Laut, the latter didn't mean anything, but our other two mates lapped up their share, and more. In the mess hall, poker and crap games drew big crowds and, for some die-hards, ran on into the daylight hours. Hundreds of dollars were lost each night by the more reckless, and conversely won by the cool-minded and calculating. Business at the wet canteen boomed. The Service Corps men in charge knew how to keep the food and drink supplies coming from some mysterious depot beyond the camp limits.

There was everything needed to fuel the debauchery, except perhaps for one normally vital element: girls. As officers might arrive at any moment, even the bolder men among us wouldn't run the risk of having girls found in the camp. That would be extremely unmilitary and good for several weeks in the digger. Instead, the adventurous just commandeered a truck or two, loaded themselves in, and went off to Victoria to seek out the ladies.

Eventually, the day of reckoning arrived. We benighted latecomers were unaware that the real nucleus of the unit had, since earlier in the summer, been located at Gordon Head, elsewhere on Vancouver Island. Heading this group was the commanding officer of Number One Canadian Special Wireless Group, Lieutenant-Colonel H.D.W. Wethey. Before August was done, Colonel Wethey, along with his officers and senior non-commissioned officers, moved in. Reality came with them, on the double.

The shabby group of men we'd first encountered suddenly vanished, and in their place there appeared quite a presentable company of soldiers with tunics done up tight, wedge caps drawn down over foreheads in regulation style, boots shining like black mirrors, and jaws shaved so close they were pink. These were the same bunch that had been slouching about camp, but what a difference the news the officers were coming made! We four from Ipperwash quickly fell in, reverting to the spit-and-polish riflemen we'd once been.

Before the inevitable general cleanup of the camp was ordered, the whole complement of the new 1CSWG was called into parade in the open space at the centre of the camp, where there had indeed once been a parade ground. After snapping to attention at the call of a company sergeant-major, we were introduced to a Captain Ralph March, our new adjutant, who addressed us and told us how it was going to be. It was to be strict discipline from now on: no more loose uniforms, unshaven faces, and no more sleeping past reveille.

Captain March then introduced the chief player, Lieutenant-Colonel Wethey. The Officer Commanding was a career administrative officer in his late thirties, dressed in a beautifully cut uniform of fine drill, the pants pressed in frontal creases that might give you a bad cut if you weren't care-ful. Everything about him represented razor-sharp precision. He gave us a quick lecture on discipline and a warning on keeping absolute, airtight security about the unit — including the fact that it existed — and its work. Then we were dismissed, feeling to a man that a great weight had fallen upon us, the weight of military authority so great that a mere pri-vate wouldn't even be able to call his soul his own. To the four of us from Ipperwash, it was déjà vu all over again.

Somewhere a bugler was found, and from now on the dawn would be split by his off-key but determined reveille call. Morning parade was at 0700 hours sharp, and you'd better have had your breakfast by then or you would be out of luck until lunch at 1300 hours. Ferguson, the languid ex-sergeant with the shadows of stripes on his sleeve, was reinstated tem-porarily to his old rank — reluctantly, as it was plain that he would have to get along with the ordinary ranks later as a lowly signalman himself. One or two former corporals were also reconstructed for a time, but, cor-porals being what they were — aspiring sergeants — they never did fit in with the other fellows when they were at last levelled down.

We shone our boots, sewed Royal Canadian Signals flashes on our tunic shoulders, put R.C. Signals badges in our wedge caps, and threw the CIC insignia into the bottoms of our kit bags to be kept as souvenirs. Now we found ourselves divided up into sections: one for each phase of the new unit's functions. We four ex-Ipperwashers found ourselves in Ops Mon Sigs Section Two. Section One was made up of the veteran wireless oper-ators who'd been in Special Wireless work for years. We were the new trainees, yet to learn what the job meant.

Readjusting to real army life was almost as tough as doing the Ipperwash obstacle course every day. At least, somebody offered, we weren't route-marching. That, we would find out soon enough, was to be a mistaken assumption. There was a lieutenant, a graduate of Royal Military College, who had other ideas about that. We'd meet him later.

Chapter 3

Top Secrets and Japanese Kana

Kana. That was what they called the Japanese military code that we former riflemen, troopers, gunners, and regimental signallers were expected to learn. We were to be trained to steal vital enemy information from the airwaves over the Pacific, though we wouldn't have to learn Japanese or decipher the code; we would just have to get it down on paper. The Intelligence Corps unit to be attached to 1CSWG — mostly Japanese-speaking offspring of former Canadian church missionaries who'd grown up in prewar Japan — would decode the messages. The I Corps would join us later.

Though there wasn't a traditional obstacle course in the camp, there was one of a different kind, which was no less formidable: a classroom. Here we thirty-five newly ordained signalmen were to be drilled into becoming radio "ears" capable of copying Kana signals as fast as their operators — oblivious to the possibility of being overheard and understood — were likely to send them. I had at least one technical advantage over the others, having spent a good part of my young life so far as a radio

announcer and operator. The major back at Ipperwash, following orders
to produce four candidates for the top-secret Far East job, must have cast
his eye over my papers and spotted the radio experience. That decision
changed my military career.

We got only a fraction of the whole story on Special Wireless, but
there was no doubt about the man around whom our daily grind would
revolve: Warrant Officer First Class J.G.K. Hollister, an imposing, gruff
old soldier with a white crewcut and the speaking style of a parade ground
sergeant-major — always at the top of his voice. He could easily have been
a veteran of the Boer War, let alone World War I. He would have made an
excellent model for a prison warden, one with the fabled heart of gold hidden somewhere underneath his chestful of campaign ribbons.

Hollister drove us at our lessons every day; there were classes in radio
(or, as he insisted we call it, "wireless") physical theory; the structure of
Kana messages; Morse code at 23 words per minute (the usual standard for
army signals was 10 w.p.m., which shocked some former tank corps men,
who'd only had to do eight); and touch-typing — first, at 60 w.p.m., and
later, for more pay, at 75. These speeds wouldn't seem spectacular to career
stenographers, but to most of this assemblage of raw talent the very idea
of running a typewriter (using all fingers and one thumb) seemed unmanly, if not bloody impossible for those with callused hands. We were lucky
that the era of the electric typewriter, with its flighty touch sensitivity, was
still in the future.

"I ain't no kitten on the keys," the Gunner grumbled. "But put some
bimbo on my lap and I'll see she does it right smart, b'jeez!"

Of course, that comment demonstrates that the era of women's liberation and non-sexist language was also very much in the distant future.
Most of us shared the sentiment that typing was women's work. I had a
slight advantage, having done a little bit of hunt-and-peck keyboarding to
prepare scripts for the radio station. I'd also done quite a bit of manipu-
lating of radio equipment without knowing what really went on behind all
those pots and VU meters on the control board.

The rumbling and grumbling was silenced instantly by the steely snap
of W/O Hollister's commanding voice, followed by dead quiet while
everybody watched the light flashing off his gold spectacles and his white
hair. A Warrant Officer One was just a notch below a commissioned officer, but with most of the privileges of an officer, including absolute obe-
dience. Rule by terror, learned over decades of handling such raw materi-

al as this scruffy group, was the fine old soldier's method. But while he was able to keep the grumbling to a minimum, he couldn't control the fact that some of the material he had to work with was simply too raw, and the class dropout rate was to swell as time passed.

Radio — er, *wireless* — theory, Morse code, and typing were all formidable challenges, but the real puzzler was the mysterious Kana. Looking back, it seems simple. But to a new young signalman the rigours of grappling with, and instantly recognizing, the dits and daws coming through a radio headset — in through the ears and out through the fingers, *accurately*, as typed letterforms — were demoralizing. Not only that, for those of us who'd dropped out of high school — as most of us had — being stuck in barracks every night doing radio theory homework instead of passing the evening at the wet canteen like regular soldiers was almost beyond the endurance of some of "the b'ys", as the Gunner would have it. Still, the spectre of W/O Hollister had some countervailing effect, and most of us stuck with the job as best we could.

But what was this Kana all about? Since our jobs as Ops Mon Sigs didn't require that we know any more than how to put down on paper what some Japanese wireless operator was sending out over the air, nobody bothered to show us how it all fitted in with the war. Given that the work of 1CSWG was classified as top secret by both the Department of National Defence and the United States War Department, the official view was clearly that the less we knew about it the better.

(The sensitivity of our task had come closer to home than we knew at the time. After the war we would find out that we had all been checked out by the RCMP, who paid visits to our former civilian homes. The Mounties were taking no chances that any of us might have sympathetic leanings toward the enemy or might be just plain talkative. While we weren't told officially that this was going on, somehow, in true barracks style, facts slipped through — sometimes in the form of "latrinograms," sometimes from even less reliable sources — and gradually pieces were added to the puzzle.)

Kata Kana was laboriously deciphered in the 1920s by H.W. Yardley and the secret organization called the Black Chamber, operating in a small office in Washington, D.C. He and his team constructed a system that assigned each Japanese ideographic syllable its own symbol in Roman form, easily copied (by eavesdroppers) as a series of Roman two-letter groups. The Kana syllables were transmitted by Japanese wireless operators in Morse code, and Allied operators could intercept and type out these double-letter symbols in continuous form.

This produced pages of doubled Roman-letter sets, prefixing a consonant before a vowel, as, for example, BA, BE, BI, BO, and BU. Subsequent groups of syllables were similarly rendered as CA, CE, CI, CO, and CU; or DA, DE, DI, DO, or DU, on through similar alphabetical groupings of vowels with prefixed consonants, concluding with ZA, ZE, ZI, ZO, and ZU. For example, BO represented the Japanese syllable *tse*; OS represented *ku*.

This provided more than enough Roman symbols to identify all seventy-two Japanese syllables, as well as punctuation and incidental control signs such as the non-syllablic *n*, which often came at the ends of words. Other endings used as controls might be *i, no, o, ni, shi, wa, ru,* and *to*. Most common Kana syllables began with *ari, aritashi, dajin, denpoo, gai,* or *gyoo* and were given Roman symbols. A message might end with *owari,* or "stop". Fillips of dits and daws called *nigoris* and *hannigoris* provided built-in clues for decoding.

In other words, the Kana character DA — "Dog Able," as we'd call it — would be transmitted as dash-dot-dot dot-dash (or, in signalman's language, "daw-dit-dit dit-daw") together as if it were one unit of Morse. There would be an infinitesimal pause between each unit. Our training required us, as we received the signal through our headsets, to trail a second or two behind the Japanese operator's "fist" as we typed so that the message could be rendered into these two-letter groups. In this form, decoding was easier and more reliable, and therefore more quickly made available in cleartext for the information of headquarters strategists.

Once a Japanese operator converted a message into Kana symbols, he encoded the message by rearranging the symbols on a "Purple" machine — an electric keyboard device developed from the German Enigma encoding machine — or an identical machine set up for the "Red" code or one of the myriad of other codes the Japanese had produced over the years before the war. He then transmitted the coded form to its distant destination by hand-operated radio-telegraph.

It was during this transmission stage that Allied signals intelligence operators, posted at monitoring stations perhaps thousands of miles away, tuned their radio sets to known Japanese military frequencies, intercepted messages, and transcribed them. Their output would then be sent to the monitoring station's unit of the Intelligence Corps, where cryptanalysts would run the messages through a copy of the Purple machine. In 1940, William Friedman, working for the U.S. Intelligence Service, had secretly reconstructed this complex device from stolen plans.

The job of translating the messages fell to Japanese-speaking members of the I Corps section. The cleartext version they produced would then be forwarded instantly to Allied headquarters in Melbourne, or to Manila or a subsection, where a decision would be made as to which Allied field commanders should receive the message.

In many instances, Japanese troops in or near the front lines lacked the Purple machine to encode their messages, and so they were forced to transmit orders in plain Kana. This was one of the reasons that 1CSWG was originally organized. Operations near the front lines could not support fixed radio intercept stations and, since intelligence on a regimental or battalion scale was just as important as that transmitted by the high command, it was desirable for signals intelligence operators to function in forward areas, too.

Once it was fully trained and organized as a mobile unit, 1CSWG was self-contained and was never intended to serve in the fixed location that it ultimately did occupy in Darwin. Besides the two operating sections — one made up of the veteran signalmen and the second of us rookies — 1CSWG consisted of the Intelligence Corps, Technical Maintenance, Intercommunication, Motor Transport, Quartermaster, and Headquarters sections. The group's equipment complement took in over a million dollars' worth (which represented a fortune at the time) of radio, transport, and other hardware. It was all kept in condition by the Technical Maintenance section for the day when 1CSWG might actually operate as a mobile intercept unit, close to Japanese lines somewhere in Asia, the Philippines, the islands — or Japan itself, if the fighting reached that point.

The war ended before that day came. Needless to say, we and all the other millions of Allied troops in the Pacific were immensely relieved when the dropping of the atomic bomb ended the war. It meant we were going to have a future after all. Had it not been for the Bomb, there may have come a time when the Allies got at Japan via the main landmass route through China, and we would have had to move further north. That probably would have entailed hopping from island to island with the Aussies.

It would have been impossible to operate our heavy mobile CZ13s and other vehicles in the humid, tangled jungles and gumbo-like mud of

the islands. One unit of U.S. Signals Intelligence, the 138th, found this
out the hard way on the tiny island of Biak, just off New Guinea, in 1944.
Unable to shift their vehicles quickly enough to get into the most strategic positions for close-in monitoring, the 138th found itself bogged down
and left behind as the action moved swiftly ahead, then back again, and,
once more, laterally. On one occasion they had to abandon their typewriters and grab rifles when Japanese paratroopers dropped in on them
unexpectedly. The Japanese, expecting to find a headquarters camp and
bewildered by the presence of typewriters and radio sets, failed to organize
their attack, and they were finally driven off by the wireless operators-
cum-riflemen. Though the wireless intercept work was only briefly inter-
rupted by skirmishes like this, the idea of having signals-monitoring trucks
slopping ineffectively through jungle mud soon lost favour among the
headquarters strategists.

At the Mills Road camp on Vancouver Island, throughout September,
October, and November of 1944, the boys of Number Two Operating
Section, 1CSWG, toiled and sweated daily under the burden of learning
Morse, touch-typing, and trying to fathom what went on inside a radio
set. Lead-swingers and all had about three and a half months to master
this. The lead-swingers began to drop out early and were assigned different duties. Others simply couldn't get the hang of it, especially the Morse
and the Kana, and were allowed to drop out. Since they now knew most
of the 1CSWG's reason for being, the dropouts had to stay in the unit in
the interest of maintaining top security.

Regardless of what section of the unit they belonged to, the signalmen
of 1CSWG were obliged, as regular soldiers would be, to serve time on fire
picquet and guard duty. In the damp, chilly October weather, all the barracks huts, from the lowliest to the officers', were heated by little coal-
burning stoves that had to be stoked continuously. This was fire picquet:
a soldier on duty visited one hut after another to tend the stoves, at any
and all times of the day or night.

The most dismal time for this duty was during the four-hour shift
from two until six in the morning. Required to be on hand in the guard-
house for instant duty, the lucky fellow chosen for this task slept on a hard
bunk from lights-out at half-past ten until two a.m., when he would be
awakened to get going. To be roused up after only a few hours' sleep at two

o'clock every morning for a week is one of the more traumatic experiences anyone must endure. That was the hour when, in Nazi-held Europe, the Gestapo would show up at the home of a suspected spy to interrogate him. Still stupefied, the subject had to struggle to gather his wits if he hoped to be let off. Thankfully, there was no interrogation with fire picquet or guard duty, but when there was a sergeant hounding you, it did take some time to collect your wits and crawl into your uniform, even with a mug of strong, steaming coffee to blast you awake.

I seemed to be one of the favourite candidates for both middle-of-the-night details, and guard duty wasn't much more fun. The trucks and jeeps and the colonel's staff car, all neatly lined up in the vehicle compound, were a tempting target for thieves — from inside as well as outside the camp. Two guards kept watch, each carrying a rifle with one live round in case they had to fire off an alarm. I spent many an hour in absolute darkness at the camp gate, the only thing in sight being the flashing searchlight that swept the sky over the Pat Bay air base. It was hypnotic. Nothing ever happened. In the dark, you might call to your guard mate way over on the other side of the compound, and he might or might not hear you. A week of seeing the dawn break every day did little for the morale, but it was, as they said, all part of being a soldier.

In the classroom, with the help of a wire recorder — the precursor of today's tape recorders — recordings of actual Japanese messages in Kana were fed through our earphones. At first we would use pencil and paper to take them down. Eventually, as we built up our speed, we could touch-type Kana at 35 words per minute, the equivalent of about 23 w.p.m. in naval Morse.

All the while, the veteran Ops Mons Sigs of Number One Operating Section were busy in the unit's wireless receiving room, copying live Japanese naval messages. Some of these veterans had been copying enemy messages in Morse numbers — a more difficult method — for as long as three years at Grande Prairie, Gordon Head, or Leitrim. None of them held a rank higher than sergeant, and most were corporals, lance-corporals, or just ordinary signalmen. All were pioneers in the fine art of eavesdropping. They had two receiving sets, one on top of the other, with which they could tune in both ends of a Japanese circuit, the sender and the receiver. They knew the Japanese radio frequencies so well that, when they picked up a signal while prowling the dial, they seemed to know intuitively where to find the responding signal and they would twirl the pots on their other receiver to copy that end as well.

This secret monitoring system had its roots in the early 1920s, when illicit copies of telegrams and cablegrams between Tokyo and Japanese diplomats abroad were made and analyzed. In the United States this was the work of the colourful H.W. Yardley, a cryptanalyst with U.S. military intelligence during World War I, whose 1930 book *The Black Chamber* caused a sensation. His book described how he and some associates operated what he melodramatically dubbed the Black Chamber in a Washington, D.C., office following that war. But in the wake of Herbert Hoover's election as U.S. president, Yardley's government funding was cut off. The new administration's view was that it was ungentlemanly to eavesdrop on the diplomatic communications of a country with which the United States had, at the time, peaceful relations.

Yardley's book delighted devotees of cryptology in all countries — except Japan. There was indignant reaction within Japanese diplomatic, military, and editorial circles against the "Yankee perfidy" that had been revealed. Some observers claim that the Black Chamber's activities were among the root causes of Japan's increasingly hostile attitude toward the United States, which of course culminated in the 1941 attack on Pearl Harbor.

Radio eavesdropping once again became respectable, though still highly secret, throughout the 1930s. In part this was because Franklin Roosevelt had replaced Hoover in the White House, but also because, as more information was gathered from Japanese diplomatic and military sources, it was becoming more and more evident that Japan was up to no good in the Pacific. The signals intelligence people paid special attention to the diplomatic messages liberally sprinkled with clues that, when put together with other observations of military preparations, gave a partial insight into Japanese imperialistic intentions.

By the time in December 1941 that Admiral Isoroku Yamamoto, against his better judgment, ordered a large naval force to cruise the Pacific under radio silence (with Pearl Harbor as its ultimate target) American, British, Australian, and Canadian signals intelligence units had gained a solid grip on some Japanese naval codes. The story has been told elsewhere about how diplomatic messages between Tokyo and the Japanese embassy in Washington were closely monitored during the final weeks before Pearl Harbor was attacked, and how last-minute warnings of coming action by the Japanese were not acted upon by the U.S. Navy. Despite a British warning of the Japanese fleet's change of direction toward Hawaii on December 6, the radio blackout from that point on made it impossible to speculate what would happen, and left signals intelligence without any solid basis to sound an alarm. As it happened, no action was taken based on the British warning, and to this day no one knows why.

By early November 1944, Number Two Operating Section — that is, what was left of it after attrition — was deemed to have progressed far enough in the Ops Mon Sigs training regime for us novice signalmen to be classified as TS or Trained Soldiers, eligible for Class B trades pay. This added several cents to our sixty dollars a month. Now that we were considered to be operationally trained, we had only to keep in practice on the typewriter and in Kana, so that we'd be ready for the job whenever — and wherever — we were needed. On that last point, we still knew only that our posting was to be somewhere in the Far East.

It was also decided around this time that we were suffering physically from too much application of the seat of the pants to the chair and a lack of bracing exercise in the outdoors. It was true that the signalmen of Number Two Operating Section were sadly out of shape. No problem: there was a simple remedy in Lieutenant-Colonel Wethey's arsenal, in the person of Second-Lieutenant J.D. "Jack" Miller, a seasoned Signals officer who remembered only too well his original infantry training as an officer cadet at Kingston's Royal Military College. Under Lieutenant Miller there was to be no rest during daytime duty — and sometimes not in the evenings, either.

All of the legendary attributes of fire-eating parade ground sergeant-majors and drill sergeants were applicable to Jack Miller. The big voice he possessed didn't truly fit the short, slightly built man who began driving us flabby Ops Mon Sigs at the quick march and snappy pace worthy of a royal honour guard. He nevertheless owned a leonine roar and red face of the traditional parade ground tyrant. But there was no doubt of his goal, which seemed to be akin to that of a sculptor in marble, using the two dozen signalmen as his own personal block of fine stone from which to chisel a frieze of dynamic bodies, strutting as one at high speed across our rough, improvised parade ground or along a nearby asphalt road. Some of us would also have to be able to function that same night, if necessary, on fire picquet or guard duty, and also pitch in with a will the next morning for a practice session in the classroom.

For much of the remainder of the day, close order drill graced the rudimentary parade ground. Then we were swung onto the road out of the forested camp and along the picturesque, rocky, and woody byways bordering Pat Bay, where there was almost no civilian presence at all. Tall firs and pines grew thick right down to the edge of the road that meandered for miles around the bay. An island rose majestically in the bay — a dark green, largely uninhabited hump that looked from the shore as if it had never been trodden by the white man. Had it been possible to access the island on foot, you can be sure that Lieutenant Miller would have had us march all over it just for the sake of doing so — because it was *there*. The improvised route march was alternated with jogging and quick-time marching. All through October, November, and even into the misty Vancouver Island December, our black boots thudded in unison to Miller's hoarse singsong: "*Lef*-rye *lef*-rye *lef*-rye… get 'em up *high*… necks straight… *backs* straight… *lef*-rye *lef*-rye *lef*-rye…"

To his credit, the lieutenant marched right along with us at the same punishing, smart quickstep, displaying the precision drill style he expected of us. His eye for proper dress in his victims was as demanding as his drill voice was commanding. Not a brass button was to be left unshone, not a whisker was to be left unshaven, no battledress pants or tunic was to be left unironed, and no boot was to be less than a black mirror into which he might gaze upon his own face if he so wished. All of this was a far cry from the warm, lazy days of August when personnel drifted in from across the country and took up undisciplined residence in the senile camp. Many of the Number Two Section Ops Mon Sigs hadn't done parade drill in years, if ever. In the barracks afterward the groans were sepulchral, the voices whining, and the language far worse than customary whenever the exhausted section members spoke of Lieutenant Jack Miller.

Miller was a dedicated officer and one of the first assigned to 1CSWG when it was formed in June 1944. As noted earlier, he was to die of acute encephalitis at the age of 28 when we were stationed at Darwin, Australia, and the facts of his death so far away would come out only fifty-four years later.

Chapter 4

The Last Trip Home

As 1944 drew to a close, 1CSWG was still waiting for National Defence Headquarters in Ottawa to issue orders to move out. In spite of our exhaustion from parade drill, the survivors in Number Two Section Ops Mon Sigs had honed our typing and Kana skills to perfection. In the meantime, of course, Number One Section had been carrying on with the unit's real work of monitoring Japanese signals, and for them the move would be no more than a change of venue with time out for travel. Japanese signals could be picked up at any point on the Pacific Rim. For the rest of us, boredom, until we at least knew where on earth or otherwise we were going to be sent and when.

The rest of us kept typing, listening to the streams of dits and daws through our headsets, and route marching and parading. Occasionally, we'd escape from camp with a twenty-four-hour pass that entitled us to live it up in exciting Victoria — and sometimes we even got as far as Vancouver. For the most part, however, we were kept tightly in hand by the officers and not allowed to stray too often or too far in case the order came to make the inevitable move.

Getting to Vancouver from our deep-woods base was just about the most adventurous journey any of us could make on a twenty-four-hour pass. One Swigger got there by conning an RCAF pilot into letting him squeeze into the space behind the pilot's seat in a Kittyhawk fighter and hopping over to the big city in record time. But for most of us it was the usual bumpy ride in a 15-cwt. truck to Victoria, then onto the ferry to Vancouver. On those slow boats the trip from Victoria to Vancouver took eight hours; if you left at night you could reserve a bunk in advance and wake up next morning just as the ferry pulled into port on the other side.

Ian Swayne, from Edmonton, had an aunt in Vancouver. One time when weekend passes were coming up, Ian suggested we pay her a visit. She was a great cook, he promised, and besides she had a car. So we got weekend passes and journeyed to Vancouver on the ferryboat *Princess Patricia*. Unlike today's ferries, which are largely car- and truck-carrying behemoths, the *Princess Patricia* and her sister ships were small ocean liners, equipped with overnight accommodations and no space for cars. A voyage on the *Princess Pat* was more like a short pleasure cruise. A big brass plaque near the stern said she had been built in Glasgow, Scotland, in 1910. Her brassbound engine room was a spectacular sight.

As I always did on the daytime trip, I admired the many islands along the way, my teenage imagination pretending that some of them could be the strongholds of pirates who might put out from shore at any time to attack us. It never happened. We marched from the landing dock, in those days near downtown, to another one where the ferry to West Vancouver was based — roughly where the hovercraft service to North Vancouver is today. We sailed the harbour to West Van.

Ian's aunt's house was in a cozy neighbourhood. Mrs. Smith (she was the sister-in-law of Ian's mother) let us in with a matter-of-fact manner. We were just in time for dinner, and Ian had not been telling tales — our hostess was indeed a tremendous cook and housekeeper. She made us the first home-cooked meal we'd had since my arrival in British Columbia, and we also had a sound sleep in the first comfortable beds we'd known since leaving home.

For a pair of transient Ops Mon Sigs, this was a whole different world. There was no blasting bugle to blast us out of bed in the morning, we enjoyed delicious meals, and in the late afternoon we all squeezed into

Mrs. Smith's Baby Austin. She took us on a hair-raising ride up Capilano Mountain, along a rough road that led to the brand new Capilano Estates housing development, to show us how those fancy places back east were outclassed by Vancouver's best. Then she sent the little car plunging down the steep road back to West Van, giving us a stunning view of Vancouver just as its lights came on at dusk.

Back home, she cooked another great meal. It was while Ian and I were helping to wash and dry the dishes that Mrs. Smith's unpleasant side began to emerge. In a long discourse that seemed to target me as a perfidious easterner, she told how she'd lived in every province of Canada and nobody was as good as the good people of British Columbia. The worst people of all, she said rather vehemently, were the ones in Ontario. She didn't give any examples, but she went on about how those lousy Ontarians hogged the world and thought they were the only worthwhile people alive.

She seemed to give her opinion with grim relish, and pulled no punches. As I polished one of her fine dishes with a tea towel, I was speechless. Surely, I thought, she must realize that one of her two guests was from Ontario, and that *I* wasn't lousy. Perhaps her aim was to gain an advantage over an obligated young visitor from the east, despite his admirable status as a double active-service volunteer.

Not much was said from then on. There was nothing Ian could contribute to defend me from her characterization of me as one of the great perpetrators of Ontario's sins, whatever they might have been. I had never before thought that there was any difference between Canadians, from west or east. In our signals unit there were men from every province — of all ages and descriptions — and our places of origin had been nothing more than matters of curiosity. I shrugged off Mrs. Smith's vituperations and decided that the better part of valour was to keep quiet. But the experience left me puzzled. Could this be what westerners really thought?

Afterward, Ian and I went to a movie. We had to catch the overnight ferry back to Victoria later, so when we returned to the Smith home we grabbed our kits, thanked Mrs. Smith for her hospitality, and dashed to the West Van dock to start out for "home." I was reminded of Mrs. Smith's views some years later, during the early 1970s, when there was an oil shortage and certain westerners expressed the sentiment that the "eastern bastards" could freeze in the dark. Perhaps Ian's aunt was ahead of her time.

Back at Mills Road, despite the uncertainty about when we were to head overseas, Lieutenant-Colonel Wethey was able to convince the powers in Ottawa to let the 336 men of 1CSWG go on embarkation leave before shipping out. Before we left, we were firmly reminded once again to keep a tight lip. About two weeks before Christmas, most of the unit fanned out across Canada for the first — and last — visit home until long after the end of the Pacific war. During my stay back in Ontario, I still didn't run into any perfidious eastern bastards.

Like anyone else, I was thankful to be home with my family and friends once again, and especially with my longtime girlfriend, Madeline. We'd been going together since 1942, through my radio career, which transplanted me from Brantford to St. Catharines, to those few occasions when I had leave from the army, and now this long absence out west for a purpose I couldn't explain to anyone. There were nine precious days of embarkation leave to enjoy while we could. We all made the most of it, even though we would have to be back at Pat Bay before Christmas.

It was my misfortune, after several months in the balmy clime of Vancouver Island and with many more months of torrid tropical heat still ahead of me, to have to spend an entire day out of my leave stuck in the Great Toronto Snowstorm of December 17, 1944. I had made what I thought would be a quick overnight visit with my pal and former school-mate, Walter Rolland, who was going through medical school at U of T and was in residence at Knox College, on St. George Street. We had a pleasant visit, and as I turned in there was no sign of the impending catastrophe. We woke next morning to find four feet of snow — an amount unheard-of in Toronto — drifted right up to the front door of the residence.

Knowing that a train for Brantford was scheduled to leave Union Station at eight a.m., I left Knox at seven-thirty to forge my way downtown. There was only a narrow footpath worn down by the few, brave pedestrians who'd preceded me. It was a struggle to reach College Street, where I hoped to catch the streetcar to Yonge. Instead, there was a line of trolleys, stalled in the snow, reaching all the way from Yonge Street as far west as the eye could see.

I made it to Yonge Street on foot, where I found a huge throng waiting for north- and southbound streetcars — this was a decade before the subway was opened — to show up. After failing to squeeze onto three cars in a row, I managed to board one on my fourth try, but it was stop-and-go all the way to Front Street. A trip that normally took twenty minutes took two hours. I hurried to Union Station to find that my eight o'clock train was still standing on its track at half-past nine. I got on board. The train sat there on the platform until four o'clock in the afternoon, when the tracks to Brantford were clear of snow. As we left behind a city slowed to a crawl by the great storm — the first train to escape Toronto that day — we chugged along at about 10 miles per hour. Five-foot snow drifts lined both sides of the track. We pulled into Brantford — sixty miles down the line — at around eight p.m., twelve hours after the train had been scheduled to depart.

The balance of my embarkation leave went much more smoothly, consisting mainly of a round of dates and dances with Madeline and some friends, and home-cooked meals with my parents and hers. There was, however, one highlight: Madeline and I got engaged. Buying her ring had been the ulterior motive behind my trip to Toronto. The announcement no doubt stunned both our families, but they were pleased, despite the fact that, as I was to go back out west immediately, there were no plans for an actual wedding for — years? Still, our parents could remember what it had been like during World War I, when they got engaged, and so everyone did the best they could to understand what in peacetime would be an inordinate delay until our big day.

Six days before Christmas I was back at the Pat Bay camp, buoyed by the knowledge that my girlfriend Madeline was now my fiancée, but resigned to the prospect of not seeing her again for a long time. Somehow, though, at nineteen, one tends not to worry about the future. Besides, I believed, with my usual naïveté, it would all be over soon.

There was no snow back in Victoria or the Saanich Peninsula — until Christmas. For the first time in a donkey's age, as the old-timers told us, an inch of snow covered lower Vancouver Island on Christmas Day 1944. The city of Victoria panicked: motorists frantically fitted their tires with chains, and those who didn't skidded around precariously. Downtown traffic was tied up. Anyone who had heavy winter clothing — and they were few — piled it on. Those of us who had just returned from the east — especially the ones who had braved the Great Toronto Snowstorm — could only grin and marvel and enjoy Christmas dinner, served up by our officers — an army tradition. On Boxing Day the snow was all gone, having melted into the usual Victoria damp.

Forced cheek by jowl into makeshift living conditions, like all soldiers the men of 1CSWG learned the realities of communal living — and we hated it. Rather than deaden individualism, the tight conditions brought out a surprising mix of character quirks and habits. Where officers such as Jack Miller would have preferred we meld into a homogenized whole, the unit turned out to be made up of rugged individuals bent on preserving their differences.

Most of 1CSWG's members were mavericks of one kind or another, and many had been bumped out of other army units by superiors fed up with their antics and striking lack of dedication to discipline. All, however, had been identified as candidates for 1CSWG through aptitude profiles that showed they had the ability to learn and do what they had to. They may have been branded incorrigible at some point, but after the war many Swiggers would go on to successful careers. Dave Corbett would become a university professor and return to Australia and marry the girl he'd met during our two-month postwar stay in Sydney; John Taylor got a faculty appointment at McGill University. There were also future teachers, lawyers, accountants, clergymen, and other professionals among our numbers. Guy D'Avignon went on to become deputy minister of Supply and Services in the Trudeau government and, later, head of Information Canada. Don Laut rejoined the army during the Korean War to serve as an officer. I became a journalist.

Some of 1CSWG's officers were trained professional engineers who returned to their professions after the end of hostilities, and at least one officer — Major J. Ross Mackay, one of the unit's founders — became a learned professor of geography at the University of British Columbia. Dr. Mackay earned international recognition and acclaim as a leading authority on permafrost in the Canadian Arctic, and he was active in fieldwork into his eighties. Others went into commercial radio and businesses of various description.

The older hands of Number One Operating Section were the real backbone of the unit, having been in the trade for many months — even years. For the most part, they brought a sense of sobriety to what often seemed to be a project that was never to fulfill itself. On the other hand, we mavericks of Number Two Operating Section were probably viewed by the rest of the unit as least likely to succeed.

It follows that alliances would quickly be formed among those of like mind, often with hell-raising results. The most cohesive alliance — and the most troublesome to the officers — was one of which I inadvertently became a member. It was made up of Dave Corbett, the professor-to-be, from Magog, Québec, who'd come over from the Tank Corps, and future deputy minister Guy D'Avignon, from Montreal. Those two were our leading adventurers and *bon vivants*. Don Laut, of Bracebridge, Ontario, and I — from Brantford — had been together since the Horse Palace, and we were the staid, non-drinking members of the group. There was also Bert Pusey, a service corpsman from Sarnia, and an avid yachtsman in civilian life; Charlie Stanes, "the Gunner," the "Newfie from Toronto," and already a five-year army man; and an assortment of others who came and went.

When the unit was isolated at Mills Road, we rarely did more than the usual mischief. But when 24- or 36-hour passes unleashed the hell-raisers on Victoria, or even Vancouver, it was a different story. Soon after Christmas, Lieutenant-Colonel Wethey announced during a classroom session that we would be going to Australia, with later plans so far unknown. There was an oblique reference to India, but he did not elaborate on that.

With the knowledge that we would be gone from Vancouver Island early in the new year, there was little to deter pass-holders from living it up in whatever way they could. On New Year's Eve, three or four of us arrived in Victoria. One of the boys, I don't remember which, located a bootlegger who sold us a bottle of Scotch. Our anonymous leader later tasted it and pronounced it greatly watered-down. Still, after we'd each had a swig, the old year seemed very redundant and the new one showed great prospects.

It was a full year since I'd had my first drink ever — at a CKTB New Year's party, when one serving of eggnog sent me into an unbelievably happy state. On the brink of another new year, I was now taking my second libation. All four of us novices in the art of drinking — no match for the Gunner — performed disgracefully on the streets of Victoria, crashing theatre lineups and getting into a scuffle with some airmen, then reeling off to somewhere else unknown, until somehow we ended up in a Salvation Army hostel for the night.

As we later discovered, we weren't the only miscreants. Another group of Swiggers had run amok downtown at three a.m., stealing an antique horse-drawn stagecoach, a historical object that belonged to the city, and running it around — accompanied by a great deal of hooting and hollering — before wrecking it down by the harbour. Police rescued what was left of the relic and rounded up the rampagers, all of whom were Swiggers. It proved to be a delicate task for the unit's officers to spring the culprits loose the next day, but they managed to convince the authorities not to jail our colleagues without letting it slip that they were about to be shipped out of the country on top-secret wartime business. New Year's Eve 1944 was not a proud night for 1CSWG. Fortunately for the mayor of Victoria, it wasn't to be more than a week later that this pesky Signal Corps unit would be on its way to the South West Pacific and a new set of adventures.

On January 2, 1945, the unit was paraded out, hangovers and all, to be inspected by Major-General George Pearkes, V.C. — the commander-in-chief of the Canadian Army's Pacific forces. Twelve years later, this man would become minister of National Defence in the cabinet of Prime Minister John Diefenbaker. A day or two later, it was Colonel W.L. Laurie, director of signals from army headquarters in Ottawa, and Colonel A.B. St. Louis, chief signals officer of Pacific Command in Vancouver, who did the honours. General Pearkes observed that our battledress uniforms were looking rather worn, but we didn't get new ones. We did, however, get to exchange our grey woollen blankets, which we'd slept in for six months in a row, for new ones. Otherwise, we apparently passed our series of inspections by the top brass with a satisfactory rating.

One morning, we got an unusual ultimatum from Lieutenant Hank Koehler, our section commander. Hank lined us up and informed us that there were thirty cases of beer at the wet canteen, and that we couldn't take them with us. They would have to be disposed of instantly. That evening's session at the wet canteen was the wildest yet.

There was a quick short-arm inspection by a team of medical officers who ordered everybody to strip, looked in our mouths and at our penises, asked how we felt, looked us up and down, and ordered us to dress, all within about a minute. We were given a month's pay in U.S. dollars — I got $46. All of our radio vans and other vehicles and equipment were loaded into a freighter, the *Bristol Park*, and sent off to Australia. Signalman Morris bounced into Colonel Wethey's office to ask permission to marry, which he got.

Strangely, just before we left the Mills Road camp, we were handed American G.I. helmets. We had no idea of why, as we already had our regulation Canadian Army "tommy" helmets. When we arrived at Camp

Stoneman, near San Francisco, we were ordered to turn in the G.I. helmets and new Canadian helmets were issued. No explanation was ever given for the brief masquerade.

By about the end of the first week of 1945, we were strapping on our full gear, picking up our kit bags, filing aboard the chartered *Princess Patricia* at Victoria, and cruising across the Strait of Juan de Fuca to Seattle. The exercise that Lieutenant-Colonel Wethey called "Operation Salmon" was under way.

By this time, fully adaptable to any and all living conditions we might be called upon to endure, some of the Swiggers decided that the best way to pass the two-day rail journey through Washington and Oregon and into the glorious sunshine of California was to play poker and shoot craps, and plenty of each. Some U.S. servicemen who also happened to be on board played with bemused looks on their faces, not sure how to take these Yankee-talking strangers in British uniforms, with G.I. helmets in their packs.

Even the porters, past masters at the games, got in on the action. Hundreds of American dollars from the month's pay we'd been issued changed hands between Seattle and San Francisco, and as much of it found its way into Canadian pockets as American. Life on board a troop train was the picture of boredom; there was no reading material on hand and the novelty of seeing palm and orange trees was quickly wearing off. The Gunner, broke from poker and not noted as a scholarly reader, exclaimed the first night: "Lard Jeez, b'y, have to pull out an old letter or somethin' to pass the time!"

Stops at Seattle, Portland, Eugene (Oregon), and Sacramento saw us put off the train for quick route marches through the streets, led by Lieutenant Miller. We amazed the locals with our "British" uniforms and spit-and-polish parade style. They must have wondered if they'd been invaded by the British once again.

Slumping back in my seat on the train, I calculated that, at age nineteen, I'd already travelled 14,280 miles by train and over salt water, when I took into account my weekly railway commutes from St. Catharines to Brantford, the cross-country trip from Ontario, the sea crossing to Seattle, and now this jaunt down the U.S. west coast. Eventually I would log over 40,000 miles of travel by water and rail across two continents, the Pacific Ocean, and a couple of seas.

Camp Stoneman, where we were finally delivered, was forty miles east of San Francisco, next to a small town called, oddly, Pittsburg. We got there late in the day, transported from the Pittsburg railway depot by trucks piloted by a squad of harried, nattily attired U.S. Army personnel, and then marched in full kit and glory, with our officers leading each section, into the camp at the smartest drill clip possible. Without stopping, we marched straight onto a vast, paved parade ground — to the mixed astonishment, sneers, and distant whoops of American G.I.'s lounging and lying around the perimeter in their olive-drab fatigues. They'd evidently been forewarned of the impending arrival of some sort of foreign troops from the far north — perhaps they were expecting Inuit, all the way from the Arctic.

Marching along smartly and with the perfect coordination Lieutenant Miller had drilled into us — arms swinging high and knees lifted smartly with each step — we clicked most of the way across the asphalt. The parade ground covered at least three acres of land. On the piercing scream of the sergeant-major, 1CSWG came to a halt in perfect unison of steel-clad boot heels hitting the asphalt: one, two, three, *halt!* The snap of nearly three hundred heels in one loud crack sounded like a rifle shot. It echoed off the faraway barracks buildings and back. All was silent until about five seconds later, when a lone American soldier's awed voice could be heard drifting across the parade ground: "Ho-oly Jesus!"

Number One Canadian Special Wireless Group had arrived and made an impression — if mostly in the asphalt. Interestingly, about twenty years later or so, a Hollywood movie was made that began its story with the arrival of a group of hardened Canadian commandos at a U.S. Army camp in California. Their arrival in authentic Canadian uniforms, complete to the swift and precise march from their train to the smacking of boots as one on the parade ground, faithful even to the awed yelp from a U.S. soldier across the parade ground, had all the trappings of 1CSWG's arrival at Camp Stoneman.

It is tempting to think that, among the hundreds of U.S. uniforms clustered around the Camp Stoneman parade ground — or perhaps even among the khaki battledress of the 300-odd Canadians of 1CSWG — there was somewhere that day a future Hollywood screenwriter who made good in the movies, remembered the dramatic arrival of these rare birds called Canadians, and considered it a fitting scene to include in a dramatic movie script.

Chapter 5

San Francisco Over the Hill

Sprawling Camp Stoneman, a major staging point for whole armies bound for the Pacific war since its start, was an international community. Besides the thousands of American troops from all over the States, it hosted military personnel from the Australian air force, Dutch West Indies, Royal Navy, and numerous other odds and ends. Most of them had probably been sent to North America for some kind of training and were waiting to be shipped back to the war zone.

Now came Canadians, the first and only unit to go west (to the East) since the ill-fated battalion sent to Hong Kong and almost immediately into the prison camps of Imperial Nippon back in 1941. Even though we were from just next door, 1CSWG was something of a puzzle and a curiosity to our American hosts.

The camp food was great, compared to what we'd been served in Canadian camps. We'd arrived just past normal suppertime mess, but we were guided into a huge mess hall anyway, where there was a long, stainless-steel serving counter with food kept hot by steam heat, flanked by several cooks. Something else we'd never seen before were the aluminum food trays with depressions stamped into them to hold different foods, similar to the sort that would be commonplace in postwar cafeterias. As we shuffled along the railing in front of the serving counter, our eyes popped at the incredible banquet we were about to indulge in. One of the cooks, hustling like a beaver, apologized profusely for the lack of selection, but pointed out that we'd arrived late and vowed, "If we'd known youse was comin', we'd a' done youse up a real feed." We burst out laughing. The spread that lay before us was better than what most of us had been eating at home, let alone in the army.

During the week or so that 1CSWG was parked at Stoneman, awaiting the order to board a troopship, most of the unit managed to get passes to visit the Golden Gate City, San Francisco, roughly thirty miles away. We were as much of an oddity to the civilians as we were to the men of Stoneman. Already used to being hailed as "the British" in camp, on the streets we were pegged as "Scotchmen," Frenchmen, New Zealanders, Aussies — everything but Canadians. After she'd absorbed the news that I was Canadian, a hostess at the Stage Door Canteen in San Francisco asked me, in wide-eyed, innocent amazement, "However did you learn to speak English so well?" Word had apparently circulated in town that Canadians spoke only French. Another lady thought our berets (not yet worn by U.S. troops) were snappy, but she didn't seem to believe that we were legitimate soldiers.

One of my oddest experiences came the day I was walking through the camp and was called to a halt by an American officer. He was black and a captain. I snapped to attention and saluted as smartly as I would have done to one of our own officers. I hadn't noticed any black soldiers in the camp, but it flashed through my mind that they would have been segregated off into another area. Stiff, motionless, and blank of face, I stood there as the captain, with a mix of amusement and kindness, inspected me up very close as if catching a specimen of one of those northern "Britishers" was something of a triumph for him. Pleasantly, he asked me a few questions as an officer inspecting a parade might do. I answered, apparently amusing him further with my Canadian accent — sounding so much like someone from the northern states and not at all like an Englishman. Then he dismissed me. I saluted again and, still the well-drilled soldier, turned smartly left and walked away. He watched me go, still amused.

The near-perfect weather — dry and 75 degrees — was a drastic and pleasant change from the mist and damp of Victoria. The excitement of being within a stone's throw of one of the world's most famous and romantic cities made us all impatient to get passes to spend a couple of days visiting San Francisco, even though we'd be moved there to board ship soon enough. Some in the non-commissioned ranks solved that one easily enough by just slipping out some back gate and finding their own way to the city, pass or no pass. The Gunner vanished on the very first day. He was later reportedly seen several times by some of the boys who wangled legitimate leaves, shambling along the streets and in and out of the joints of San Francisco's entertainment and red-light districts, oblivious to his surroundings. He may as well have been back in Victoria, or St. John's. He eventually returned to camp, unscathed, several days later when he had run out of money. Not a single military policeman or 1CSWG officer was the wiser — or, at least, none admitted to knowing about his absence.

For the first couple of days at Camp Stoneman, we of Number Two Section were trotted out for parade square drill, presumably to keep the Americans suitably impressed. In the evenings, groups of us roamed the camp, which was almost a complete city in itself, with its own first-class movie theatre, bowling alley, swimming pool, and most of the other features of a comfortable holiday resort. The conditions that the U.S. troops enjoyed never ceased to boggle our minds. The two-storey barracks blocks could well be considered high-end housing in some underdeveloped parts of the world, even today. And the camp's paved roads, gardens, and airy, screened recreation hall made the place one that any lowly Canadian soldier might have been happy to inhabit for the duration of the war. The food was first-class, and even ice cream cones were available.

As the days passed, the glow of the Golden Gate City seemed to beckon us from beyond the nearby Sierra Nevada hills. But most of us didn't get off Scot-free the way the Gunner seemed to. Twenty-four-hour passes to go to the city were handed out according to some obscure plan so that some of us would always be in camp, or theoretically so. After some time it became clear that Number Two Ops Mon Sigs was the last part of 1CSWG still camp-bound. With only a few days before we were to leave — although we didn't know that yet — word got out that passes were available. Available to all, that is, except for a hapless half-dozen. It turned out that there were approximately three hundred Lee-Enfield .303 rifles — ours — to pack in grease for the Pacific crossing. We quickly held a draw for the passes, and I was one of the six who missed out. The boys who did secure passes vanished like snow in a Chinook.

Greasing by hand the unit's three hundred rifles, a task that seemed to us to belong more to the Technical Maintenance section, was akin to mud wrestling, with the difference that mud can easily be washed off, while rifle grease has to first be scraped off, then scrubbed with soap, and finally boiled out of one's clothing. Our coveralls were soon coated and saturated with the green-black grease, as were all bits of exposed skin and hair.

My coveralls actually remained in that state until long after we reached Australia. We had been told that we could get passes to San Francisco as soon as we'd completed the grease job, so, when the chore was done, I hastily stuffed the filthy clothes into my rubberized ground sheet and stowed it away in the bottom of my kit bag. There they stayed for nearly four months, when I finally was able to hang a large cooking pot over a campfire and thoroughly boil out the grease, leaving the khaki cloth white as bone.

The six of us who wallowed far into the night in the grease pit of one of the camp's garages — under the watchful eye of an unfortunate corporal — ran through every known curse word in the English language and some frilly French expletives from our bilingual buddies, despite D'Avignon's claim that to swear the worst he had to do it in English. It wasn't enough to relieve the horror of the evening. We even tried singing uplifting wet canteen ditties such as "Friggin' in the Riggin'," but our spirits stayed down in the grease pit. Finally, sometime after two a.m., the job was finished. Rolling up our grease-monkey outfits and dousing each other with gasoline to get the black gunk off our skins, we showered and scrubbed for another half-hour or so, then stumbled away at last to our barracks where we fell into our bunks like the walking dead.

Although still exhausted, we somehow managed to rise at eight o'clock that morning and reel off to breakfast. There were about a dozen of us who'd drawn various types of fatigue duties, and there were no other Canadian uniforms visible among the masses in the huge mess hall. We all had our twenty-four-hour passes, now partly used up because of our midnight ramble with the rifles, and we were determined to get to San Francisco without further ado.

When we arrived at the bus station in Pittsburg, outside the camp, we were in relatively good spirits, despite the fact that it was now raining. One or two of the boys were nearly sidetracked by the scantily dressed hookers who lurked around the station in their come-hither stances, each swinging her loop of love beads in one hand while the other hand rode on a hip. Then someone discovered that there were no more buses for San Francisco that morning. The soggy air went blue with strings of curses that caused even the hookers to back away. For a while, there was a push to commandeer a bus and drive it to the city ourselves, if need be. But the proximity of some hard-boiled U.S. Marine Corps service cops was reason enough to drop that idea.

Finally, one of the more brilliant among us suggested that we *charter* a bus instead. And that's what we did. A group of drivers was loitering a little way off, and it was easy to find a volunteer to take us bumpkins, dressed in funny clothes, anywhere we wanted to go. Over the Sierra Nevadas and down the Pacific slope to Oakland we went. We got off the bus somewhere in Oakland, then hopped onto the electric train that whisked us across the San Francisco–Oakland Bay Bridge — the world's longest at the time, and the one that partially collapsed in the 1989 earthquake — and into the fabled city by the bay. On the way the rain clouds cleared, the sun shone, and we burst into song.

One of the hazards of visiting a foreign city in a strange uniform is that you are so conspicuous. As we wandered along downtown sidewalks searching for the glamour that was rumoured to be at every corner (most of which were tarnished by hookers), we kept attracting the attention of passers-by. The Canadian change in our pockets was accepted only with great skepticism, along with suspicious looks at our uniforms — in particular, our berets.

However, we managed to take in all the sights and drink in the exquisite California air (yes, it was exquisite then). By evening, the six original refugees had dwindled to four, the others having drifted off at one of those glamorous street corners. Those who remained were, coincidentally, all jazz fans, and we spent the evening prowling streets where it seemed as if bars featuring a small combo could be found through every second doorway. The ever-present hookers loitered around the doorways, eyeing us with hope and interest. Don Laut had a habit of clucking his tongue at me in such situations to remind me of my recent commitment back home; he did the same to Bert Pusey, who was married. (Ted Allen, the fourth member of our group, had a girl-friend in Vancouver and seemed impervious to the ladies.) Don needn't have bothered at this point. We were only on one-day passes, so we would have to be back in camp by eight the next morning if we were to avoid arrest.

Eventually, we picked a saloon from which some good jazz was emanating. Almost instantly a bouncer appeared and demanded our

I.D. cards. The roughneck in a tuxedo informed us that no one under twenty-one could drink in the bars — and none of us was even twenty, except Pusey, who was twenty-three. Our I.D. cards couldn't lie. As we hit some of the other spots, it became a challenge in itself to dodge the bouncers long enough to take in some jazz — and even grab a quick drink — before they moved in. But it was never long before we were "invited" to leave.

So, once more navigating past the hookers, we headed for the Stage Door Canteen and snacked and danced with the respectable young matrons and debutantes of San Francisco — who were forbidden, we found out, to date the servicemen they met there. Still, we had a great time. A leader in swing, Charlie Barnet, was on the bandstand, which excited those of us who knew his band's music.

The night, and the Canteen, were filled with a swirl of deafening big-band music and jitterbugging bodies, male and female, in every kind of uniform imaginable: sailor suits from the U.S. and Royal Navies; Dutch Army pinks; Women's Army Corps (WAC) and Women's Navy (WAVE) outfits; U.S. Air Force tans; and Royal Australian Air Force blues. There was also a kilt or two and we even caught an occasional glimpse of the alien Canadian khaki. Everywhere, legs, arms, and heads bobbed franti-cally to a red-hot boogie beat in the semi-darkness. The entire room was lit only by myriad flashes of light reflected from a great mirror-covered sphere that hung from a ceiling hidden high in the darkness above.

The few drinks we'd had during our tour of the bars were catching up as we hadn't had dinner. The edges of the evening grew less and less dis-tinct, our companions less identifiable, and our whereabouts more ques-tionable. So we four — augmented here and there by a few Yanks who would join us briefly and then drift off — headed out to look for some solid food. The evening seemed to culminate in our joining forces with a gang of American sailors off one of the battleships anchored in San Francisco Bay who knew, as all sailors do, where a great party was going on. It was happening in a bar where the bouncers didn't care how old you were. Needless to say, we never did get a proper meal into our stomachs, and things shortly became very disorienting. With some help from our sailor friends, we found a service hostel where we bunked for the night. The Great San Francisco Adventure was over — for the time being.

Groans. More groans and grunts. Somebody had woken up in the room where six of us slept like supine statues. He was swearing at his wristwatch. It was nine o'clock in the morning. The mellow California sunlight was streaming through a window. Only a few of the rest of us also woke up, while the others lay still as chiselled stone.

"They'll be looking for us at camp," Bert said, swinging himself out of his cot and sitting on the edge in his shorts. He lit a cigarette and got the reviving drag of nicotine into his lungs as quickly as possible. "We're supposed to be back there by now."

Our passes had expired and here we were still in the middle of San Francisco, hardly even awake yet. Being absent without leave (AWL) didn't seem so strange after all, at least not yet.

"What the hell," Ted grunted, "they won't be going any place today," then he groaned and grasped his rocky head with both hands. The morning after had come too quickly in the wake of the night before.

"Well, we're all in it now," somebody said from under his blanket. "I'm for staying till noon."

Despite the lack of logic in that remark, and after someone else recalled how the Gunner had gotten away with his extended visit, we all slid into agreeing that we might just as well stay and enjoy life. After all, what could be worse than an evening greasing rifles? The sergeant-major couldn't find a worse job than that to punish us for overstaying our leave. And they couldn't court-martial us all, could they? Getting up at noon, having a leisurely brunch in one of the fancy downtown restaurants, and heading out to see the sights of San Francisco by morning light would be a pleasurable way to wait for the real opportunity of serving our country, we reassured ourselves with great bravado. Surely we were owed a break after being picked so arbitrarily to grease rifles.

There were shows still to be seen. We found a huge burlesque theatre where the humour and language were actually rawer, if at all possible, than the average day's conversation in the barracks. After that, we moved on to another theatre, where Ella Mae Morse, the star swing vocalist of 1944, was featured along with Johnny "Scat" Davis and his band, whose star was then high but has long since set. By the time we got out of that show, we had just enough time — and money — left to make the late afternoon bus back to Camp Stoneman. We kept our eyes peeled for military police who would want to look at our passes, now as ancient as the Sphinx. We eluded them.

"Jeez, are you b'ys in shit!"

That was the kind greeting we got from the Gunner as we silent four Ops Mon Sigs tried to slip unseen into our barracks block two hours late. The Gunner was all slicked up, and what's more, he was wearing his steel helmet with a big number 6 chalked on the front. More incredibly, he was cold sober and was acting every inch the good soldier. The whole unit was in battledress and steel helmets, all with the number 6 on the front. Most were striding out of the barracks block with their full kit slung on. It was plain that something big was up. We soon found out what.

Sergeant-Major John Addy was near the point of exploding as he broke the news to us. He lined up all four offenders, his face already nearly purple, and blasted out the news that during our absence an American general had come to inspect the unit. Lieutenant-Colonel Wethey was very angry with us. He would see us in the morning. (I hadn't previously thought the colonel was even aware we existed.) Meanwhile, we were to get our kit packed and get our helmets chalked with the number 6 and turn in our bedding to the quartermaster's office, because we were being shipped overseas the next day! Wouldn't you know it!

All through the process of getting "registered" for the ocean trip, we kept running into our buddies, all of whom grinned tightly and took their turns at different, smug ways of telling us that we were in the deep-six with the colonel. One or two knew what they were talking about, because they'd already gone through the process of coming back from AWL and been paraded before the C.O. They'd had pay docked. A couple of others, namely Boombaw and Pierre deMal, were sickeningly gleeful at the prospect of what awaited us the next morning. This pair had actually vanished from the camp without passes the same day as the Gunner, stayed in town nearly a week, and gotten back into camp without anybody knowing they were gone. And now they had passes for our last evening at Camp Stoneman and were about to head out for a final fling. How they'd snagged the passes was top secret, they said. But there was this little WAC in the orderly office…

At 0900 hours the next day, nine nervous soldiers marched at quick pace, with the sergeant-major barking behind them, headed for Lieutenant-Colonel Wethey's office. Three of the gang were corporals from the favoured Intelligence Corps section. Two others were from Motor Transport and Technical Maintenance. We other four were from Number Two Ops Mon

Sigs. All in all, it was a broad cross-section of 1CSWG. We were brought to a smart halt in the anteroom outside the colonel's office and lined up along a wall. The sergeant-major called me out first — I had no idea why, unless I was held to be the ringleader — snapped an order to hand over my beret, did a snappy about-face, and, with me behind him and two corporals behind me, marched us into the office in precision form.

The window blinds were drawn. Ranged around the room were two or three lieutenants, all of them wearing Browning .45s in holsters as if to warn that I would be gunned down if I made the slightest move to attack the colonel. With a spring-loaded salute to the C.O. seated behind a desk, the sergeant-major rapped out my name — "Signalman Murray, G.S., *sah!*" — and stepped aside to let the culprit be fully scrutinized. I stood at rigid attention, bareheaded, awaiting the caress of the axe on my neck. Even thus paralyzed, I was still able to take in the melodramatic scene. Lieutenant-Colonel Wethey, grim-faced and decked out in a uniform that looked crisp enough to crumble if he bent one inch, his brass rank insignia — a crown and crossed swords — glittering on each shoulder, gave me a regulation withering stare. On either side of him, standing at ease, was a captain. I found myself actually shaking in my boots.

I was impressed for the first time how fiercely the officers were taking this breach of iron discipline. I wondered bitterly what they would have done had they only known — or if I could prove — that a couple of dozen others of the unit had gone AWL for days on end, compared with our two hours. But, I supposed, they had to make an example of this nineteen-year-old, blond, blue-eyed criminal who seemed to have put 1CSWG in some sort of great peril. The implication seemed to be that to go AWL just as the unit was about to embark for overseas constituted desertion, which would have carried a very severe penalty — in the U.S. Army it would mean twenty years in prison.

The colonel asked if I had anything to say. As I'd been coached before-hand by one of the miscreants disciplined the day before, I answered that it was "unavoidable, sir," and that I would accept the C.O.'s punishment. The sentence: I was docked thirty days' pay. I thanked the colonel for this outrage, another tip from my barracks-room adviser.

The sergeant-major rapped out an "About face!" and I spun around in classic Miller parade-ground style, then, on "Queek march!" strode out of the darkened office in regulation form. Outside, I got my beret back and was shooed away to barracks. In the open, free from the oppression of the dark chamber full of brass, I puzzled over what it was all about. Although I'd been asked if I had anything to say, and had followed my buddy's advice, it occurred to me that there should have been, perhaps, an officer assigned to defend me. I could have briefed him on the unfairness of the assignment to grease rifles even though my buddies and I had already been granted twenty-four-hour leave.

After all, who among our superiors had failed to order that the greasing job be done earlier in our Stoneman stay, instead making it necessary to be done at the last moment? Surely if this could be brought up it would have been a mitigating circumstance. But this was the army, not a democracy. I didn't care much about the docked pay, because I knew we'd be travelling for the next month or so and there wouldn't be much need for ready cash anyway. Still, I resented being made an example for such a trivial matter as overstaying leave by two hours where others had been gone for days.

I didn't know it at the time, but that loss of thirty days' pay would represent thirty days I was technically not in the army. Long after the return home, I would find out that the blank month deprived me of a proportionate number of "points" needed for army discharge, delaying my departure from the army and reducing my demobilizing "cash entitlement." Then, upon entering my second year of university, I would learn that I wasn't going to get any more tuition money from my "re-establishment credit" to continue my education. That was a severe blow. I had to struggle to complete my degree on my own meagre finances, never forgetting Lieutenant-Colonel Wethey's dramatic little bureaucratic charade and his heavy-handed punishment, which was akin to killing a fly with a sledgehammer.

Such was our reward for trustfully volunteering twice for active wartime service, for the filth and the hours spent in the middle of the night greasing rifles that were never to be fired in anger, and for the hard construction labour we would be forced to do later at Darwin. I and the other punished active service volunteers would, once our wartime usefulness was over, re-enter civilian life very late and with few enough dollars to rub together for a long, long time.

An element of irony was added to the whole episode when, later in the day, the order to get ready for embarkation was cancelled. That meant all the Swiggers, and the thousands of U.S. troops, who'd gone to such lengths to suit up with full pack, steel helmets, kit bags, and everything else they had to carry, now had to dump all that gear or sleep in it. The next day, the order came all over again to get ready, and the suiting-up ritual had to be repeated. This delay rendered moot the whole question of our apparent desertion at the time of embarkation. We wouldn't have missed the boat after all.

Chapter 6

The Troopship as Floating Theatre

The USAT *Monterey* — a prewar luxury liner owned by the Matson Steamship Line of San Francisco — and her sister ship the *Lurline* had cruised the Pacific in exotic splendour for over a decade before the war, taking the wealthy on holidays to Hawaii, Fiji, Bali, Sydney, Manila, and even Tokyo. The ship's wireless officer on the *Lurline* had, in fact, detected strange coded signals while on a cruise to Hawaii on December 7, 1941 — as well as frantic plain-language signals from Honolulu saying that Pearl Harbor was under attack by Japanese aircraft. These signals were among the earliest, if not *the* earliest, news of the assault.

As the United States went to war, both liners were converted to troopships, and they shuttled tens of thousands of American military personnel across the Pacific — in the early days mainly to Australia, and later, as the fighting moved northward and new Allied bases were established, to deepwater ports in the Pacific islands.

If anything resembles a floating theatre in which the audience is also the cast, it is a troopship in wartime. In mid-January 1945, with the war in the Pacific at fever pitch, the *Monterey* would become our home and stage. We were joined by five thousand U.S. troops, most of whom were headed for the new battlegrounds of the Philippines. Only two weeks beforehand, General MacArthur's forces had made their first landing at the Lingayen Gulf, and the Battle of Manila was just about to begin. Two thousand of the Americans were black — mostly "pioneers" whose job would be building roads, bridges, and airfields in battle zones. For us Canadians, to whom black people were for the most part a novelty, the sight of so many filing onto the lower decks where they'd been billeted was astounding. The white troops were mostly paratroopers, as young as we were and hard as hickory. In about a month they would be dropping from the skies over the Philippines to whatever fate they were to meet on the ground.

Getting to the ship from Camp Stoneman had been a trek in itself. The Americans did everything in a style of their own. After breakfast — at 0530 — we'd been marched for two or three miles at the rear of an immense double column of shambling G.I.'s to a dock on the Sacramento River where, in relays, we filed onto a large riverboat. We were played aboard by a military band which blared out marches and swing tunes from the dock. The riverboat trip was made all the more interesting by the old tub's tendency to tip to one side whenever there was something particularly special to be seen along the riverbank. And there were some spectacular sights in the form of young women who sunbathed and waved gaily at the brave boys going downstream. As three or four hundred men all trotted from one side of the deck to the other in hopes of getting an eyeful, the captain's voice would boom out over the public-address system: "Everybody to port!" or "Everybody to starboard!" as he tried to keep his ship trimmed and avoid capsizing. His pleas were usually drowned out by wolf whistles. Somehow we sailed down the river without incident.

As we passed through the mouth of the Sacramento and entered San Francisco Bay, there ahead of us on the starboard side crouched "the Rock": Alcatraz, the famous escape-proof prison for America's most hardened criminals, which was still very much in use in those days. It was a grim sight, despite the sunny skies and silky air. There were no signs of life from our vantage point. Resigned to our fate in the Pacific, we could relate to the plight of the convicts who, we imagined, were no doubt staring back at us through their barred windows.

Next we saw the masses of aircraft carriers, battleships, cruisers, and destroyers anchored in the bay and awaiting sailing orders. We had an excellent view of the Bay Bridge and later the underside of the Golden Gate Bridge, which was only fourteen years old as we sailed beneath it.

A brass band played "Stardust" and ladies of the United Service Organizations (USO) greeted us on the dock to serve us coffee and cookies as we disembarked from the Sacramento riverboat and made our way to the *Monterey*. Laden with packs, mess cans, steel helmets, and kit bags, we were herded up the gangway and a couple of flights of companionways to B Deck — which was luxury class in the old cruise-ship days — where we were in for a shock. What was once the ship's ballroom was now a jungle of horizontal canvas sheets laced to an intricate structure of vertical plumber's pipes to create a system of bunks a foot and a half wide and six feet long, stacked four high, one above the other. Narrow aisles ran between the double rows. As many bodies as possible could be crammed into this gigantic seagoing barracks. The wealthy holidaying folks of the 1930s would never have tolerated such overcrowding. The rugged soldiers of the '40s had no choice.

For the next three weeks, about 250 Canadians would be stored in this space at night like unrefrigerated sides of beef. Even in San Francisco's temperate climate, the "ballroom" was already hot and sticky. The closer we came to the equator on our South Seas voyage, the more unbearable these quarters were to become. Finally, no longer able to endure lying in our bunks naked and bathed in sweat, we would try sleeping on the bare deck outside. There we would not only still be sweaty, but also covered with soot from the ship's funnel when the engineers put on extra speed (and more smoke) at night. By day, smoke was cut to foil Japanese submarines.

Even the deck and its soot would have been better than sleeping head-to-head and feet-to-feet, if not head-to-feet in some cases. We did manage to create bizarre, semi-private worlds for ourselves within our one-and-a-half by six-foot domains by hanging our web-belt packs and other rig on the cross pipes. A side effect was that this helped to further reduce the circulation of air. Of course, there was no air conditioning. You just had to sweat it out, literally.

The 1CSWG officers were quartered on the deck above us, an appropriately symbolic placing. In peacetime, those were the most luxurious quarters. We took some satisfaction in knowing they would likely be as crowded as we were because of the great numbers of American officers who would be quartered up there as well. It was unlikely, however, that they'd be sleeping in canvas cots stacked one above the other. This satisfaction was dampened by the knowledge that the girls of the USO entertainment troop, the nurses, and the female army and navy officers were also billeted only on the boat deck. That was the army: take and take.

Despite our lowly status as mere signalmen, four or five of us contrived to amble out onto the boat deck during our exploratory wanderings about the ship. The U.S. service police hadn't yet learned — and probably never did — to tell the difference between officers and other ranks in Canadian uniforms, so we managed to get some long, close-up looks at the sunbathing USO girls. Of course, whenever any of our own officers came into view we made a rapid descent to the lower decks. There were plenty of these: B, C, D, E, and F decks — and even, down below the waterline, G deck. That's where the two thousand black troops were billeted. I supposed their officers were somewhere down there, too.

There were only two meals a day, breakfast and supper. We ate standing up at waist-high counters fixed to the deck, after bringing our meals up from the mess hall, which was about six decks below. The mess hall could only be reached after joining a lineup that wound down six flights of stairs and along corridors rich with the odours of army cooking — and military bodies. The discomfort index rose higher as long as we obeyed orders issued over the P.A. system and wore our Mae West life jackets at all times. This practice died out as the air temperature got warmer and warmer with each passing day.

When dusk began to fall and all had gone ashore who were going ashore — which amounted to almost no one, as the military cops kept steely eyes on all the ship's decks — the liner cleared the dock and cruised through the bay and under the Golden Gate Bridge, just as she had done — with a more genteel passenger list — countless times in the '30s. We left San Francisco Bay for the open sea with all the ship's outer lights doused in a blackout that would last all the way to New Guinea. The city lights threw the *Monterey*'s bulk into silhouette, which would make the ship easy enough to spot for the Japanese submarines that slunk up and down North America's west coast looking for such a juicy target as a heavily laden troopship.

While the U.S. Navy probably had firm control over enemy submarines near the mouth of the bay, we'd be on our own once we entered the open sea. The plan was for the *Monterey* to make a quick, zigzagging, solitary dash across the Pacific — without an escort and not as part of a convoy. With a top speed of 32 knots, she was certainly fast enough to carry off the feat.

The night sky over the Pacific was perfectly clear; the moon's reflection shimmered over the water's surface and the stars blinked the way they always had over Canada — except that they were all shifted to slightly different positions. Aside from the novelty of the steady heaving of the deck, like an endless up-and-down ride on a forgetful elevator, onboard life didn't seem all that great a change to us. The Pacific was, so far, living up to its name.

The boat deck and its girls were the preserve of the officers, so there was no choice but to confine our sightseeing to other parts of the big ship's insides. Signalmen Corbett, D'Avignon, Kerfoot, Wolfe, and Murray went on the hunt for some kind of entertainment. The decks were blacked out, but the noise made by more than five thousand troops seemed as if it could have reached Tokyo. Hundreds of newly minted sailors in khaki and olive drab bumped and groped their way around the outer decks, stumbling around, laughing and shouting to their buddies as they sought out doorways hidden in U-shaped light traps, marked only by faintly luminous arrows labelled "Exit." Smoking was prohibited on the darkened decks. It was actually brighter out on the ocean than it was on the ship until we finally stumbled through the light traps and into the dimly lit interior saloons and cabins, most of them furnished with the same pipes-and-canvas bunk system that we had in the ballroom.

We came across one room that was full of smoke and servicemen of all kinds. A group of black soldiers from the Dutch West Indies sang in Spanish and played guitars and maracas, spreading a rich mixture of Caribbean sounds over the Pacific waves. The ship began to sway slightly, the deck coming up to meet our feet before we were quite ready. Combined with the chatter of several different languages and the cigarette and cigar smoke lying thick in the air, there was an atmosphere unlike anything else on earth. From out of thousands of packs came bottles of Scotch, bourbon, rye, rum, and brandy that always appear magically at such gatherings.

There was a huge, floating party going on all over the ship, with about five thousand guests and the ship's crew as hosts, or at least onlookers. It would be impossible to guess just how many gallons of liquor flowed through all those thousands of kidneys, but it probably would have been enough to sink the ship if it were poured directly into the hull. Fortunately, the ship's capacious latrines, ever-flowing with salt water pumped from the ocean and back, helped in their own way to keep the *Monterey* afloat. There must have been, though, an alcoholic content to the ship's wake that would have given a monstrous hangover to any dolphins that happened to be following.

We moved on to another long, narrow, low-ceilinged room in which the rich vacationers of the 1930s had once crowded around roulette and chemin de fer tables. Now the bare floor was obscured by rings of soldiers, white and black, sitting and squatting, bare to the waist, surrounded by tall stacks of money, shooting craps with great gusto. In one corner, a black soldier played jazz music on a baby grand piano. He was accompanied on guitar, industriously and expertly, by one of our own Canadian Intelligence Section corporals, who also broke into song sporadically. A mostly black crowd gathered around the two of them, shouting encouragement ("Go, man, go!").

Around three or four in the morning, by which time just about all the oxygen had been exhausted from the room, we groped our way out to the deck, getting entangled with unseen people in the darkness of the light traps and even on deck, where you could see your hand raised to your face only if it were held up against the starry sky. We were under orders to go to bed partly dressed on the chance that a sub might do some target practice during the night, so we got down to our shorts and slid horizontally into our bunks in total darkness for a reasonable night's sleep.

Despite its size and the aid of gyroscopes, the big ship was rolling around in the water next morning. We were well out in the open ocean, with no sight of land anywhere — it would be about a dozen more days before we again saw a coastline. The sunlight was red hot and flying fish were skimming over the deep blue waves. Three or four of our boys were seasick. I had been finding the voyage quite palatable until I tried to shave in the seawater that poured out of the latrine taps. Not even the saltwater soap we'd been provided would lather in it. And there were no freshwater showers — except perhaps on the boat deck. Being left with a coating of salt after bathing sure didn't help ease our discomfort.

Incidentally, the long row of latrine toilets ran constantly with a steady flow of seawater — after all, there was no need to flush in the middle of the ocean. There were no laundry facilities, as the soap wouldn't lather anyway, so our uniforms, filthy from rolling around on the dirty decks, had to stay that way.

Down in the mess hall, about six decks below B deck, the thick, super-heated air killed one's appetite for the scrambled eggs and thin porridge that were offered up for breakfast. There being no other meal until supper, however, I gulped what I could and stuffed an orange into my pocket to snack on later. Don Laut and I bolted for the nearest open deck. The fresh sea air brought us back to partial health. We found ourselves standing on a deck full of black soldiers stripped to the waist, as far as the eye could see. They sat on the deck in circles, their legs crossed, and they shot craps, as they and their buddies had been doing the night before. Curious, we walked among them carefully, but none of them looked up, so intent were they on winning.

A slender, fully dressed man in a civilian cap saw us and approached, bouncing slightly, and asked, with a twinkle in his eye, what a couple of white Englishmen were doing on this deck. Didn't we know this was Harlem afloat? Then he launched into a great, good-natured guffaw and began bragging about the boxing matches he'd been in. Next he made a fist and showed us the great brass ring just below the middle knuckle on his right hand. A short, sharp metal stub projected from it, mutely hinting at the devastation that a punch from this fist would do to someone's face. He laughed again and threw a shadow punch in the air with it. Laut and I laughed, too — if only to mask our nervousness — shook the hand that wore the ring, and made a quick exit from that deck.

This deck and the next one down — below the waterline and literally in the bilge — were the quarters for the black soldiers. It wasn't hard to imagine that, if a torpedo were to hit, the two lower decks would be the first submerged. I suppose this reflected the U.S. Army's priorities.

There was absolutely nothing for us to do aboard the but wander about or read whatever books we had with us or could scrounge. There weren't even kitchen fatigue duties: the owners of the Matson Line had actually paid a hundred or so U.S. servicemen to work in the kitchens, serve food, and clean up. Otherwise, it would have been a sure bet that all of us San Francisco AWL miscreants would have spent the whole voyage in the kitchens.

There was no wet canteen on board for carousing. The private enterprisers among us bought cases of beer at the P.X. (post exchange) down on E Deck, then sold the individual bottles to the violently thirsty G.I.'s and Canadians at a dollar apiece. The well-paid G.I.'s would give anything for a bottle, while the Canadians had to conserve their depleted reserves of U.S. cash.

We weren't the only Commonwealth servicemen on board the *Monterey*. Sharing the ballroom with us were four or five Royal Navy sods and a half-dozen Aussie air force non-coms on their way to operations Down Under. None of them would divulge what their business was. And neither would we. There was that top-secret thing again. Still, relations between the three different Commonwealth services were raucous but good-natured, except for an argument or two between Bert Pusey and the Aussies as to who actually had an accent. Pusey maintained that Canadians had no accent, and that the Aussies, Englishmen, and Scots put them on for show. That bit of mischief almost led to a fistfight, but the potential combatants were cooled off with beer.

The days and nights passed with no break in the routine, while the *Monterey* stayed on its zigzagging, southwesterly path, changing direction slightly every twenty minutes or so to spoil the aim of any Japanese sub commander who might be trying to draw a bead on her. From aboard the ship you could plainly see it happen — for a while the moon would be over your left shoulder, then, when you noticed it again, it would be over your right.

One benefit to the daily monotony, however, was that we hardly saw our 1CSWG officers during the entire trip. We and they were having a welcome vacation from each other. They knew that there was zero chance of our going AWL again, and we knew that they had more to occupy them on the boat deck.

On one of our evening rambles around the ship, we came upon a band of jazz musicians practising down on one of the lower decks. They were the USO band, civilians going out to the war zones to entertain the troops. Trombonist Snub Mosley, a famous New Orleans jazzman who'd played with Louis Armstrong, was the leader. The bass player had been with growl-trumpeter Cootie Williams's band. The alto sax man, Bill Johnson, was the band's arranger. He had been a member of Erskine Hawkins's band from 1936 until recently and he co-wrote the famous Glenn Miller hit "Tuxedo Junction." Johnson lived in Canada for a while after the war. We never learned the full name of Sam the pianist, but despite a strong resemblance he wasn't Dooley Wilson, who played Sam the piano player in the movie *Casablanca*, made only four years before. Nor did we identify the rest of the band, but from the way they performed we could tell they were obviously jazz veterans. Those who shared my appreciation of jazz and swing couldn't believe our good luck to be in the presence of such greats.

From then on, the ship seemed like a series of floating Hollywood sound stages, as the musicians filled the blacked-out nights with spontaneous New Orleans and Chicago jazz in the "lounges." Meanwhile, thousands of crap-shooters and poker players could be seen sprawled about the decks. U.S. Navy gunners slouched alongside the amidships Oerlikon .50-calibre antiair-craft machine guns and the eight-inch cannon at the stern, their round white sailor caps down over their eyes. Beautiful USO, WAC, and WAVE girls sunned themselves on the edge of the boat deck, tantalizingly visible from below. American brass chomped cigars as they strolled in groups around the crowded decks, peering blindly through their black sunglasses.

During the daytime, the waters of the ink-blue Pacific frothed white alongside the ship's hull as flying fish sailed along the wave crests. Under the hot daytime sun one might have expected, against the art-deco back-drop provided by the 1930s luxury liner, to round a corner and come upon Groucho Marx and his brothers tormenting Margaret Dumont or panicking some waitress along the open-sided, covered deck. Instead, now there were just more sweaty, half-clad bodies, all of them male. By night, the sea was sinister and beautiful as its raggedy road of silver reached toward the moon and heaved under the inverted bowl of enor-mous stars that seemed to come all the way down to rest on the wire-straight horizon. Phosphorus flickered and flared along the ship's hull at night as it sliced through the black water. We constantly battled to sup-press the thought that, somewhere beneath that enchanting seascape, a hostile submarine might be slowly poising itself to take all five thousand of us down into those depths.

The sun rose farther off to port each morning as the *Monterey* made its way along its southwesterly course each day. Its line of navigation was, of course, secret, but we were sliding south of Hawaii and toward the Gilbert and Ellice Islands, with the Solomons and New Guinea our ultimate destination. The punishing daytime heat forced the Commonwealth troops into regula-tion shorts, an item the Americans lacked. Lying around in their long pants, they spoke enviously of our khaki shorts. Had they been allowed to wear them, they probably would have paid top dollar for our extra pairs. Our sleeping quarters were so hot we could have baked bread on the bunks, as Boombaw quipped. The mess deck was worse. Sunburn was a constant threat to our fair northern complexions. Unexpectedly, my own skin went gradually went from light to dark brown without a burn, which I would certainly have sustained back in Canada.

The only other object we saw in five days of fast sailing over the mirror-like sea was a small freighter we passed. The monotony of perfect, tropical weather was relieved from time to time by a grand practice show put on by the gunnery crews, who would send up gas-filled balloons and pick them off with their tracer-firing Oerlikons, Brownings, and a three-inch cannon. The grand finale to the show was marked by the eight-incher sending a shell or two over the rudder at a box set adrift in the wake. Their accuracy was reassuring. It gave us hope that there would be at least some retaliation against whatever we might encounter as we entered the South West Pacific war zone.

Our uniforms were becoming even more abominably filthy, but they'd have to stay that way until we landed somewhere on solid ground. Sudden rainstorms, though, gave us a chance to strip down and shower in the falling fresh water, which also gave our discarded clothes a rudimentary rinsing, but these occasions were rare and brief.

We crossed the equator almost exactly where it is bisected by the International Date Line southwest of Tarawa, and passed among the Gilberts. As we crossed the date line we leapfrogged from Sunday, January 28 to Tuesday, January 30. Most of 1CSWG hailed this event, mainly because it meant gaining a day's pay without having to put in the day itself. We San Francisco vagabonds earned nothing, however, as our pay for the month had been docked.

As we crossed the equator, the *Monterey* was suddenly boarded by some outlandishly dressed individuals, who turned out to be King Neptune and his court. Over the public-address system came the belligerent declaration that Neptune had arrived to punish the landlubbers who'd dared to enter his domain. It seemed that all who'd never before crossed the equator were subject to trial by His Majesty — who, under his false beard, crown, and sarong was a member of the ship's crew who had made many crossings and was thus a veteran "Shellback". All of us newcomers were to be turned into Shellbacks and subjects of Neptune without delay.

Neptune's authority was challenged by thousands of landlubbers who yelled, waved "the finger," and crowded along the rails of the top four decks, overlooking the giant notch amidships where the hull deck was exposed. At this display of impertinence, the king's henchmen seized a number of seasoned crewmen. As punishment for bringing so many landlubbers with them, Neptune announced, he sentenced these veteran Shellbacks to a dunking in a makeshift pool of seawater created by dipping a huge hatchcover canvas over the side of the ship and hauling it up by crane to the wide expanse of deck that the king declared to be his court. They were then paddled with oars and slapped with brightly coloured calcimine paint for good measure. Every now and then a court devil — in fiendish costume — aimed the swab hose at the tiers of yelling and waving landlubbers hanging on the deck rails above and gave us all a good dousing of seawater.

At last enough landlubbers had been punished to appease King Neptune. He brandished his trident ominously at the new Shellbacks and, with his entourage of devils, went over the side and down a rope ladder into a ship's boat tied below. The boat then slid back along the hull to a point out of general sight at the stern, where its inhabitants, crewmen once again, climbed back aboard. Thus were five thousand landlubbers inducted into the Ancient Order of Shellbacks in one fell swoop. We all were issued with cards testifying that we had indeed been initiated. I still have mine.

Chapter 7

Magic in the Torrid Zone

The *Monterey* zigzagged on, southwest through the Gilberts and the Santa Cruz Islands, then bore due west, just to the north of Espiritu Santo and to the south of San Cristobal, the most easterly of the Solomon Islands. We were now in the war zone. While the focus of the fighting was the Philippines, all of these island archipelagos were still riddled with Japanese troops that Australian and American forces were "cleaning up."

One by one we passed the Solomons. Some were tiny islets bearing one or two palm trees, just like you'd see in a cartoon. A couple of miles to starboard was Guadalcanal, where U.S. forces made their first landing in the South West Pacific, and where fierce fighting — on land and sea — extended from August 1942 until February 1943. Next was Bougainville, where the plane carrying Imperial Japanese Navy Admiral Isoroku Yamamoto had been shot down by Lockheed Lightning aircraft, thanks to the interception of Japanese radio signals by Allied Special Wireless. We passed a strangely shaped craft that turned out to be a U.S. Liberty ship

— a type of hastily built armaments supply freighter which sometimes broke in two at sea.

We veered through the deep waters of the Solomon Sea toward the slot between the north coast of New Guinea and the southern tip of New Britain. On this island, Australians were engaged in a ferocious struggle to gain possession of the peninsula on whose point perched Rabaul, a major Japanese base which had long since been deprived of aircraft and naval support and was now in the final stages of the Japanese Eighth Army's dwindling defence. On the New Guinea side of this slot, the Vitiaz Strait, the same process was going on against the remains of the Japanese Second Army under Lieutenant-General Fusataro Teshima and part of the Eighteenth under Lieutenant-General Hatazo Adachi. Here, Australian and American units had crammed the Japanese into a pocket between the Sepik River and the town of Wewak.

We were close enough to this shore that we could easily see the surf breaking on the white strand that separated turquoise ocean from the dark green jungles of New Guinea. High above humped the Owen Stanley Mountains, carpeted over by the jungle and running in irregular bumps to form a 15,000-foot-high spine along most of the island's 1,400-mile length. It was their disastrous attempt to surmount the Owen Stanleys by means of the Kokoda Trail — in a bid to capture Port Moresby on the south coast — that stopped the Japanese land advance in the South West Pacific before it reached Australia. Retreating to the north coast, they were eventually out-manoeuvred by combined Australian and U.S. forces under General MacArthur and largely annihilated. As we progressed along the north coast at night, we saw vivid flashes light the sky as Allied bombers pounded the Japanese Eighteenth Army's last major stronghold at Wewak, isolated by the Allied offensive of six months earlier.

Other signs of battle began to appear. A Dakota cargo plane flew low over the *Monterey*, followed by another, and then three Corsair fighters. We began to feel that we hadn't been sailed off the edge of the world after all. An Australian Beaufighter circled and then paced us at a couple of thousand feet, vanishing and reappearing now and then for most of a day. We zipped on past another freighter, came alongside a couple of Australian Navy frigates in jagged black-and-yellow camouflage, and left them behind, too. We were in what our crew told us was the hottest spot in the world. Even the simple effort of scribbling down some facts in a notebook were enough to break out a sweat. Snub Mosley and his boys played jazz on the after deck, glistening with sweat, their instruments looking hot as stoves.

Even though we hadn't seen land in twelve days, the view of the green-carpeted mountains of New Guinea on one side and the lower-lying New Britain on the other began to bore us. The USO troupe tried to mount a full-scale show on the hull deck, for which an American officer of junior rank had lined up a whole series of acts. He took the stage (the main hatch cover) to announce, "This show is being put on for the mortification of our enemies and the enjoyment of friends." Before the first act could go on, an order came down from a U.S. colonel — said to be a Southerner — that no act could take place in which both blacks and white appeared on stage at the same time. This, of course, stalled the show. Negotiations between the officers resulted in a compromise: in the dancing acts, blacks and whites could perform together — as long as they didn't touch. Mosley's band refused to play at first, but after more talks — which included some of 1CSWG's officers and men — they agreed to go on.

In spite of the limitations, quite a creditable show did come off. Some of the Canadians joined the fun, doing the jitterbug with the USO girls and performing in singing acts and even on guitars. The audience of thousands, hanging over the deck rails above, sent up a roar that the Japanese and the inhabitants of the nearby islands must have taken to be some sort of tribal rite. The show did end on a bitter note; the junior officer acting as master of ceremonies closed with: "I retract what I said at the beginning. I'll say now that this show was put on for the mortification of our friends and the enjoyment of our enemies." We didn't learn what fate befell the young man as a result of his barefaced frankness.

At night the blacked-out coastal villages were as invisible as our darkened ship. A "latrinogram" circulated that we were going to put into a port late that night, but the destination was unknown to the rumour mongers. Next morning, we woke up to find that the *Monterey* was indeed alongside a dock. The high, jungle-covered hills of Dutch New Guinea sloping down to within about a hundred yards of us. An incredibly tall Papuan native, imposing in a fantastic costume and headdress of grasses and beads, with a bone through his nose, stood alone on the dock below, holding up a fish-flat full of native jewellery for us to buy. He wasn't a tourist prop. He was the real thing, an indigenous entrepreneur, showing that private enterprise was flourishing even as war roared nearby. Some twin-fuselage P-38 Lockheed Lightnings dodged around above the harbour. We'd apparently arrived overnight at our first stop in the South West Pacific: Finschhafen, New Guinea.

The view of Finschhafen from the decks of the *Monterey* struck us as something out of the pages of a Joseph Conrad novel. The high, green hills descended almost to the water's edge, hiding mysteries under their heaps of steaming vegetation. Air as hot as a blast furnace, was saturated with the rancid smell of the sodden jungle. Enormous royal palm trees lining the shore, dwarfed everything around them. A clearing in the jungle, on the far side of the harbour, where bamboo huts on tall stilts were crammed together, was ominously devoid of life. A harbour filled with rusting tankers, fore-and-aft sailing schooners, brigs and luggers, lay among rakish modern fighting ships.

Decidedly foreign to the world of Conrad's *An Outcast of the Islands* were the Allied fighter planes constantly buzzing about, giving a clue to the existence of the airfield lying just over the hills. The whole scene was no less foreign to a green Canadian youth. At night the heavy, wet smell of rotting vegetation was made even more oppressive by the falling of a light rain.

We were delighted, however, to learn that we had arrived at our landfall just as the military in this part of New Guinea was declaring an end to blackouts. The Japanese, though still toughing it out in pockets like Wewak — along the coast to the west of us — and over on nearby New Britain, were almost completely out of aircraft, thanks to the activities of the same friendly fighters buzzing around us and their colleagues based on U.S. aircraft carriers farther north.

Recaptured just a little over a year before as part of the massive Allied assault on the eastern end of New Guinea, Finschhafen was a busy supply port. Small launches sped around between the anchored ships like puppies around elephants, sputtering, barking, and gurgling. Also cruising among them were the unusual-looking "Alligators" — wheeled, amphibious craft. It was a strange sight to see one of these vehicles come racing down a road that ended at the water's edge and just keep right on going across the water. At night, when flares marked the meeting of road and water, we might see a pair of headlights approach through the dark of the land, sweep down toward the harbour, hesitate for a moment between a pair of flares, and then continue smoothly over water toward a ship anchored far from shore.

On our first night without a blackout, the movie *Louis Pasteur* was shown on deck. It was the first movie we had seen since San Francisco, and there was Paul Muni, spread large across the silver screen. Beyond him the South Pacific night sky, sparkling with stars that seemed to hang down lower and larger than they ever did in the northern hemisphere, provided the backdrop.

In the morning, the heat left us weak and listless even after a reasonably good night's sleep. The temperature was well over 115 degrees, with humidity probably close to 90 percent. The metallic voice that usually came over the ship's loudspeakers countless times a day to give out endless orders clicked on and intoned: "Attention please, attention please… hear this! United States military forces have just captured the Philippines capital of Manila…" It was February 5, 1945. The news had little impact on us. It was just another battle in what seemed a lifelong series that had gone on forever and would go on and on. It was just as well: the announcement was the product of wishful thinking on the part of some information officer. Manila did not actually fall until three weeks later.

We hung over the ship's rail, panting in the heat, staring at the green world spread around us, entertained mainly by the loudspeaker system, which had resumed its work of calling Loo-tenant so-and-so to Room 11, please. We'd become familiar with the names of these unseen officials. One of them was, quaintly, Corporal Woodrow Wilson. The old U.S. president's namesake was called upon frequently.

A steamy, soul-destroying day was spent in the still heat of Finschhafen harbour, as the ship's crew no doubt awaited orders as to where the *Monterey* should head next in light of the latrinogram about the fall of Manila. The New Guinea mosquitoes found us, but we'd already been issued atabrin tablets to thwart the malaria bug that the pesky insects carried. Atabrin turned one's skin yellow, which, combined with our suntans, gave our bodies a strange bronze hue. When we were in Sydney immediately after the war, it was easy to recognize Australian veterans who'd served in the islands by this same residual yellow-brown skin tone.

All around us, the harbour's business carried on. Landing craft troops (LCTs) chugged around, piled high with heaps of green camouflaged boxes, while Alligators sliced through the water like pleasure launches. A fore-and-aft-rigged schooner hove into sight, laden with heavily armed, sun-blackened Australians in digger hats, shorts, and boots. Some of them wore reddened bandages around heads, arms, ribs, or legs. They looked out morosely from under a makeshift sun canopy of canvas sail on the foredeck, their rifles and Bren guns across their knees or being used for support. They were returning from action on New Britain, and were headed for the Finschhafen army hospital.

When we awoke the next morning, Finschhafen was gone — the *Monterey* was cleaving its way westward through deep blue water along New Guinea's north coast. To starboard was the big island of New Britain, which, with a couple of smaller islands, crowded close to New Guinea to form the narrow passageway of the Vitiaz Strait, linking the Solomon Sea with the Bismarck Sea. About three years before, all of these waters had been the scene of savage naval warfare as the Japanese navy destroyed the sea power of the Dutch, who had owned the East Indies for centuries. As well, they eliminated the sparse British and U.S. naval forces scattered around the Bismarck and Solomon Seas.

Twenty-three months before the *Monterey* approached the eastern end of the Vitiaz Strait, all the Allied air forces in the South West Pacific had converged upon a major Japanese troop convoy of between eight and twelve transports and the same number of destroyers. There were nearly seven thousand men aboard the ships. Using a then-new technique known as skip-bombing, in which delayed-fuse bombs were dropped almost at water level so that they bounced and skimmed along the surface and hit the enemy ships' hulls side-on, the Allied squadron of Flying Fortresses, Liberators, Mitchells, Havocs, Lightnings, Beaufighters, and Kittyhawks rained machine-gun and cannon fire on the wildly manoeuvring Japanese ships. In turn, the Japanese filled the air with antiaircraft fire until the skip bombs crippled them. All but four destroyers were finished off by seven American torpedo boats. Six Allied aircraft were lost.

Known afterward as the Battle of the Bismarck Sea, the encounter actually took place in the Vitiaz Strait at the point where it joins the Solomon Sea. The battle was an example of how Allied Special Wireless was able to pick up details of Japan's plans for the convoy by closely monitoring their signals and thus enable the Allied forces to concentrate a massive striking force at the right time and place. As a result of this loss of thousands of their troops, Japanese Imperial Headquarters ordered that no more troop or supply convoys be sent to New Guinea on surface ships. Instead, their armies were to be supplied by submarine wherever possible. Detecting more of these kinds of enemy operations would be the role of Number One Canadian Special Wireless Group once we were operating in Australia.

Shortly after the Battle of the Bismarck Sea, again tipped off by Australian or American Special Wireless, Allied Mitchell bombers and

Lockheed Lightnings destroyed 100 Japanese Fourth Air Army aircraft lined up neatly on the airfield at Wewak. The commander conceded in his (monitored) communiqués that the Allies had achieved a "decisive victory." Thereafter, with the aid of Special Wireless, the Allies began to get the upper hand in the Solomon Islands and New Guinea.

In April 1944, only about ten months before the *Monterey* slipped through the Vitiaz Strait with 1CSWG aboard, Australian and U.S. forces landed at and captured nearby Aitape, halfway along the New Guinea coast, and Hollandia, our next stop. This lengthy campaign, which broke up the Japanese Eighteenth Army, was cited by General MacArthur as one of his most important strategic victories; he later said it "initiated a marked change in the tempo of my advance westward." If that momentum could be maintained, he believed, prospects for the liberation of all of New Guinea were promising. Japanese General Adachi, whose army was pocketed below Hollandia, waited helplessly and in vain for help or some word from headquarters about what to do next. After two months of this, he called on his troops to make a suicide breakthrough at Aitape, on the coast between Hollandia and Wewak. His regimental communications were intercepted by Australian and American Special Wireless and the plan was detected. The Japanese Eighth Army ended up completely surrounded and chopped into three segments. Their suicide rushes resulted in wave after wave of Japanese troops being cut down by machine-gun and artillery fire. Every move that General Adachi made, as well as every detail about the number of troops he had and their supply situation, had been mapped by Special Wireless.

Aboard the *Monterey* it was a beautiful day — a fresh breeze was blowing, there was a sizzling sun high overhead, and there was none of the stickiness to which we'd grown accustomed. But though we'd escaped the close heat of Finschhafen, we were still on the sun's anvil, having the sweat pounded out of us. Prickly heat rash was epidemic. A box of large Hershey chocolate bars that I'd bought in the P.X. held nothing but a mess of liquid chocolate floating in dark blue wrappers. I dumped this exotic treat overboard for the local marine life to enjoy.

A day later we were sliding between two great rocky heads into the vast harbour of Hollandia, a former Dutch trading centre known today by the Indonesians as Djajapura, and one of the best deepwater ports among the islands. The harbour was so big that there were even islands in the middle

The *USS Monterey*, anchored at Hollandia, New Guinea, after transporting ICSWG across the Pacific from San Francisco in February, 1945. The Canadians were transferred here by LCTs from the *Monterey* to the *Shawnee* for the trip farther south to Australia.

of it. As at Finschhafen, it was stocked with former ocean liners turned into troopships, merchant freighters, destroyers, cruisers, and at least one aircraft carrier, all in port for supplies, repairs, or transshipment of troops. Even filled with all of these seagoing giants, there was still open water.

Several Black Widow night fighters — the latest word in fighter aircraft and the first to carry on-board radar — zoomed low over the harbour, looking suitably vicious in their black paint. Many LCTs moved about among the ships, ferrying personnel, ammunition, weapons, and other supplies. Later, when night fell, signal lamps flickered their dots and dashes of silent light from ship to ship, from ship to shore, and back, transmitting a multiplicity of orders. This stealth was a byproduct of the radio blackout maintained for the benefit of our opposite numbers, the Japanese wireless monitors.

Hollandia's most notable feature besides its harbour — as there seemed not to be any town or village near the water — was a red gash in the steep, towering green hillside. This was a road, which laid bare the red soil of New Guinea as it wound it way up over the hills from the harbour. A continuous cloud of red dust seemed to hang over it as endless convoys of trucks nosed their way up or down, carrying supplies and ammunition to the Allied fighting units a few miles inland. The red road dust coated the jungle all around this traffic artery, creating what from mid-harbour showed as a great pinkish smudge on the green landscape.

On our first afternoon at Hollandia we got orders to be ready to disembark. We rushed to pack up our kits. Sweltering from the exertion in the heat, all of us in 1CSWG were completely rigged out in tropical battledress — our fifty pounds or so of web belts, web packs, kit bags, and helmets — and were starting to file out on deck when, in typical army style, the tinny loudspeaker crackled: "Attention please… attention please… designated personnel will not disembark until tomorrow a.m.…." We slept on deck that night — having surrendered to the heat and the mosquitoes — fully rigged out, ready for the call whenever it might actually come.

We repeated the procedure the next morning, and again it turned out to be a false alarm. We got the order a third time that afternoon, and this time the army meant it. In full pack, we climbed down the side of the *Monterey* and onto a couple of LCTs as they shuttled us, in groups of a dozen at a time, across the harbour to our new temporary home, a U.S. Navy troop carrier called the *Shawnee*. We wouldn't see the *Monterey* again until a year later, when she turned up in Sydney harbour after the war. As we chugged away from the *Monterey* we waved an energetic goodbye to the people we'd met on board and who now lined the rails, waving back just as enthusiastically. Among them were the RAAF men and Royal Navy sailors we'd befriended on the Pacific crossing. We expected we would never see them again.

One of the sailors was a midshipman named Jimmy, from Dundee, Scotland. He had served in the Royal Navy since the beginning of the war, mainly in the Mediterranean. He told stories, laconically but vividly, of his rambles throughout Egypt, Palestine, Turkey, and Cyprus after his ship had left him behind. In the autumn of 1942, Jimmy was in a Cairo military hospital with a case of pneumonia he had contracted while his cruiser lay off Tobruk. Then General Montgomery's El Alamein campaign began, and the cruiser made a quick exit. Upon his release from hospital, Jimmy took a train to Palestine. He had some worthless German money he'd picked up from a wounded Australian, and he had a good time spending it among trusting merchants — and girls — in a Jerusalem bazaar.

He hitched a ride on a truck convoy bound for a British outpost in Turkey. After a while, he caught on with another that was going to Haifa. Stranded there, he held up a thumb to an approaching truck and was picked up. The driver was, incredibly, one of his shipmates from the cruiser, which was now anchored in Haifa harbour! Back on board, he found out about the action his shipmates had seen near Gibraltar while Jimmy was doing his circle tour. In return, he told them of the Turkish girls who wore only "bloomers," and how he'd stayed several jumps ahead of irate Turkish husbands. Jimmy's tales of his Arabian adventures made many an evening on the *Monterey* more entertaining than a movie.

The *Shawnee*, our new seagoing home, was a much smaller ship, and had spent, the crew told us, many months transporting troops among the islands on landing operations. It hadn't been in dry dock in all that time, as was evident from the ship's filthy condition. Since we were already so filthy ourselves, however, it didn't matter much. Boarding the *Shawnee*, we tottered under the weight of our packs — which by now seemed to weigh a ton — up three decks. Our perspiration splashed like big raindrops on the planking.

The first surprise was that we now had cabins — each of which housed four men in a space of about eight feet by ten — and the bunks actually had some headroom. On the other hand, the cabin had a sink with two taps — but no water. And the cabin was stinking hot. Before dumping my packs I flung up one of the window sashes — not a porthole, as you might expect — which instantly came right back down on the first joint of the middle finger on my left hand. I was the first among the new boys on the *Shawnee* to need first aid.

We soon found out we were to share our passage to Australia with another army: the cockroach brigade. They were everywhere. The Gunner wanted the ship renamed *La Cucaracha*. We were also to find that the durable little beasts made their homes primarily in the life jackets supplied us as we came on board. Later, we would ceremoniously heave the life jackets — and their cockroach residents — overboard; they sank immediately. The infestation of the ship slackened considerably after that.

Our next surprise came when we found that, bunked in on the next deck down, were the RAAF, Dutch West Indies, and Royal Navy men we'd thought were remaining on board the *Monterey*, including the aforementioned Jimmy. Much handshaking and backslapping took place. There were about two hundred of these fellow voyagers in all. The five thousand American troops had stayed aboard the *Monterey*, their next stop being the battles in the Philippines.

We were to linger in Hollandia harbour for a couple days more. From the *Shawnee*, we could see the goings-on from a different angle. Signal beams from the dozens of ships were busy again that night, striping the heavens, flashing a tangled web of flickering, anxious light probes across the sky, tying together communication links for brief instants, asking questions, sending orders, gossiping. The old hands of our unit, who knew all forms of telegraphic signalling, could read them. One flashing beam asked, "Anybody aboard from Cleveland?" "No, but I'm from Missouri," the reply went back. A strong beam flashed from somewhere behind one of the harbour islands, repeatedly calling "KQXY," which were the *Shawnee's* call letters. *Shawnee's* signaller replied over and over to go ahead, but with a much weaker beam that seemed to be invisible to the caller beyond the island. At last, a signaller on a third ship, who could see both *Shawnee* and the caller, flashed a signal that he'd act as a go-between. He then relayed signals from our ship to the unseen one, in a code our people couldn't decipher.

Aboard the *Shawnee*, a smaller world than the *Monterey* and one whose crew had been around the islands for many months, the latrinogram service improved. We learned that, some time before the *Monterey* entered Hollandia harbour, a Japanese sub had sneaked in and fired torpedoes at the anchored ships and a dock. The story was that the torpedoes bounced off and did no real damage. The sub had made its way out of the harbour and was now believed to be lurking somewhere under the Bismarck Sea or the Vitiaz Strait, territory through which we would again soon be passing on our way farther south. Looking back, the blackout on the *Monterey* while we were at sea may well have kept us from being spotted by the sub as it headed out from Hollandia at the same time as we drew near. Had the sub seen us, more than five thousand Allied troops might have gone to the bottom of the strait to join the six thousand Japanese and their ships sunk months before.

After the war, Mochitsura Hashimoto, one of the last Japanese sub commanders to survive the war, would publish his book, *Sunk*, the story of the Japanese Submarine Fleet from 1942 to 1945. It was a tale of total calamity, but one that featured many triumphs and heroic endeavours. One of his accounts described how, in January 1945, the Japanese Imperial Navy formed the Kongo Unit from the six large submarines of the latest type that they had left. Each of the subs was assigned a target along an arc formed by strategic island bases recently captured by the Allies; this arc represented a curved line of defence that the Japanese intended to hold west of the Philippines. The sub *I.36* was to proceed to Ulithi, the *I.58* (commanded by Hashimoto) to Guam, the *I.56* to the Admiralty Islands, the *I.53* to Palau, the *I.48* to attack Ulithi later on January 20, and the

I.47 to attack Hollandia. They were also to attack shipping along the way.

While the others proceeded with either no or limited success, the *I.47* "penetrated safely Hollandia harbour during daylight on January 11. She got in while enemy patrol craft were in the midst of firing practice. She reached the launching position and launched all of her torpedoes at intervals of half an hour from four a.m. At daylight the shore base W/T (wireless telegraph) station was heard transmitting a succession of 'SS's,' which was thought to indicate a submarine attack or sighting. Consequently, *I.47* left on her return trip with no doubts concerning the success of the attack." By the time the *Monterey* arrived in Hollandia, there was no sign of damage from the *I.47*'s torpedoes. But there was no doubt the sub was still lurking in the vicinity of the Vitiaz Strait when the *Monterey* passed through. Fortunately for us, the Japanese sub seemed to have used up all its torpedoes in Hollandia harbour.

The *I.47* had more adventures before Hashimoto last mentioned her. She was one of the four subs, each carrying six *kaitens* (one-man suicide submarines), that formed the Tatara unit, which left the base at Kure, Japan, on March 29, 1945. She surfaced at one point and was attacked by "over fifty small aircraft which she had thought to be friendly," and crash-dived. At 2:30 a.m., while cruising on the surface, she sighted two warships at 6,000 yards, dived for an attack when the lookout reported them as cruisers, then discovered by periscope that they were actually destroyers. Too late to rectify the mistake, the *I.47* endured four hours of depth-charge attack before escaping. She surfaced after sunset, and her crew was busy trying to find an oil leak when she was again attacked by aircraft and crash-dived. The oil leak got worse, and the *I.47* returned to Kure.

Next, she was part of the Amatake unit. Leaving the Kure base on April 12 and April 20 respectively, the *I.47* and *I.36*, making up the two-sub unit, headed for the waters around Okinawa. Eight of the twelve *kaiten* suicide subs they carried were launched, and each of these, Hashimoto says, accounted for a transport or a destroyer. After that, there is no further reference to the *I.47*.

Only one Japanese submarine — Hashimoto's — survived the war intact. Again, the success of the Allied anti-submarine forces against the Japanese can be attributed in part to Special Wireless, as orders radioed to the Japanese subs from Imperial Navy headquarters were closely monitored and provided a relentless pattern of their whereabouts. Of course, when the subs observed radio silence they were capable of surprises such as the *I.47*'s adventures in Hollandia harbour.

Chapter 8

Bogged down in Brisbane

Throughout the campaign to wipe out the Japanese in New Guinea — and thereby provide a massive base from which to supply the Philippines invasion thrust — Allied air and sea power had been hammering Japanese airfields and supply convoys under the guidance of Special Wireless monitoring. In June 1944, for example, General Adachi's Eighteenth Army was found to be in a perilous state after an intercepted message to Tokyo from Southern Army headquarters stated clearly that, because of shortages created by the attack on Aitape, the army would have trouble carrying on if 28 tonnes (31.1 tons) of supplies were not delivered by two RO submarines.

A later signal picked up by Special Wireless said that an all-out attack would be launched near Aitape around July 10. It also contained the information that the 20th, 41st, and 51st Divisions would be involved, that about twenty thousand troops would be thrown into the battle, and it gave out key Japanese unit locations. As a result of these revelations — transmitted from Tokyo in complete ignorance that they were being decoded by Allied monitors — Adachi's attack was a disaster from which the Eighteenth Army never recovered, despite the tenacity of its troops in hanging on until most of the way through 1945.

When we first laid eyes on the sad collection of American soldiers who were helped onto the *Shawnee* as we lay anchored at Oro Bay, near the eastern end of New Guinea, we realized that as badly off as we thought ourselves to be, we could have been much, much worse. Burned almost black from the sun — and where they weren't burned they were bright yellow from prolonged intake of atabrin to fend off malaria — our new shipmates numbered about five hundred, and were some of the wounded, burnt-out casualties of the battles that were slowly wearing down the remnants of General Adachi's troops. They seemed to be faring little better than the trapped Japanese who were holding out fanatically at Wewak despite disease, starvation, and dwindling medical and food supplies. The Americans' ragged uniforms hung from them as if they were scarecrows as they limped, hung onto the ship's rail and fumbled along, or had to be helped aboard by medics. Some seemed to be blind. Many were heavily bound with red-stained bandages, some had plaster body or arm casts. Some just walked along glassy-eyed, with vacant expressions on their faces, apparently shell-shocked or simply robbed of their sanity by the incredible conditions of fighting a war in the superheated New Guinea jungles.

The appearance of these hundreds of terribly wounded G.I.'s puts the lie to statements published elsewhere that General MacArthur moved his American troops from Hollandia to points west along paths of glory to the Philippines, leaving the Australians alone to mop up the remaining Japanese. In fact, American troops were still in the eastern end of New Guinea on February 12, 1945, when the *Shawnee* touched in at Oro Bay.

Meanwhile, the signalmen of 1CSWG found that, aboard the *Shawnee*, we were to become galley slaves. We were no longer under the umbrella of the Matson Line, with its own paid staff of G.I.'s to handle kitchen fatigue. Workers were needed for kitchen and cleanup duties, and the logical patsies — from the official view — were the low men on the totem pole, the Canadians. We were shanghaied into the detail, for which we drew no extra pay. No apologies were made. We just had to follow orders.

I was serving time in the superheated, below-decks mess hall the day the wounded G.I.'s came aboard. Outside on the deck, the very air burned on the skin, but down below it seemed to burn the lungs as well. The heat was enough to cause the butter on a slice of bread to melt instantly and run across the table in a yellow, oily stream. My post in the food line was on the sugar can, where I stood clad only in the now-customary dirty shorts and sneakers, doling out spoonsful of sugar into enamelled tea mugs as each soldier came by with his mess cans. Shirtless, we still perspired copiously enough for our shorts and even our canvas sneakers to be soaked. I did my best to keep the sweat that was bursting out all over my body from rolling down my arm and into the sugar, but none of the jungle casualties would have been alert enough to notice, nor even care.

The walking wounded limped along, seemingly oblivious to the heat — or at least putting it down as the least of their problems. Some mumbled incoherently, their eyes closed, while others moved mechanically like zombies, their heads up but their eyes blank, trying their best with shaking hands to hold out their mess trays for food, aided by white-jacketed medical orderlies.

When we kitchen workers got our chance to eat, the sweat ran into our eyes and mouth, robbing the food of all its taste. Washing down the hot food with hot tea didn't make things any more comfortable. At the end of a ten-minute meal I would feel kitten-weak. This was a far cry from the sumptuous meals at temperate Camp Stoneman. And after meals, there was no escape from the incredible heat, as the mess hall deck still had to be swabbed.

Perhaps the most dramatic — and dangerous — task was getting the dixie vats of boiling hot soup or stew up from the galley onto the next deck, just below the mess hall. The companionway from the galley to the deck above was a steel ladder that led straight up through a round opening measuring about two feet across by three feet deep — just big enough to take the brimming dixie vat, but not if a human body were also trying to get through at the same time.

For this manoeuvre the Canadian sweats had to work in teams of two. One galley slave had to go up the ladder first, extending one arm down to grasp one of the vat's handles. Once he'd made it up through the hole he would reach down for the other handle. Meanwhile, a second man struggled to steady that other handle far above his head while he inched his way up the ladder. He ran the greater risk of being scalded if the vat tipped its burbling, volcanic contents. Naturally, we took turns being the top or bottom man on the ladder.

Once we were up the ladder and through the hole — understandably, a slow process — the team still had to carry the vat and its payload of between fifty and a hundred pounds of hot lava to the serving counter, which was at least another fifty feet away. Then we heaved the dixie up onto the serving counter and lowered it into a hole made for it. Our bodies quickly gave up trying to protest the superhuman effort required to complete our chores in the 120-degree heat of the mess hall. (The thermometer reached 150 in the galley, and of course the vats of soup were near the boiling point at 200 degrees.) We simply collapsed when the ordeal was over. I began to think that volunteering for active infantry service might have been a better choice than this hellish servitude.

The galley was a hellhole of a kind all its own. Large, black U.S. Navy cooks in chef's whites worked in the torrid heat over long, coal-burning stoves, singing dolefully to themselves most of the time, oblivious to the plight of the Canadian boys who had to tote the dixies. They would step back from stirring the soup or stew just long enough for us to lift the dixie off the stove, barely glancing at us from the corners of bloodshot eyes, and then hoist an empty dixie onto the stove to fill with another batch. I wondered at first why they didn't open the row of portholes that ran at about eye level above the stoves to cool the galley down a little. Upon further examination I saw why: the blue waters of the Bismarck Sea were sliding by just a few inches below porthole level. Keeping out the sea — in the event that the *Shawnee* careened to port slightly — was more important than getting the temperature down.

The *Shawnee* had taken us out of Hollandia, into the Bismarck Sea, and back east again toward Finschhafen and the Vitiaz Strait. Australia would be our ultimate destination. We passed through the strait about nine o'clock at night and, with our ship blacked out, sailed past Finschhafen. The scattered lights of the town stretched out across about two miles of the dark hulk of land at sea level. Casting a sheen over the sea that rivalled any lunar reflection, the planet Venus hung low and bright over the black cutout silhouette of the Owen Stanley Range against a sky of deep blue. Next to the moon it was the brightest celestial body I'd ever seen in a night sky.

On the water between us and Finschhafen there loomed a dim hulk showing one red riding light. From the erratic way the light shifted, first here, then there, it seemed that some odd kind of vessel was twisting and turning as it slowly warped its way toward Finschhafen. Jimmy, our Scottish naval chum, hung over the *Shawnee's* rail beside me as we watched the hulk's progress into the darkness. "Anything queer-acting on the water," he said, "you can bet it's a Yankee."

Oro Bay, where we had taken the American wounded aboard, was close to the scene of one of the bloodiest Allied shore landings in 1943. Buna Beach, on the shore of Oro Bay, was captured early by the Japanese. From there they attempted their move along the infamous Kokoda Track and over the Owen Stanleys toward their target: Port Moresby, on the southern coast. More than six thousand Japanese troops were sent up the almost perpendicular, switchback track, but they were bombed and strafed so successfully by Australian aircraft that they abandoned the attempt and the survivors — shot-up, starving, malaria-ridden, and emaciated — struggled back to Buna. A supporting Japanese naval force, which had landed marines at Milne Bay on the eastern tip of New Guinea, was so heavily attacked by Royal Australian Air Force planes that it had to evacuate its troops out to sea again. It was the first major defeat of a seaborne invasion that the Japanese had suffered to that date.

Milne Bay, our next stop — where we were to drop off military personnel, wounded or otherwise, and take on others — was the farthest point southeast that the Japanese Imperial forces reached on land, and their repulse marked the end of the Japanese advance in the Pacific.

The 200-mile strip of New Guinea coast from Buna to Milne Bay betrayed no signs of war damage when we passed by. The jungle was quick to mask the scars that bombing had left, and the waters were deep enough to swallow without a trace any sunken Japanese invasion craft. We could see jungle animals coming down to thrash about in the shallow water near the shore. There were nothing else but the heat, the insects, the rough-and-ready docks, the lagoon-like green water, and the eastern extremities of the Owen Stanleys, now just foothills, rising quickly from points near the water's edge everywhere we looked. Milne Bay was several times bigger than the harbour at Hollandia, which we had thought was oversized, but here there were very few ships. Instead, the harbour was full of sharks.

When we left Milne Bay we left New Guinea behind. We passed through the low-lying Louisade Archipelago by way of the Jomard Passage, following almost precisely the route taken three years before by the Japanese aircraft carriers *Shokaku, Shoho,* and *Zuikaku,* together with two or three troop transports and destroyer escorts, when they entered the Coral Sea to round the tail of New Guinea and attack Port Moresby. Again, Allied Special Wireless detected and followed their progress. A smaller U.S. Navy task force, made up of the navy's only aircraft carriers to survive Pearl Harbor — the *Lexington* and the *Yorktown* — as well as a few destroyers, intercepted the Japanese fleet. In the famous Battle of the Coral Sea, the U.S. aircraft sank the *Shoho,* badly damaged the *Shokaku,* and inflicted minor damage on the *Zuikaku,* succeeding in turning back the attempted seaborne invasion.

The *Lexington* was extensively damaged and was later sunk deliberately by a torpedo from a U.S. destroyer. The *Yorktown* was also damaged and thought by the Japanese to have been sunk, but she was miraculously repaired in two days at Pearl Harbor, thousands of miles away. She was back in action in time to take part in the Battle of Midway in June, a month later. The Japanese withdrew their troop transports to their stronghold of Truk Island, and Port Moresby — and therefore Australia — remained free.

The Battle of the Coral Sea was the world's first carrier-to-carrier sea fight — the rival ships never even saw each other — and although it ended in a draw the Japanese Navy never again attempted to carry its fight beyond New Guinea's southeastern tip. When we sailed over the spot where the sunken *Shoho,* and later the *Lexington,* lay buried at sea, the Coral Sea was glassy, silent, and empty, with no indication of the site of the historic sea battle.

Somewhere on the South Coral Sea, someone aboard the *Shawnee* discovered a shipboard cache of swing records. As we steamed through the night toward Australia, all lights ablaze now, the strains of the Benny Goodman Sextet playing "Time on My Hands" and "Stompin' at the Savoy" surged through the ship and over the waves. It was the first jazz we'd heard since leaving Snub Mosley and his boys on the *Monterey.* It eased shipboard life somewhat.

Now, two days and two nights out from Milne Bay, the Aussies among us could smell home. Away to starboard, the darkness was pierced here and there by the odd pinpoint of light — lighthouses marking the jagged edges of the Great Barrier Reef that runs for 800 miles up and down the coast of Queensland. The Australians greeted each with whoops of delight. On the other side of the equation, we Canadians had come about as far from home as we possibly could without leaving the planet.

Twenty-seven days after leaving San Francisco, Number One Canadian Special Wireless Group and company steamed into the harbour at Brisbane, where the *Shawnee* was just one more ship in Queensland's chief port, to be manoeuvred and worried to the dock by two scrappy little tugboats. We had arrived Down Under. It had taken nearly a month for 1CSWG to transit the Pacific via New Guinea, a distance of nearly 11,000 miles. Today's tourists casually fly that distance in less than twenty-four hours. *Sic transit* the world.

Saying goodbye to the *Shawnee* — with its cockroaches and hellish galleys — was not all that heartbreaking to 1CSWG as we tramped down the gangplank under full pack. If any sentiments were uttered at all, they no doubt included a general muttering of obscene wishes over the shoulder at the floating roach and lice farm as our boots touched solid ground for the first time in four weeks.

The Brisbane docks were devoid of life. We hadn't expected crowds of well-wishers to greet us, but we did expect at least to see a busy waterfront, teeming with wartime dockyard activity, as we'd witnessed in the war zone at Hollandia. There we had seen huge cargo cranes swinging ominous loads of war materiel onto ships; stevedores sweating, swearing, and heaving boxes off trucks; bosses shouting and cursing their charges; quiet men in shirts and ties, carrying clipboards and carefully checking off war goods as they moved hither and yon. Here, apart from the tramp-tramp of Canadian parade drill boots and the snarl of the sergeant-major, there was peace and tranquility.

The scene was a stark contrast to Hollandia and Finschhafen, up on the firing line, where an occasional torpedo or two might liven up an already overworked and overcrowded harbour. If one were fired at the Brisbane docks, it wouldn't have killed anyone but a few new arrivals from Canada and perhaps some seagulls. As it turned out, the Brisbane dock workers were on strike — a labour hiatus that would be significant to 1CSWG in the very near future. Apparently, in the union's view, the war raging in the waters and islands to the north took second place to the longshoremen's grievances. Nothing moved unless it had its own feet. No one was in sight. I thought of the schooner full of wounded Aussies at Finschhafen and the burned-out Americans we'd picked up at Oro Bay who would be disembarking from the *Shawnee* at any moment.

A convoy of American trucks with Australian Army markings was lined up nearby, their motors cooking and grumbling in the heat as they waited for us to heave ourselves on board. We'd barely gotten used to solid ground after a month at sea, and now it was once again being yanked from under our feet as we prepared to travel the army way: by truck.

On that blazing February afternoon, the silent parade moved through the back streets of Brisbane — as if we were to be hidden from the populace as plague carriers — and on out through the pretty, semi-tropical countryside. All of the little frame houses we passed sat about eight feet off the ground on stilts designed to tire out any ants or termites who might wish to climb up for a visit.

Suddenly it dawned on us that we were slowing down in the midst of a strange-looking assortment of tin-roofed, Beaverboard huts scattered around a former farm field, overshadowed here and there by towering eucalyptus and gumwood trees. Without having passed through a grandiose gate or ceremonial camp entrance — as would have been the case in the States or even in Canada — we had arrived, we soon learned, at Chermside Camp, about five miles outside Brisbane. To herald our arrival, a tropical downpour immediately roared down and the camp became a porridge of puddles and mud.

After we'd had a few nights of sleeping, accompanied by the odd wandering lizard or two, on the huts' splintery floors on the two blankets each of us had carried in our packs all the way from Canada, the Australian quartermaster stores issued us each a big burlap sack. These were to be filled with straw and become palliasses — straw-filled mattresses. Lamentably, a truck dumped off enough straw to fill only about ten sacks. The Australian quartermaster's idea of a palliasse must have called for only a thin scattering of straw inside each bag. We Canadians were hardly spoiled after our long journey, but to us a reasonable straw mattress would be at least four inches thick. So, ten early birds slept in blissful comfort, while more than 250 signalmen and corporals would have to sleep on their two blankets — with an empty sack underneath. Naturally, the officers and non-coms, segregated from us in their own section of camp, slept in luxury on regulation wood-and-canvas cots.

Luxury barracks at Chermside camp near Brisbane where I CSWG marked time for two months, waiting for The Wet to end in Northern Australia so their trucks could use the primitive, bog-like roads. Seen here at a dry moment, the camp was usually a near-swamp.

Brisbane was no San Francisco, but we all wanted to get there anyway, if only to escape the bad food, mosquitoes, mud, and kitchen fatigue of Chermside — soon known to us as Germside. This time, 24-hour passes were not hard to get, and for eight pence each a bunch of us rode an open-air tram from Chermside to downtown Brisbane, which we soon were taught to pronounce "Brisbin." An apparently sizeable city with a fair quota of tall buildings, Brisbane brought to mind the strangely familiar — if slightly outdated — image of a North American city of the 1930s. For instance, our first observation was, naturally, of the girls' skirt lengths; to our amazement, they came down to halfway between the knee and ankle — a decade-old style which we saw as a hangover from the days of the Great Depression. (It would also turn out to be a forerunner to the "New Look," which, to our chagrin, would be the rage among Canadian and American women two or three years later.) Canadian and American girls in 1945 were wearing their skirts to exactly one inch below the kneecap, so our first sight of Australian girls, even with bobbed, marcelled hair, was somewhat of a letdown. The disappointment was eased by the occasional sight of American Red Cross girls and WACs, whose khaki uniform skirts met the current North American fashion. Eventually, we would discover that the Australian girls had numerous other attributes that were quite palatable. Nevertheless, I kept my betrothed status firmly in mind.

Emulating the locals, we hopped off our scenic railway tram while it was still moving at its normal sleepy pace along a narrow, cobblestone downtown street. It trundled off around a bend, and was very nearly the last moving vehicle we would see that day, aside from the occasional tiny English car — of early-1930s vintage — rattling along the bricks. We'd picked Saturday to visit the big city; back home, it was *the* day to go downtown. In Australia, we learned, it was the custom on Saturdays to close shops, and everything else, up tight and take a train to the nearest racetrack. We found out in time that we were in the midst of a nation of racetrack touts.

There were still a few people who didn't play the ponies to be found around the main shopping district. A few shops and one or two movie theatres remained bravely open. As we had been in San Francisco, we were taken for anything but what we were. "Hello, England!" one cheery Aussie called out as he passed. We whirled and called back, "Never been there — we're from Canada!" It worked a wonder. He came back to us, a look of amazement on his face, and eagerly wrote down his address on a card. He would not let us go without a promise that we come and visit him that very day. He told us — to puzzled looks all around — that his daughters were used to entertaining Americans, so they should be able to get along with us quite well. We pledged, with all the insincerity of itinerant soldiers, that we'd drop in. As he went cheerily on his way, Boombaw rubbed his hands in glee until Pierre DeMal pointed out that the daughters might be all right but, with father presiding, it wouldn't be exactly like San Francisco.

By evening, having knocked about the quaint city and taken in a movie, we were headed for the American Red Cross entertainment centre when an Aussie sailor told us we'd be better off at the Trades Union Hall. At the steps to this smoke-blackened nineteenth-century building, we encountered an alert Australian Army commando, hard as flint and yellow from atabrin, who nearly made us regret our choice. Still in his jungle greens, his digger hat pinned back on one side, the commando had his back to us as we approached. When Bert tapped him on the shoulder, he spun around with blinding speed and, in a blink, was facing Bert in a commando crouch, about to slice him with the edge of one hand. We yelled out to him to hold off the attack.

Suspicious and confused by the North American accents coming from what looked like British uniforms, he straightened up but remained ready for action. There had been, we were told later, a few incidents between Yanks and Aussies, mainly over women and money, and this hard case was posted at the Trades Union Hall to keep out the high-rolling G.I.'s. He had orders to keep not only the Yanks at bay, but also "pommies," as the Aussies called Englishmen. He couldn't quite sort out which category we were in as he cast his yellowed eye over our British-style khaki shirts, shorts, and brown berets, and listened incredulously to the words coming out of our mouths. Then he caught sight of "Canada" on the loops of our shirt epaulets (we'd actually been issued Royal Canadian Navy flashes) and broke into a wide grin. "Good on ye, mytes! In ye go!" he cried before wheeling around once more to take up his vigilance against any potential Yank or pommy invaders.

Once inside, we could see we were out of our depth. Entering the main hall at the top of a broad staircase one level above the dance floor, we found ourselves overlooking about a hundred couples who, ranged in rows across the floor, were gracefully — and in perfect unison — going through a highly formal, slow-tempo dance to the ear-smashing sound of a six-piece band that featured a persistently loud and strident snare drum. The couples faced each other with joined hands and, still in rows, circled grandly about in time to the snare drum in long, sweeping steps. Had the men not been dressed, except for the absence of digger hats, like the commando outside the building, while the girls sported calf-length frilly frocks, it could have been a scene out of an eighteenth-century formal ball. The numbers the band played weren't that old, but they certainly dated from the early to mid 1920s and into the '30s.

As we watched in awe, the couples switched to placing arms around each others' waists, and the rows moved back and forth rhythmically in a few intricate, perfectly coordinated kick steps. Then the dancers broke up the rows in a quick single movement. Each man whirled his partner in sweeping circles all around the floor, nobody coming even close to colliding. We gaped. There were waltzes, one-steps, and other dances we'd never seen, all executed with a polish that suggested they'd had formal training since childhood. Hollywood's Busby Berkeley couldn't have choreographed a better dance sequence. We four club-footed Canadians wouldn't stand a chance.

We were just about to clear out for the Red Cross when the band broke into a foxtrot. We hurried down the stairs in a twinkling. The girl

I danced with followed my sloppy footwork bravely, never letting her smile drop. It was in the jitterbugging that followed later that she left me standing still.

Chapter 9

Secret Tricks of "Magic"

War or no war, the dock strike must go on. It had apparently closed down most, if not all, of Australia's seaports. There wasn't a glimmer of hope of a settlement anytime soon, and the Labour government in power was making no real effort to bring it to an end. Fortunately, a steady flow of strategic supplies was now going directly from North America to the South West Pacific and eastern Pacific theatres of war. So, even though nothing was moving out of Brisbane, not much damage was being done to the war effort. Although inconvenienced, even the Australian forces on the islands just north of Australia, such as New Guinea and New Britain, could get supplies from North America with little trouble.

However, a ship that was of top priority to 1CSWG had just arrived in Brisbane. This was the *Bristol Park*, a Canadian merchant freighter of about 10,000 tons — hardly bigger than a Lake Ontario coal carrier. But the cargo she held was vital to 1CSWG's odyssey: all of the unit's radio equipment, trucks, jeeps, rifles, Bren guns, huge electric generators, and sundry other military luggage, with a total value of around a million dollars. The *Bristol Park* had made the 7,000-mile crossing from Vancouver directly to Brisbane while we were navigating the South Pacific on the *Monterey* and *Shawnee*. Now, having arrived only a few days after we landed, she lolled at the dock, there being no stevedores to relieve her of her cargo.

The solution to that problem quickly made itself apparent. Through camp cleanup and guard duty in Victoria and rifle greasing in San Francisco, or as kitchen help or general-duty navvies aboard the *Shawnee*, the men of 1CSWG — or some of us, at least — were always available to be thrown into any breach that might threaten the Group's front line. And there were fellows in Technical Maintenance and Motor Transport who were handy with machinery and could operate the dock derricks. Number One Canadian Special Wireless Group was transmogrified into a special dockworker brigade.

First off the ship were a few of the flat-nosed Canadian Ford 15-cwt. trucks, designed to carry a dozen or so troops each in their canvas-covered back boxes. A Canadian corporal, at the controls of a dock derrick, hoisted them high into the air. From a height that made them look like toys, the trucks descended to the dock. After about five or six were landed, the Technical Maintenance men examined them for roadworthiness.

Next out of the hold came wooden boxes — make that boxes and boxes and boxes — all sealed and stained dark green, in sizes ranging from the same rifle containers we'd packed in San Francisco, which two men could handle, to great, two-and-a-half-ton wooden structures that only a derrick could lift. These contained everything from the unit's standard short-wave wireless "52" sets to spare parts to cables to two-ton gasoline-driven electrical generators. To us signalmen who had to manhandle the dozens of smaller boxes, they might as well have been loaded with scrap iron, so heavy were they to heave up onto the half-dozen trucks liberated to that point. In the heat, they seemed to take on more mass. As more and more boxes appeared it seemed incredible that this small freighter could hold all of this heavy equipment, including so many full-sized trucks. We laboured on until it was almost dark, loading truck after truck with green boxes.

There would inevitably be stretches when the flow of man-sized boxes would temporarily stop. During these times we would stand by in our still-greasy coveralls. We were all alone on the docks. There weren't even any picketers — so completely was everything in the harbour shut down that they weren't needed. The union must not have considered the little contingent from Canada a likely strike-breaking threat. Anyway, we weren't involved in commercial business, we were only chasing a war.

Five or six of us got so bored standing around that we wandered off into the city's back streets in our greasy coveralls. After about an hour one of our trucks, carrying a staff sergeant and two corporals, came around a corner. We were spotted and instantly carted back to the docks, and we were no doubt once again suspected of desertion.

We loaded a couple more of the trucks, which then drove off for camp, and while we waited for their return the ship's crew — all Canadian — invited us aboard the *Bristol Park* for a bite to eat and some coffee. The evening was spent mostly in a comic routine in which a number of us piled into a little delivery truck for the ride back to camp, then got crowded out as the truck's springs sagged. When it returned to pick up another load, we crammed into it once more — I was the first one aboard and could prove it because I'd grabbed the only cushion in the truck. Then I was forced out once more after losing a coin toss, which I'd originally suggested. Finally, we commandeered one of our half-load trucks and drove it to camp ourselves. We'd missed supper. Grabbing a sandwich at the nearby Australian Army canteen, a few of us tramped through the Aussie camp to a spot where an outdoor movie theatre was supposed to be showing *Casablanca*. The place was dark and silent. We went back to camp and, exhausted from the day's workout, crashed onto our two-blanket-and-empty-sack "beds," tired and hungry.

In the morning we were granted a change of pace. Instead of going to the docks right away, a dozen or so of us were set to the task of unloading the trucks we had loaded the previous day. Later, though, we had a real treat: about twenty of us were dispatched aboard the empty trucks to the docks once more, and there we found a sight to behold: about five officers and three or four sergeants working like mad to unload more trucks and more two-and-a-half-ton boxes. We were transfixed by the novel spectacle of seeing officers actually pitching in and doing hard labour. We had never witnessed such a thing.

They paid no heed to our arrival, and we all sat down on stray boxes to watch. Along came a sergeant, however, who shooed us briskly over to a pile of two-man boxes to load onto trucks. It was half-past midnight before we left those deserted docks and got back to camp. Once more we flopped down, exhausted, on our pseudo-beds, and slept as we were, in our sweat-soaked, grease-coated coveralls, despite the heat, just like back in San Francisco. There was some satisfaction, though, in knowing that now at least some of the officers knew what it was like to slave like navvies for the sake of good old 1CSWG.

Shortly after daybreak, Sergeant Long woke us up with the news that the colonel was going to be coming through at 0900 hours on hut inspection. Of all the times to hold an inspection: we were socked out from loading trucks, with only about four hours' sleep and we had had no time to clean up! Barely conscious in the grey dawn light, we struggled to shave, change, get properly dressed, and straighten up our belongings scattered all about the hut floor — there being no furniture nor beds — in time for the C.O.'s arrival. Right on time, Lieutenant-Colonel Wethey, accompanied by an entourage of officers and Company Sergeant-Major Addy, entered the hut. All of them looked spic and span in clean, crisp, neatly pressed uniforms; they also seemed well rested and hostile, looking as though they were seeing one of these Beaverboard huts for the first time.

As we stood at attention, the C.O. spoke very critically of the hut's — and our — appearance, and gave us a lecture on the army's requirements of neatness, alertness, and orderliness on the part of each and every member of ordinary ranks. No slacking of duty or disorderliness of dress could be excused. If the hut wasn't cleaned up, there would be penalties. There was no mention of — nor words of appreciation for — our Herculean efforts at the docks over the previous two days. When he finished, we saluted our C.O. respectfully, and he turned to set out for the next hut. For several moments there was no sound in our hut but the grinding of teeth.

After we'd piled up the last of the green boxes in a nearby field, life at Chermside Camp offered all the excitement and stimulation of sitting in a steam bath while watching a turtle race against a snail. We hadn't been paid since San Francisco, so there was no likelihood yet of carrying on any red-hot leaves in Brisbane. As the Gunner said, "All we're goin' to do here is sit around scratching our mosquito bites." As usual, he was mostly right. The latrinogram service told us that we were to wait in this swamp until "the Wet" ended in Northern Territory. Until that happened and "the Dry" arrived, there was no way that our trucks and Jeeps could get through the dirt roads around Darwin, our ultimate destination. We could appreciate that; our camp was now getting daily torrential downpours, the rain roaring down on our tin roofs like Niagara Falls. It was then that I learned the true meaning of the old New Orleans jazz piece, "Tin Roof Blues."

Boredom began to set in, as there was little to do but swat the oversized mosquitoes that emerged. Any attempt at going for a stroll in the long grass near the camp caused hordes of the anopheles mosquito to fall upon us like a pack of hungry piranha. Normally this breed was a malaria carrier, but the Australians had carefully removed everyone who'd ever had that sickness from the general area, leaving the predatory insects without access to the virus and rendering them incapable of transmitting it from one human to another. To be safe, however, we were ordered to continue taking one atabrin pill a day. Despite the precautions, the mosquito bites were savage, and the only safe place — especially around sunset — was under the mosquito netting we were finally issued. Without these we would have been eaten alive by morning.

Complementing this airborne plague were the ground troops of big red ants who lived under the floorboards and who emerged in crowds to snap up any morsel of food that was dropped. When none was available they liked to walk all over our mess cans, licking up whatever might be left from the latest meal.

Even the birds flitting among the trees seemed to mock us. One whistled a pretty good version of "The Campbells Are Coming, Oh Ho, Oh Ho!" Others sang more lilting songs, but there was one mysterious variety that sat in the trees and snored all night. And we were fascinated but a little skittish at the sight of spiders with bodies like fifty-cent pieces and legs like matchsticks, to say nothing of a praying mantis six inches long which we found clinging to the door of our hut as we returned one night. Told by an Aussie that they were poisonous, we killed it before it got into the hut.

For some reason that wasn't explained to us, we were moved from our tin-roofed Beaverboard huts into tents. The roaring rain now came coursing down the alleys between the tents and under the wooden floor. We'd thought the floors were a luxury when we first saw them, but during our first night under canvas another cloudburst nearly floated us away. Recognizing the need to do something, we got busy digging trenches around the tent to channel the deluge on down the line. It was pure self-defence. The next tent group did the same. For lighting, kerosene lamps — "Soldiers, for the Use Of," in quartermaster's terms — were issued, one to a tent. Each tent slept six.

Rain and heat or no rain and heat, the urge among the Swiggers to seek out the party life was strong. The colonel loosened up enough to grant us passes to go into Brisbane, and instantly DeMal and Boombaw produced the address given us by the enthusiastic father who'd invited us to visit with him and his daughters. We decided to take him up on his offer.

The girls turned out to be overwhelmingly charming but firmly aware of soldiers' weaknesses. This, of course, was only a "cheer up the troops" visit, and we knew that Father was somewhere in the house. Sitting on the floor of the small living room, we played card games and flipped coins in the traditional Aussie two-up style to great peals of laughter. One of the girls who won heavily collected her coins and handed them to me with the casual order to "put them up." I, as a literal Canadian only just learning Aussie slang, obediently put them up on a nearby table. That provoked shrieks of laughter and the hilarious admonition, "No, not that — *count* 'em!"

The evening went by quickly, and despite DeMal and Boombaw's persistent attempts to get the girls to leave the house with us "for some larks," they gaily refused, well aware of the subterfuges of soldiers from their experiences with oversexed Americans in the past. Late that night we left, all in good humour, and hied ourselves off to the American Red Cross hostel for an overnight stay. Next day, as Brisbane was no San Francisco, we wandered back to Chermside camp.

In March we got the stimulating news that the unit was going to be inspected by Major-General Sir Thomas Blamey, commander-in-chief of the Australian military forces. The general was, in fact, the instigator of our Australian posting, having asked Prime Minister Mackenzie King for help in monitoring Japanese signals. Consequently, Lieutenant-Colonel Wethey and his officers viewed his projected visit as the most important event to hit 1CSWG since the inspection at Victoria by the top Canadian brass. All members of the unit were to be turned out in our very best form, with no exceptions.

As it turned out, however, there would be one exception. Signalman Murray, G.S., awoke that morning with a fantastic fever and feeling like he'd been run through the stomach by a Japanese bayonet. I couldn't even get off my straw-filled sack when the sergeant-major and two corporals arrived at my tent to see what could possibly be the matter. The sergeant-major was furious that one of his flock would have the audac-

Shortly after the Canadians arrived in Australia, Major-General Sir Thomas Blamey, Commander-in-Chief of Allied forces in the South West Pacific Area, inspected the signals group. General Blamey was instrumental in having I CSWG assigned to the Pacific theatre. Lieutenant-Colonel H.D.W. Wethey, C.O. of I CSWG, is seen on left.

ity to get sick on the day of the great inspection, when he was to have the honour of shouting out orders before one of the Allied world's great military leaders.

Even though I could barely stand, he ordered me into my uniform and at least make the effort to get better. All ranks, he barked, were to be on parade for the major-general as the C.O. had ordered — with no exceptions. The two corporals hauled me to my feet. I was on the edge of falling over from weakness, but I did manage to get into my shorts and a shirt before sinking down onto my palliasse again. I seemed to be suffering from an attack of some kind of sickness worse than any flu I'd ever had in Canada. Finally, the sergeant-major had to admit that I was sick. Still, he ordered the corporals to get me to my feet and march me, weaving and even staggering a little, through the camp to the medical officer's shack, where the M.O. gave me a going-over.

To the sergeant-major's exasperation, the M.O., an Aussie, declared that I was suffering from dengue fever, a malady transmitted by mosquitoes. I was to go back to my tent, lie down, and stay there all day and possibly the next. He gave me some kind of medicine and sent me on

my way, marched back by the fuming sergeant-major and the two corporals striding behind.

And so, on the occasion of the great inspection of 1CSWG by
Major-General Sir Thomas Blamey, commander-in-chief of Australian
Forces, one man — Signalman Murray, G.S. — was unable to attend
parade. That was the least of my worries. Under the influence of dengue
fever, I was ready to accept death without resistance. After two days of
dengue misery, I recovered, and my missing out on the historic inspection was quickly forgotten.

It was impossible for us to set up any kind of quarters where we could
carry on training and practise in Kana and Morse. As a result, the sergeants'
ingenuity was taxed as they tried to come up with joe jobs that would keep
us busy and alert. On one morning parade, Lieutenant Hance Legere asked
how many hadn't cleaned their web belts and web packs. I'd done mine the
day before, but, along with almost everyone else in the section, I raised my
hand. He dismissed us with the order to get it done. I disappeared with my
ground sheet, some books, and a supply of newly issued mosquito repellent
into the nearby woods for the rest of the morning while the rest tackled the
cleaning of their web packs. The army did owe me a break.

Once the 250 equipment boxes, still sealed, were all piled away under the
trees and tarpaulins (and, in fact, stacked twice more by the faithful young
operator/trainee/labourers of Number Two Ops Mons Sigs until the job
was done to the sergeant-major's acute satisfaction) there wasn't much else
for us to do but keep the camp cleaned up, as ignorant O.R.'s (Other
Ranks) are universally expected to do — or were in those days, at least.

Once we had been given our pay in Australian currency, we got more
chances to get into Brisbane for leave, and we came to know more
Australians. The Aussie girls were grand, and for the most part were well
bred, although for those Swiggers who preferred the fire-ship kind, those
could be — and were — found in the juicier parts of the seaport. The
Aussie men, most of them in the armed forces, were tough-talking, friendly, and ready for a dust-up if their national honour were taken too lightly.
All in all, they were a loveable group of people.

The pet hatred of the male Aussies was, of course, the Yanks. But the
females loved Americans. Hundreds, maybe thousands, of Aussie girls
married them. Many had already gone to the enchanted land, the United

States, to await their hubbies' return home. This didn't endear the Yanks to the Aussie soldiers one bit. In fact, pitched battles, sometimes involving weapons, frequently broke out. The Yanks also had a penchant for paying merchants about twice what a given piece of merchandise was worth — perhaps because they, like us Canadians, confused the Australian five-pound note with a five-dollar bill, when in fact it was actually worth $25. Some merchants were quite happy to profit from this misunderstanding, which drove prices to absurd heights. The Yanks did rankle us somewhat by having bought up just about all the souvenirs worth sending home. The leftovers were on sale for absurdly high prices.

In any event, shopping wasn't at the top of the Swiggers' priority list. Next to the girls, the most sought-after commodity was Australian beer. You could even get it ice-cold — probably at the Yanks' insistence. The dark brown fluid came in quart-sized bottles, was twice as powerful as its Canadian counterpart — which in turn was twice as potent as American brew of the day — and we quaffed it by the gallon. The cursed heat just wouldn't let up, we protested. The beer, therefore, must continue to flow.

On March 3, we were jolted by the news that one of our number, Signalman D.J. Green, drowned while surfing at Maroochydore Beach. He was buried at Woombye-Palmwoods Military Cemetery near Brisbane. The irony was that Green had come with us all the way with from Canada, via California, across the Pacific to New Guinea and Australia — only to drown on a weekend pass, thousands of miles from home. It was a sobering thought.

As with any clandestine military unit, 1CSWG had ulterior and hidden "other motives" for what it appeared to be doing. The official story was that the unit was lingering in the Brisbane area for almost two months while it waited for the northern rains to stop. The Allied security blanket, however, covered up the fact that Brisbane — specifically 21 Henry Street, next to the Ascot racetrack — was the home of "CB," the Central Bureau. CB had been set up early in the Pacific war as the pivotal clearing-house for all Japanese wireless massages intercepted in the South West Pacific Area (SWPA). Formed originally from an Australian Intelligence unit recalled from the Middle East in 1941, CB was expanded after General MacArthur retreated to Australia from the Philippines, after which it continued as a joint intelligence centre for the Allied counteroffensive in the

South West Pacific and was manned half-and-half by Australian and American military personnel.

The U.S. Signal Corps unit of CB was headed by Colonel Abraham Sinkov — an associate of William Friedman, whose team had constructed an American duplicate of the Japanese "Purple" encoding machine just before the outbreak of war. The Australian Army Intelligence Corps commander at CB was Lieutenant-Colonel A.W. Sandford, and his second-in-command was Major S.R.I. Clark, commanding officer of Australian Signals Traffic Analysis. Colonel Sinkov was also chief cryptanalyst of the Special Intelligence Service, U.S. Air Force. Heading the Royal Australian Air Force unit of CB was Wing Commander H. Roy Booth of Australian Air Intelligence. In actual operations, leadership was provided by either Australian or U.S. personnel, depending upon who was best qualified for the various functions of CB.

Cloaked in tight secrecy in its old building next to the racetrack (it was said to have been a sporting house at one time), CB operated in complete obscurity in its backwater location in Brisbane. Inside, however, thousands of Japanese messages — mainly naval communications — were received each day via coded radio-teletype from far-flung monitoring stations throughout SWPA. After processing them further, CB would relay them, by the hundreds of thousands, to Allied headquarters in Washington and Melbourne — and, whenever time was a key factor, directly to military command units on land or sea.

Operating throughout dozens of points — in Australia, at Hollandia, the Solomons, the Admiralty Islands, SWPA headquarters at Morotai and later at San Miguel, the Philippines, and everywhere that Allied operations against the Japanese were actively going on — Australian and U.S. Special Wireless monitoring units fed intercepted Japanese signals traffic into CB around the clock. Cryptanalysts and traffic analysts sifted them for the snippets of information that gave away enemy plans for fleet movements, reinforcement and supplying of their island defence garrisons, and all kinds of orders that revealed any new Japanese attempt to group their forces for counterattack. Even coded messages that couldn't be cracked because of a code's recent introduction could reveal profiles of stepped-up activity or a change in the use of supply routes. Volume of a given type of coded message was often as important as the information it actually contained.

Since 1CSWG was destined to take over and expand the Australian Army's intercept duties at Darwin, one of the most northerly points in

Australia and a strategic location for signals monitoring, the period at Chermside allowed the veteran operators of Number One Section and the members of the Intercom section to spend time at CB, learning some additional tricks of the signal-snooping trade from the masters themselves. At the same time, Intercom was made familiar with the Typex coding machine, which would be used at the Darwin station to encipher and radio-teletype 1CSWG's message harvest back to CB.

CB was such a tightly dedicated group of intelligence officers and non-coms that, for decades after the end of the war, a Central Bureau Intelligence Corps Association consisting of the operation's survivors was still active as an informal club in Sydney, Brisbane, and Melbourne. This organization assisted greatly in the research for this book.

Australia had become the base for signals intelligence in the SWPA early in 1942. This was due not only to Australian Army Intelligence's own initiatives, but also to the influx of U.S. and later British (not to mention Canadian and New Zealander) military intelligence units.

One of the first groups of Americans was the U.S. Navy's "Cast" code-breaking unit which had to pack up and leave Corregidor in the Philippines when the Japanese all but overwhelmed the garrison there. Lieutenant-Commander Rudolph Fabian, a colourful character, got his seventy-five-man group to Australia by submarine and relocated them at Melbourne in the Monterey Building. Fabian's unit was important mainly because it brought with it the only Purple machine in Allied hands anywhere in the Pacific to that date. The unit, renamed "Belconnen," joined forces with that headed by Commander R.E. Nave of the Royal Navy, an Australian who in 1941 had set up intercept stations in Darwin, Melbourne, and Canberra.

As noted earlier, a book called *The Emperor's Codes*, written by British journalist Michael Smith and published in 2000, claimed British credit for breaking the Japanese JN25 code as early as 1939, the knowledge of which was passed on to the Americans. The U.S., he said, then "lost interest in further co-operation with the British." The "true heroes" of the Allied code-breaking effort, he maintained, were Eric Nave and John Tiltman, a British cryptographer. The close-knit working relationship between Australian, American, and British personnel at the Central Bureau seem to conflict with this allegation. American co-operation in getting 1CSWG to Australia and helping to get it established in Darwin also seems to contradict the claim.

When SWPA headquarters moved to Brisbane from Melbourne late in 1942, its makeup included — in addition to Australian Army and American

Signals Intelligence people — the RAAF; the Australian Women's Auxiliary Air Force; the Australian Women's Army; Commander Nave and his group; a Major N. Webb, representing the British Army; and the only civilian, a Professor Room of the University of Sydney. The overall commander of intelligence operations under General MacArthur was U.S. Major-General Spencer B. Akin, chief signals officer of SWPA H.Q. Second to him was U.S. Colonel J. Sherr, another associate of Friedman of the Purple machine. Sherr was killed in a plane crash on a visit to India and replaced by Colonel H. Doud, C.O. of the Special Intelligence Service of the U.S. Air Force.

It was Major Clark, the Australian Signals Traffic Analysis C.O. at CB, who on behalf of the Australian High Command first started talks with the Canadian Army's Department of Military Intelligence in Ottawa that led to the formation of 1CSWG and its ultimate posting to Australia. Major Clark was one of the originators of CB, having himself served before the December 1941 Japanese attacks with the Australian Number 1 Special Wireless Section in Greece, Syria, and Crete. He was also attached to Number 2 Wireless Company, Royal Corps of Signals, British Army, in Palestine and at the Air Ministry Wireless Station at Heliopolis, near Cairo. By the time 1CSWG arrived in the South West Pacific, Major Clark had moved from CB at Brisbane to the Advanced Echelon at Hollandia. He was busy supervising the cracking of enemy messages at the time that 1CSWG was switching ships there early in February.

Although operating on a small scale, the Australians had in 1941 broken the code used by the Japanese mission in Australia and sent the key to Bletchley Park, the British Ultra headquarters in England, and to Washington. In September, they picked up a message telling the Japanese consul-general in Australia to find another neutral country to look after Italian interests on whose behalf they had been acting. The Australians also detected on December 4, 1941, three days before Pearl Harbor, that the Japanese diplomatic staff in Canberra had been told to burn all their codes and ciphers. Thus, early in December, Australian authorities were expecting an imminent Japanese attack somewhere. But the time and place remained unknown until "the day of infamy" arrived.

Most experts on the Pacific war now agree that radio intelligence was by far the most effective of the whole range of worldwide intelligence and security activities of the Allied war effort. It has been regarded as critical to the success of many crucial occasions in the European war. Allied forces made heavy use of British Ultra information in most major European operations, from the Battle of Britain to the Atlantic U-boat war and even beyond D-Day. In the Pacific, where the interception of Japanese communications by American, Australian, Canadian, and New Zealander signals intelligence units was lumped together under the code name "Magic," radio monitoring played a more significant role than in any other theatre of war. Without it, the vast sprawl of the Pacific theatre would have continued to conceal the roaming Japanese fleets which, in the earliest days of the war, ranged over thousands of square miles, from Asian waters east to the Gilbert and Marshall Islands — not to mention Pearl Harbor — and far into the Indian Ocean. They attacked seaports from Ceylon to the Solomons Islands virtually unchallenged — the shattered Pacific sea forces of the British, Dutch, and American navies could do little at first to stop them.

Special Wireless monitoring around the Pacific Rim drew a picture of this rampage and of the placement of Japanese land forces throughout the Philippines, the Dutch East Indies, and the myriad islands to the north of Australia. Air strikes guided by Special Wireless monitoring were able to give the Allies a chance to hit back at strategic points and inflict great damage on the Japanese forces. Subsequently, shortages of rations and equipment among the Japanese forces would often show up in routine administrative communications. Some strategic signals provided an overall picture of Japanese plans and operations in the whole of the southeast Asian and South West Pacific theatres of war. The Coral Sea battle, which thwarted the Japanese navy's attempt to pass around the southeastern tip of New Guinea and attack Port Moresby on the south coast, was initially made possible by Allied Special Wireless cryptanalysis. So was the Battle of Midway, which followed weeks later and which marked the beginning of the end of the Japanese expansion. Prior to this latter skirmish, the U.S. Air Force learned through Special Wireless that Admiral Yamamoto's plane would visit Bougainville, enabling Lockheed Lightnings from Espiritu Santo Island to deal a major psychological blow to Japanese morale.

Major Stan Clark, the veteran Far East traffic analyst, was one of the thousands of members of the Australian forces who had come home in 1942 to help defend their country from what seemed to be certain invasion. He would play a key role in creating and establishing the Allied operation at Brisbane as well as its later echelons in Hollandia and Luzon. His initials — "S.R.I.C.," for Stanley Robert Irving Clark — gave his American colleagues at CB the impression that he was operating under a code name: "Special Radio Intelligence Clark."

As second-in-command of the Australian section of CB under Lieutenant-Colonel Sandford, Clark was as deeply immersed in cryptography and the tracking of Japanese military movements as anyone in Allied special radio intelligence operations. He launched into training Australian Army, RAAF, and U.S. Army "E" Branch personnel for base and field duties at CB. "E" Branch was concerned with traffic analysis, not cryptography. Clark served as C.O. of "E" Branch; CB Task Officer; C.O. of "I" Branch for British services; a member of the CB operations planning committee; and C.O. of the Advanced Echelon when it was relocated to Hollandia and San Miguel. During Clark's service with CB he represented the organization at Empire conferences held at the Government Code and Cipher School at Bletchley Park. He was also second-in-command of the Australian Army Radio Security Service. In short, he was a figure deeply involved in most aspects of the wireless war against Japan, and before that, the German armies threatening the Middle East.

For this book, Major Clark recalled with great clarity the expansion of CB in late 1942 when it was set up in Brisbane. Decryption and analysis were aided by two banks of IBM computers. The Australian Army's Number 1 Special Wireless Section was expanded into a group. The RAAF combined a number of wireless units into one and the U.S. Signal Corps provided the 126th and 138th Special Radio Intelligence Companies.

The 138th was the unit that found the gumbo mud on Biak Island north of New Guinea too much for their mobile radio trucks when they attempted to operate close to Japanese lines, forcing the military to rethink the viability of mobile Special Wireless units in the island jungles. Nevertheless, 1CSWG was originally formed along the same lines as the 138th, with roughly the same complement and diversity of personnel and mobile equipment. New Zealand's army also had an intercept unit, but no evaluation personnel, so they fed their intercepted Japanese radio traffic to CB.

"Add to these units Number One Canadian Special Wireless Group and you have the picture," Major Clark said.

CB's network of intercept stations, from which messages poured in at the rate of 100,000 or more each day, embraced enormous areas of the South West Pacific. In Australia alone, there was a station at Canberra; an RAAF station in the Darwin area; a Dutch station in a hidden location in Northern Territory; the U.S. Army's 138th Signal Company's main intercept and direction-finding (DF) group; a Royal Australian Navy (RAN) monitoring station; the U.S. Navy intercept and decoding station at Melbourne under Lieutenant-Commander Fabian; monitoring facilities at Watsonia, near Melbourne; the U.S. Army radio intercept station at Townsville, Queensland; the RAN monitors at Perth, Western Australia; the U.S. intercept station at Brisbane; and the British Secret Intelligence Service (SIS) post in Brisbane, to which was attached a Special Liaison Unit, SLU-9, one of the Bletchley Park branches handling *Ultra* information.

With 1CSWG's ultimate construction of the large new intercept station outside Darwin, another knot was added to the net. With so many hundreds of people involved in these top-secret operations and scattered so widely over the face of the earth (including those who were monitoring in Canada and the United States), the wonder is that the Japanese military could have remained so ignorant of the massive hemorrhaging of their battle plans and troop movement data into Allied hands.

At CB, radio traffic analysis was code-named "Thumb" when it was mentioned in communications between Allied intercept centres and those who were required to act on the information. Thumb consisted of knowledge of enemy activities derived from many sources: by inference, from analysis of the frequency and flow of radio traffic itself; from the use of direction-finding to pinpoint the locations of Japanese communications centres; from enemy wireless operators' chatter; and even from an individual Japanese operator's "fist" — his characteristic touch on the sending key. If a particular enemy operator was transmitting from a new location, it might indicate that his wireless unit had been moved for strategic reasons.

Intelligence derived from the breaking of low- and medium-grade codes, such as those used in air-to-ground communications, was code-named "Pearl." Both Thumb and Pearl intelligence could be intercepted by field monitoring units and relayed to local Allied unit headquarters for appropriate military action.

Japanese military messages denoted the particular service involved — naval, air, ground, or transport — by the first group of ciphers in a given message. For example, 3336 was the Japanese Air Code insignia; 2468 was Japanese Army Water Transport. Major Clark recalls that CB's "main claim to fame" in code-cracking was the solution of the 2468 system and the ATP (*A*ddress in *T*he *P*reamble) system. The 2468 system was of key importance in the tracking of Japanese plans to ship troops and supplies between islands. The volume of traffic indicated whether a major attack or a massive reinforcement of Japanese-held positions was about to begin and by what route they might move. Relaying this information to an Allied air strike group could pay off in a crushing air attack on an otherwise secret Japanese offensive.

The blanketing of Japanese radio communications by Allied Special Wireless units was made possible only by co-operative links formed among the Australian, British, Dutch, and American military services early in the Pacific war. The U.S. and its British Commonwealth allies combined and exchanged information on Japanese and German codes. The U.S. supplied Magic information on Japanese communications and the Purple machine, while Britain made available Ultra information on German signals and the Enigma machine. Australia provided American, British, Dutch, and later Canadian forces with locations for intercept stations.

Equally important was the absolute secrecy of these operations and the total protection of the fact that, not only could Japanese codes be broken, but that the Allies possessed in the Purple machine the means to intercept the very highest level of commands that Japanese Imperial headquarters was sending via radio-telegraphy to its forces throughout the new — if only temporary — Japanese empire that extended over the vast regions of the western and southwestern Pacific.

Chapter 10

By Train and Truck to the Outback

As our train rattled along in the 100-degree heat, the scene that suddenly rose from the stone-strewn Queensland plain could have been created by a team of Hollywood set builders. It looked like a ghost town from North America's Wild West: a dusty main street wide enough to drive a herd of cattle through, flanked on either side by a row of false-fronted wooden commercial buildings on either side, weathered grey and smooth. In front of the buildings there were raised, covered, wooden sidewalks running the length of the street, wooden watering troughs and hitching posts for horses — even tumbleweeds rolling down the main drag. There were no automobiles to be found, but there was what looked like a livery stable. I half expected Wyatt Earp and his friends to appear in the middle of the street, striding grimly toward the O.K. Corral.

As a final touch, a barely legible sign reading "Silver City Saloon," mounted on the wooden sidewalk canopy, stretched the new arrivals' credulity even further when we noticed the bullet holes that peppered the faded text. Beneath the canopy could be seen a pair of batwing doors. We looked at each other and laughed. This really must, we thought, be an old set for a Wild West movie. Walter Brennan and John Wayne would have been right at home.

But we were wrong. It was the real thing. This was Mount Isa, a once-booming mining centre — and one which would boom again after World War II, when the population returned to resume digging silver, lead, and copper out of the nearby hills.

Australia's north, a huge continental expanse roughly equal to Canada's prairie provinces and the Northwest Territories combined, had been almost completely evacuated of the ordinary civilian population in 1942, when the threat was strong that the Japanese might invade Australia. The Coral Sea battle, followed by the humbling — largely by Aussie troops — of the heretofore invincible Japanese land forces on New Guinea's mountainous Kokoda Track, at Milne Bay, and at Buna, eased that threat, but the evacuation remained in effect until after the war.

Mount Isa was the last centre that might be called civilization that 1CSWG would see for the next eight months. Some of the civilian population was either still there or had returned when it was plain the Japanese invasion threat was over. Small shops and bars and an army hostel catering to the itinerant troops were open, though the legions of Australian and American troops were thinned out now. Most of the shops were boarded up — not to fend off invading Nipponese as much as to withstand the ravages of the "friendly" soldiers who worked off their resentment against being consigned to this harsh environment by staging frequent rampages through the place.

The bullet holes in the sign were easier to account for when we learned that the town had been, during the transient residence of American forces in Australia over the previous two or three years, at the centre of a huge spread of U.S. army camps, and the G.I.'s had been very free with the use of their weapons, especially during a Saturday night on the town.

One remarkable piece of evidence of the troops' unbridled and rowdy habits was a patch of arid plain right next to the town, where once had sat the tents of thousands of U.S. and Australian troops. This patch stretched off far to the west and east of the town to the low, flat-topped hills on the horizon. Off in the distance beside and beyond this former tent city was a stretch of stony desert where thousands — nay, *millions* — of bits of broken glass glinted in the hard sunlight. This had been the "shooting ground" for the hundreds of thousands of trigger-happy troops. Whether to practice their aim for later encounters with the Japanese or just for the sheer hell of it, they would toss beer bottles in the air for their mates to fire at. Two or three years of this "skeet shooting" had scattered glass shards and splinters over an enormous expanse of desert, equalling, in the familiar modern comparison, two to three football fields in area, perhaps more.

The ancient, clanking, jerky train ran on a narrow-gauge track, the kind of contraption one associated with movies about tropical colonies in the backwaters of the world. Today such antiques — as this train was even then — are more likely found covered with spanking new coats of paint and ferrying sightseers around Disneyland or some other amusement park. The three-foot-wide track had no doubt played an important part in opening up the Outback forty to fifty years before, but it didn't come close to the day's luxury trains of North America or Europe. (Canadian standard track gauge was five feet ten inches, and in New South Wales it was over six feet.) The "other ranks" were crammed in, fifteen to a tiny compartment, like vertically stacked logs, forbidden and in any event unable to move except to climb over the others to get to the washroom. We slept sitting up in full kit. The first leg of the journey from Brisbane lasted four days.

Pulled along by a battered engine that groaned, clanked, and puffed out huge volumes of greasy black smoke from its fuel of soft coal, the train's twenty or so carriages had hauled 1CSWG halfway across Queensland to Mount Isa and the end of the line. From here until Darwin we would travel in trucks, jeeps, and some personnel vehicles on loan from the Australians.

Our seventy-five vehicles, including our own 15-cwt. trucks, three-tonners, our big mobile CZ13 radio vans, our dozens of jeeps, and the colonel's staff car, had ridden this far on flatcars on the train that brought us to Mount Isa.

The enormous, flat expanse of the eastern Australian Outback would have been easy country for a large and powerful Japanese tank-supported force to traverse in short order. It would have been another desert war, as in North Africa.

In 1942, Australia's defences — as far as equipment went — were much like Britain's. And the bulk of its fighting men were campaigning in North Africa against Rommel's Afrika Korps. As it turned out, thanks to the quick retaliation against the Japanese in New Guinea and other islands, it would be necessary only to build fighter and bomber bases on the north coast, enormous army staging camps on the routes to the northern defence points, a better north-south highway, and of course, secret locations for Special Wireless interceptor and direction-finding (DF) stations.

Brisbane was a thousand miles behind us now, with over nine hundred still to go to Darwin. We'd left Chermside camp on April 7, almost two months after we disembarked from the *Shawnee* and after once more loading those 250 green boxes and equipment crates onto trucks. Then the more than three hundred men of 1CSWG were loaded onto the first of the two midget trains that carried us as far as Mount Isa. Our whole world was a single seat on a thinly-padded, springless bench. We sat in twos, our booted feet crammed tightly against those of the pair sitting on the opposite bench. When the train passed though a series of tunnels in the Brisbane suburbs, the men sitting next to the windows had to move smartly and pull them closed, or else the donkey engine's smoke would rush in.

Dave Corbett, always inventive, fashioned a hammock out of his blankets, slung it across the carriage from luggage rack to luggage rack, and hoisted his solid, six-foot-two frame into it. Earl Cole, about five-foot-seven, climbed up into another luggage rack, grinned down at us, and spent most of the trip there in relative ease. In my window seat, I sometimes woke in the middle of the night to find myself half-leaning out the window with one arm hanging down the outside of the carriage.

After a day or two, having become as grimy as coal miners from the soot, we gave up trying to wash in the miniature washroom, despite an Aussie's assurance that these were rare trappings for this line. The climb over bodies was hardly worth it, unless nature forced the issue.

There was of course no such thing as a dining car, so we had to climb out of our diminutive railway carriages at certain stops along the way where lunchrooms provided sandwiches or plates of bully beef. At one stop, just before we hit the desert, we found ourselves drawn up beside a sizeable pineapple plantation whose rows of squat plants stretching away from the track were the most orderly sight we'd seen on the journey. There on the railway station platform were several young Aussie entrepreneurs ready with a plaintive "Buy a piney, myte?" and brandishing something Canadians rarely got to see: freshly picked, succulent pineapples, soft to the touch.

Through the windows we bought out the young hawkers' stock, each of us taking two big pineapples and paying some kind of king's ransom for them. In the 90-degree-plus heat the juicy, golden slices we cut with our dirks made life seem worthwhile once more. As the train rattled off again we had a moving feast of the heavenly fruit. But orgies have their penalties: the washroom was heavily in demand over the next several hours.

The lunch stops were marked by a Hobson's choice: get off the train for the bully beef, coarse bread, and green ginger jam and fence with the millions of flies that sought to cover the food and ourselves with their little black bodies, or take the food back to the train, close up the windows against the flies, and eat in the choking heat. Staying outside seemed the better option as we had to wash out our mess tins in the hot mineral water that spouted from the artesian springs that were usually nearby.

More prairie-like grasslands than we'd ever seen in Canada kept slipping past our windows, compounding the boredom of sitting at attention all day. But there was visual relief, in the form of dozens of kangaroos, emus, parrots, and large long-necked birds. The kangaroos, some of them seven or eight feet tall, literally flew alongside the train at full tilt, as baffled and bemused by the contraption as we were. Most of them outdistanced it easily. Twice, a group of two or three kangaroos got hemmed in between the train and a wire fence that paralleled the track for a few miles — one of them actually took to the track, ahead of the engine and, although panicked, outran the big machine for several minutes before bounding off to the left and over the fence into the field, where it made for the low scrub trees. The presence of this wildlife clarified for us the reason for the big yellow sign fixed inside each carriage compartment, which said: "Do Not Fire Guns Out of Train Windows!" Shades of our gun-happy American and Australian predecessors.

Hopes of at least some comfort were raised, then dashed, after our conveyance nosed up to what had once been a bridge across a fairly wide river but which now rested in broken chunks on the riverbed, apparently undercut by a flash flood. We were roused out of our carriages and into half a dozen army trucks that appeared seemingly out of nowhere and took us, a load at a time, across a Bailey bridge, a temporary military structure erected for the duration. We talked hopefully on the way across about the chances of being transferred to a "real" train. But on the narrow track on the far side sat a duplicate of our unlamented silver streak. The same bunch who'd shared the compartment with me on the other train got into an identical compartment on the second — all but two, who had to find room elsewhere. That left thirteen of us per compartment.

Upon reaching Mount Isa, it took us two days in the Silver City to get ourselves cleaned up after the trip of the previous four. It was a tough job, too, because our many feet kicked up a continuous, hanging cloud of dust every time we took a step on the sand floors of the tin-roofed huts where we were billeted. But the sun shone relentlessly and dried our laundry quickly.

We were free to take a turn around the town, which took about ten minutes, and to flop down in the only outdoor theatre. That was where we had our first view of aboriginal Australians. Several men, women, and a few children were in the audience; they worked on the nearby cattle stations and were outfitted in ordinary civilian work clothing, which dimmed for us our vision of the Outback as a last outpost of the noble savage. No doubt they were noble, but in their overalls and checked shirts — or brightly coloured skirts and blouses — and wide-brimmed hats they looked anything but savage.

There was an otherworldliness to this edge of the desert, a surrealistic clarity in the stark, dry sunlight, in the empty, arid plains that stretched west toward the hills in the distance, and in its scattering of tiny, desert-stunted mulga trees. Salvador Dali couldn't have depicted it better. There were no limp watches draped over parched logs, but our clotheslines loaded with shirts and shorts — dry the instant they were hung up — substituted nicely as they drooped immobile in the breezeless air. Dali's brush might have been responsible, if this were really just a painting, for the snaking, black streak — narrowing and disappearing into the actual desert — that was the asphalt road we would soon be traversing to Darwin.

Lining a dried-up riverbed behind our transit camp was a grove of paper-barked ghost gum trees of respectable size, their tiny leaves casting a salt-and-pepper shadow on the sand below, their white bark seemingly lit from within because of the intense reflection of sunlight from all directions, even into their shade. They leaned at crazy angles, some touching the ground with their branches, as though they had given survival a good attempt but were slowly bowing to the chronic absence of water in the dry bed amidst them. The dreamlike unreality of this small white forest conjured up the vision of a prehistoric tableau of life arrested and preserved in mid-collapse in this petrified and still landscape. It was real-life T.S. Eliot.

Nothing would do but that I make a mark on this ancient scenery, one that itself would likely remain static for a while into the future. With my dirk I carved my name and the date into one of the white trunks. But I swore to myself that if it meant travelling again in the cursed, clanking, calamitous contraptions that had brought us across this land, I would never, *ever* come back to Mount Isa to see whether my carving had survived.

Along the road to Darwin there was no place to stop and smell the roses. Nor were there any roses, or any desert flowers. There were, however, prickly pears, tumbleweed, cactus, spinifex, and even tinier mulga hardwood trees. And there were rock lizards. No kangaroos or emus ventured into this waterless waste. There was colour, though, across the flat seas of pulverized rock that frequently dominated the scene. Every hue of the spectrum was present in the hen's egg–sized pebbles that layered these seas of stone, truly a rock hunter's heaven. Every non-precious metal must have been represented, and perhaps there were some valuable bits that we weren't equipped to recognize. Whenever the trucks stopped for natural relief breaks, we collected a few of the more spectacular stones as souvenirs.

Our mixed convoy started out from Mount Isa along the blacktop military highway built by the U.S. Army Corps of Engineers early in the war to give access to the Darwin staging areas. The blacktop, an engineering triumph, was the only man-made artifact along the 900-mile

Stretch of the 2,000-mile "Bitumen" road running south from Darwin in Northern Territory to Alice Springs. Branch of about 1,000 miles through Queensland and Northern Territory took I CSWG to junction a few hundred miles south of Darwin.

On the way north to Townsville, Queensland, from Brisbane, I CSWG switched to an antiquated train, then to trucks to their ultimate destination of Darwin on the north Australian coast. The troops endured extremely cramped accommodation but got rare chances to stretch their legs during stops.

trek to Darwin, except for the rough transit camps that we reached every day just before dark. Even under the full daily blast of the sun, undimmed by any filtering air pollution, the asphalt remained solid. God knows there was enough rock beneath it to bear the weight of the thousands of trucks that must have rolled over it in the three years of the road's existence. This highway, and the "Bitumen" — which ran from Darwin to Alice Springs at the dead centre of the continent — which we would travel after war's end, were the thin, black lines of supply for the Flying Fortresses, Liberators, and Spitfires that, early in the war, had carried out their raids on Japanese concentrations in the islands from the Darwin air base. In peacetime these same routes would carry people and goods north to rebuild Darwin as the Australian gateway to Asia, and bring products such as Rum Jungle uranium to the south.

Crossing the bleak Barkly Tableland northwesterly to join up with the Bitumen was a three-day marathon for the trucks, one which paused only for relief breaks or lunch along the way and at transit camps when dusk closed in. On April 13 we arrived at Camooweal and then at Tennant Creek, near the junction of the road from Mount Isa and the Bitumen. Farther up the Bitumen, Banka Banka and Larrimah were two more rough-and-ready camps consisting of hardly more than collections of tin roofs on stilts — no sides, and the floors were the good earth itself. All of these places existed only because of the need for strategically placed stopovers for desert travellers, probably originating with the explorers of the nineteenth century.

The meals, everyone agreed, were disgusting, consisting mostly of stew smothered in curry to mask the taste of decaying meat — refrigeration was as rare in the desert as snowflakes. But, as we constantly reminded ourselves, this was the army — it didn't matter which army — we were in the desert, and there was a war on.

We Canadians, so overgoverned by officers and non-coms, marvelled at the fact that the whole convoy was in the hands of a few Australian Army corporals, with one jeep-borne lieutenant in nominal command. The jeep buzzed up and down the convoy at times, but the scheduling, driving, feeding, and care of the troops and the seventy-five vehicles were conducted by the corporals. Almost as black as the road itself from months in the desert sun, grinning from under their cocked Aussie hats and wisecracking with a "Good on ye, Bluey" as they manhandled the convoy, the corporals determined where and when the hourly ten-minute relief stops would take place. They masterminded the lunch stops, inspected the trucks once a day, marshalled them into formation to park for the night at the transit camps, and ran breakfast and got everyone on the move in the mornings. Steering the convoy in the right direction, of course, did not tax their decision-making skills, as the lone highway went for hundreds of miles in the same direction with no sideroads or crossroads to confuse the drivers.

In this Never Never land of the Barkly Plain, the grasslands were absolutely devoid of trees in many places. We knew that there were cattle stations of incredible size — the Alexandria Downs station, for instance, occupied 7,250,000 acres and was the world's largest — somewhere in the heart of this territory, but no buildings, steers, or sheep ever came within our view. They must have been some place where the grass was greener.

At the merging of the road from Mount Isa and the one from Alice Springs there were no landmarks to speak of. All that was required was that the drivers bear right to navigate the curving junction, and it wasn't even necessary to look to the left or right as they did so — there was no other traffic within at least 500 miles.

From the start, I'd been put in the lead truck, along with eight of my mates. This paid off for us at Katherine, about 160 miles south of Darwin. There was actually a sprinkle of rain as we arrived, and we knew then that we were beginning to leave the desert behind. Everyone agreed that Katherine was the worst camp along the whole stretch from Mount Isa. Luckily for four of us, one of the Aussie corporals, Ned Kilcullen — a rotund, sweating digger whose twangy tongue never stopped cursing "the flymin' lorries" or "the flymin' Yanks" or "the flymin' cockabillies (officers)" — appointed us to guard the trucks that night. This was fortunate for us because for some reason the trucks had to be parked at another camp down the road — the truck drivers' own camp. So our food was better that night, there were bunks to sleep in, and, while our fellow Swiggers at Katherine slept under leaky roofs, we fortunate four kept dry.

The thought that out there, hundreds of miles from the celebrated nowhere, there might be anyone with theft on their minds, was laughable enough. Even if they did steal a truck, there was only one road. No matter whether the thieves went north or south, they would eventually have to gas up at one of the transit camps. The order to apprehend them would

Trucks carrying ICSWG to its new home at Darwin pause for a break along "The Bitumen", the single north-south highway through the Australian Outback north of Alice Springs.

have been radioed to the camp military cops long before they arrived. In the vast Outback, there really was no place to hide.

Following this reasoning, the Aussie corporals took us along to a patch of ground where a big white sheet had been hung between poles as a makeshift movie screen. Aussie soldiers from odd local units were already sitting around on logs and upended oilcans, some contentedly smoking pipes, waiting for the big show to start. These outdoor theatres were a standard fixture in all the Northern Territory camps, movies being the only source of entertainment aside from the wet canteen. We found our own oilcans to sit on and tried to blend in. We wondered at first why the cobbers had draped themselves in rubberized groundsheets and their wide-brimmed digger hats.

We soon found out. By the time the mobile projectionist turned on the movie, Bing Crosby in *Going My Way* — which, of course, we'd all seen before — the rain had turned itself on. Minus our groundsheets, we Canadian four were soon drenched, while the Aussies huddled under theirs, some — probably old hands from the islands' rain-soaked campaigns — managing to keep pipes and cigarettes going even while the heavens opened. Having come to see a movie, we weren't about to give in

Not quite the Royal York, these huts at Barrow on ICSWG's way north to Darwin sheltered the group from the tail-end rainstorms of The Wet on a stopover. Quarters lacked the comforts of home, but Swiggers were used to sleeping in their own blankets anyway.

and let the Aussies witness a retreat by greenhorn Canadians triggered by a perfectly ordinary tropical cloudburst. Stone the flymin' crows! This was, after all, the Outback, and it was the tail end of the wet season. So we stayed put and, there on the raw edge of nowhere, sat through the Crosby epic, slapping at mosquitoes, battered and drenched by the deluge, and straining bravely for an hour and fifty minutes to enjoy the novelty of watching an old movie through a curtain of rainwater.

On the final leg to Darwin, the number of deserted army camps began to increase, more evidence of the tremendous number of Allied troops that had been quartered over huge patches of bush during 1942–43. These would have included air and ground crews from the bomber and fighter squadrons as well as ground troops carrying on training exercises in the earliest days and waiting to be ferried across the Arafura Sea to Port Moresby, New Guinea — or perhaps over the treacherous Torres Strait to circumnavigate New Guinea's eastern tip for the landings in the Solomons. There had been wireless operators and intelligence personnel — and there still were, somewhere in the apparent emptiness — engaged in a variety of communications work. Number One Canadian Special Wireless Group would be the latest of these.

Closer to Darwin, the camps were almost as derelict, but some were actually inhabited by the still-extensive air force and communications population. It was clear that life would continue to be primitive in Arnhem Land: shorts and boots; tin-roofed, open-sided huts; plenty of mosquitoes and crawling life forms; warm water to drink and bathe in; heat; spiky-fronded pandanus trees; six-foot-high anthills; dry, scrubby bush with towering, rock-hard gum trees to cut for kitchen firewood; and prison-style food — Devil's Island couldn't have served better.

It was the middle of April. Our last significant rain had been the night we watched Bing Crosby through the raindrops. Our arrival had been timed perfectly, when it came down to it: the Wet was over until next October. Credit must be given to Harry Wethey for his planning abilities. When 1CSWG's convoy rumbled slowly over the washboard MacMillan's Road, a few miles into the bush west of Darwin, and reached our new home, everything was bone dry, the sky was blue again, the sun shone, and 336 Canadians gladly jumped down from the trucks for, we dearly hoped, the last time. The Australian Northern Territory Band played "O Canada."

Despite the rude state of the MacMillan's Road camp, within two weeks, after a feverish effort by everybody in the unit, the place was up and running. Using temporary antennae, the operators of the first and only Canadian Army wireless interceptor station in the South West Pacific Area were copying Japanese signals from anywhere between Tokyo and Rabaul and Singapore and sending them to the Central Bureau — and, ultimately, to Allied headquarters.

The Number One Canadian Special Wireless Group camp outside Darwin, Australia, is seen here from the water tower. On far left is the outdoor movie theatre. the messhall and the "Darwin Rocket" are visible in the upper right. Some barracks huts can also be seen.

At this point, Canada and its allies had been at war since I was fourteen years old. Now I was nineteen and the fighting raged on, having reached a staggering height of ferocity, with frightful devastation and loss of life on all sides. In April 1945, for all most of the world knew, the wars in the east and the west might both go on for another decade yet. It was a bleak outlook for all involved, including the men of 1CSWG, who might just as well have been marooned on a desert island.

Stranded seemingly in limbo between the peacefulness of the southern part of the Australian continent and the desperate, savage sea battles amidst the pressure-cooker tropical islands to the north, we of 1CSWG

Veteran 1CSWG operator listens to incoming Japanese signals and copies down
messages on his typewriter. Two radio sets are stacked in front of him, one tuned to
the Japanese sending operator and the other to the receiving end.

felt part of neither world. Our veteran operators were at least doing positive work against the Japanese, their long electronic reach contributing as
much to the war in the islands as the Allied ground and sea forces who
responded to the key intelligence being stolen from under Japanese noses.
It was not yet the turn of the juniors of Number Two Operating Section
to use the skills we'd laboured so diligently to learn.

While the stillness of Arnhem Land's coast created an outward appearance of peaceful tedium, in reality the very air itself was filled with the noise of wartime traffic that only became apparent with the aid of electronics.

Almost from the moment of our arrival, the Number One Section operators, their skin turned deep brown from the sun, sat in khaki shorts, sneakers, and headphones in a big, steamy tin-roofed hut, their fingers jabbing at typewriter keys. They got down on paper a typed record of the frenetic beeps picked out of the air by banks of short-wave radio sets piled on a long bench. As described before, each monitored two radio sets, one tuned to a Japanese sender, the other to the receiver.

Working in shifts around the clock, they listened for sounds that carried coded Japanese messages of enemy strategies, troop and supply statistics, transport information, and orders from Imperial Headquarters in Tokyo which spilled across the airways with the arrogant confidence that had taken the Japanese forces thousands of miles into enemy territories.

At first there had been no stemming of the military flood that propelled the "Co-Prosperity Sphere," as the Japanese called their plan of conquest, far afield. By now, in April 1945, the enemy was being rolled back toward Japan's home islands. The last major land battle of the Pacific war, Okinawa — perhaps the most savage of all — had just begun. Yet the naval and air war went on at full pitch wherever the Japanese held someone else's lands. Filtering through it all were the wireless messages to and from Japanese command centres, the contents of any of which might carry a key to a decisive victory over the enemy.

For the rest of us, the outward silence of Arnhem Land was often broken audibly and violently by the thunder of the engines of the Spitfire fighters that took off from the airfield next to our camp and flew at treetop level, on their way to deliver a shaking-up to the enemy garrisons on Timor, about 300 miles away, and to other jungle sites where Japanese units held on tenaciously. Though the threat to Japan's home islands was mounting, there were still several Japanese armies occupying quite effectively the islands that sprawled for more than 2,000 miles across Australia's northern shore. Their air support gone, their naval support half-destroyed and withdrawn to defend the homeland, they no longer posed an invasion threat to Australia. Nevertheless, their troops were well entrenched in the heavy jungles, probably the most difficult battle terrain in the world, and they were still numerous and well enough armed to withstand Allied assaults.

Another ICSWG veteran eavesdropper takes notes on an enemy signal by hand.
Part of the extensive switching equipment of the wireless intercept station is in the
background. The station operated around the clock, often in smothering heat. There
was no such thing as air conditioning. In those days before transistors, radio sets had
electronic tubes, whose heat added to the sweltering conditions.

At the Darwin camp, water was pumped up from artesian wells into these tanks, filtered
to remove alkalines. The water was sent across the camp through pipes laid on open
ground baking under hot sun. Camp showers were thus guaranteed water temperature
of about 135 degrees Fahrenheit (54C), but a cold drink of water was hard to find.

Given their fanaticism, it wasn't out of the question that a suicide task force might at some time try to cross from Timor and erase a choice military target — the 1CSWG signals intelligence station at Darwin, for instance, or any of the other eavesdropping installations within range. That was why, we came to realize, that sixty Spitfires were always at the ready on the RAAF air base across the road from our new 1CSWG camp, and why they spent much of their time in the air above us.

Lieutenant-Colonel Harry D.W. Wethey was a man with a mission: to build the best, grandest, wireless station in the South West Pacific theatre, one whose ears would pick up the electronic chatter of *all* Japanese military radio traffic up and down the Pacific and whose voice could also be turned southward to tell Allied strategists in Melbourne, Washington, and, of late, Manila, what that traffic was saying. To achieve this goal, when we first arrived at the MacMillan's Road camp in April, Lieutenant-Colonel Wethey put us all to work to build just such a facility. He couldn't hire Australians because of the secrecy behind 1CSWG's assignment; his sole alternative was to use the muscle he had under his command: the signalmen and lower non-coms of the group. All but the essential personnel needed to run the camp were pressed into action.

It seemed to be the eternal destiny of the young Ops Mon Sigs of Number Two Section to be a indentured force of coolie labour under the smelting heat of a Torrid Zone sun. Darwin, just twelve degrees south of the equator, had a climate that brought steady downpours during the Wet, from October to April, and parched, sun-drenched drought throughout the Dry, from April to October. Both seasons had one thing in common: temperatures in the nineties, which quite commonly broke the century mark. During the Wet, the jungle sprang up almost overnight and the rains turned the ground to mud. During the Dry, the ground dried up, as did everything else.

There was already a camp of sorts when we arrived on MacMillan's Road at the tail end of the Wet. Set in a forest of gumwood trees, pandanus palms, scrub bushes, and grasses already becoming desiccated, the land was just beginning to turn into semi-desert. Under a sun that relentlessly baked the red ground and the humans on it every day until the earth quietly rolled over and put it all under shadow, the camp was a real-life working model of all the backwater settlements depicted in literary tales of the white man stranded in a tropical hell. The dry heat turned the ground, a reddish clay closely related to lava, rock hard.

In the Dry, most of the fauna disappeared into hibernation until the Wet returned. The exceptions that seemed to enjoy the Dry included a few species of lizards a couple of feet long, snakes, centipedes six inches long and an inch wide, flies, mosquitoes, and vast rainbow clouds of parrots and cockatoos. Several varieties of large ants, coloured variously on their hind ends according to the army they belonged to, ignored both the Wet and the Dry and continued with business as usual no matter what the season. Kookaburra birds streaked through the bush, hoo-hoo-hawing madly. Wallabies — grey-furred, dwarf kangaroos — kept on the hop. Thankfully, the white ants that built their earthen skyscrapers as tall as eight feet, took a nap until the October arrival of the Wet, when they would re-emerge and invade anyplace they could find something dead to feast on. Their menu included the wooden supports of man-made buildings into which, being termites (mastotermes darwiniensis), they loved to burrow into and consume from the inside out, leaving a wooden two-by-four stud looking solid but actually just a shell that could be easily crushed with one hand. As a tour de force of sorts, the creatures also made short work of the long stretches of lead-covered cable we'd buried in trenches carved out of the lava between two camp huts. The colonel sent sections of the ravaged "bugproof" cable back to headquarters in Canada for the experts to mull over and marvel at.

Tall, wafer-like homes of termites dot the landscape of Cemetery Plains near Darwin. Each faces east and west, apparently to catch as much of the sun's heat as possible on its daily transit.

Signalman Murray, left, suggests to Signalman Wolfe that sitting on a Northern Territory termite hill might not be a good move. The termites built their odd homes out of local sand and hibernated through The Dry, coming out in The Wet to chew on dead organic material such as wooden building supports and even buried lead-covered cable.

Chapter 11

Under the Spitfire's Wing

Three months before, we had left a camp at Pat Bay, British Columbia, which we had rehabilitated from near ruin. Now we had arrived at another reclamation project; our new home away from home wasn't fully ruined, but it had barely progressed beyond the Stone Age. As we reminded ourselves for the umpteenth time, this was the army, even if it was the Australian Army that was now calling the shots.

As we found it, the camp was a scattering of long, narrow huts with corrugated steel roofs and tarpaper-and-wood panels running along the sides to deflect the rain. Otherwise, the huts were at the mercy of any and all snakes, lizards, centipedes, mosquitoes, flies and bugs that wished to crawl or fly in and out. The hot breezes or occasional willawaw (mini-whirlwind) blew red dust into our midst as well.

Just before our arrival, a civilian work crew had — undoubtedly with much puzzling over and cursing about the assignment — installed a concrete floor in each hut at the advance request of Major Ralph Pick of Ottawa, our own resourceful facilities genius. There was no chance of fly screening for these Other Ranks huts, but we did have our green mosquito netting to hang over our flimsy wood and canvas cots. Each night when we went to bed, we tucked the bottom fringes of the netting into the edges of our blankets from the inside. The Aussies, we noticed, were just as careful about that as we were.

Among the camp's amenities was the outdoor "bathhouse," a roofless enclosure a short walk downhill from the huts. The bathhouse was surrounded by a seven-foot wall of corrugated steel for concealment — from whom? We hadn't seen a female of any variety who might want to ogle us. Water came from deep-drilled artesian wells; alkalis had to be filtered out before the salty water was fit to drink or even to shower in, and then it was pumped to a big water tank set high up on stilts. As the water was piped at ground level to the showers, mess kitchen, and officers' quarters, it was about 85 degrees under the full blast of the tropical midday sun. In other words, there was no such thing as a refreshing, cold drink of water.

Another camp highlight was a truly ingenious pair of latrine buildings set a longer hike in the other direction, near the edge of the bush. Aussie-designed and built, these latrines were monuments to military sanitary engineering. Outwardly, with their corrugated tin roofs, they looked much like the barracks huts, except that the walls were enclosed but for an open strip along the top of each for ventilation. Wonder of wonders, these open strips were *screened*. Another surprise was the concrete floors, but in this case concrete was necessary for the latrines' function.

The latrines each featured a three-foot-deep trench, dug below floor level and running the length of the hut's single long room. Lined with concrete, the trench was exposed at both ends so that long tree branches could be stuffed into it from outside — more on the reason why in just a moment. The trench was covered with metal plates, to which a row of about a dozen sheet-metal thrones, set on holes punched out of the metal plates, was welded. The open tops of the thrones were rectangular, with the sharp metal edge curled over reinforcing rods.

The latrines had been originally designed to have wooden seats set on top, but in the rugged North of Australia these, like fly screens, were considered suitable only for "I-waws" (or AWAs, the women's army) and "'orspital patients." Besides, if proper care were not taken to remove them first, the wooden seats would have vanished in the first sanitizing of the latrine. Herein lay the beauty, myte, of the latrine's design. Once it was quite obvious that full use had been made of the latrine's facilities, the long tree branches previously stuffed into the trench — and now contaminated — were set afire, accomplishing the desired end: sanitation. A warning notice was always posted on the door of the latrine when it was being burned out. Potential users were directed to visit the alternate, freshened-up one next door. Usually, though, the aromatic smoke that drifted toward the barracks was warning enough that "sanitation" was ongoing.

It was incumbent on the "sanitary engineer" — a chubby lance-corporal who'd dropped out of Ops Mon Sigs training and volunteered to do "anything" instead — to make sure that no user was perched on one of the metal thrones when he set the trench afire. An experienced Aussie said that, during this hellish operation, flames shot up through each throne with howling fury to a height of about two feet, turning the metal red hot. So it was wise not be caught *in flagrante delicto* when the lance-corporal began his grim task. It was also wise not to visit the freshened-up latrine too soon afterward, as the metal thrones stayed hot for quite a long time. Even Major Pick couldn't improve on this system.

Not to be completely outdone, the major did adapt a portable gasoline burner — a kind of flame-thrower — meant for cooking in the field, for the lance-corporal and his assistants to start the fires more surely and quickly, thus successfully bringing a touch of Canadian technology to Australian Outback sanitation.

Even the major couldn't solve the smoke problem, however. Normally, the prevailing winds blew the smoke away over the bush to the desert beyond, toward the wallabies and emus. But sometimes the wind would shift, bringing to the camp a reminder of past deeds, and letting everyone know that Lance-Corporal Bender was performing his sacred duties, like a high priest at some holy rite.

Major Pick did achieve an advance over the Aussie engineers in a related project. Because of the distance that the latrines lay away from the huts, it was a needless waste of time for the Other Ranks to trudge all that way when the purpose was merely to relieve the kidneys. The camp being a male-only domain, it was quite proper to meet this problem right out in the open. Behind each barracks hut, Swiggers dug a large pit by hand — no easy task in that petrified ground. The pit was then half-filled with empty tin cans and assorted debris. As the pit was refilled, a device of the major's own design was installed, made from a large filling funnel that tapered down to a metal pipe about five feet long. The end of this pipe was buried in the tin cans and the pit was filled in with earth around it. The funnel and pipe stuck out of the ground about two to three feet, a comfortable height for most men of nor-mal size. The subterranean pit needed no burning out, and the device allowed the utmost freedom to achieve fast relief in the invigorating open air while watching the cockatoos at play in the nearby trees. The communica-tions-minded Ops Mon Sigs quickly dubbed these devices "pissophones." They became instantly popular and were the solution to a problem in a way that the Aussies had apparently not thought of.

One thing we Canadians hadn't accounted for, however, was that the main road ran behind some of the huts. This provided a panoramic view for anyone passing by, such as a truckload of AWAs or nurses. If an Ops Mon Sigs happened to be using the pissophone at that moment, he was sure to get a chorus of wild female cheers and waves before he could duck for cover. It was just another hazard of living in an active theatre of war.

In this environment, the signalmen of 1CSWG were put to work with picks, shovels, saws, and axes to construct what should already have been built and made ready for us to move into so that we could do the jobs we had been painstakingly trained for. Our standard uniform had long since become shorts and boots. Without shirts, we were now as brown as any Aussie. But where the Aussies wore their broad-brimmed digger hats pinned up on one side, the Canadians were issued with pith helmets. We were glad to get them, for the brown berets we'd been wearing seemed to do nothing but concentrate the sun's heat on the head. For me, there was a touch of home in the helmets. They were made in Brantford, the city I came from.

One of the first assignments for some of us Number Two Ops Mon Sigs was to create a supply of firewood for the cook stoves. Half a dozen of us stalwarts were outfitted on our first full day in camp with axes and crosscut hand saws (chain saws had yet to be invented, and there was no such thing as safety equipment) and sent out into the nearby bush. No one seemed to consider the fact that there were among 1CSWG's numbers ex-lumberjacks who could have done the job more efficiently and easily.

I'd used an axe to split firewood at some time during my brief past, but taking one to a gumwood was not quite in the same league. Gumwood trees are so hard that, once you have succeeded in chopping one down and getting a piece of it onto a powered circular saw, a thin stream of blue smoke shoots up from the slot being cut by even the sharpest blade, which must burn its way through as well as cut. Among the towering specimens,

Two signalmen of ICSWG puzzle over the purpose of a newfangled device installed behind each barracks hut at the Darwin camp. They soon found these a welcome convenience that saved trekking all the way to the latrines.

Outdoor cooking facilities of the ICSWG messhall at Darwin featured improvised cookstoves, left, and the tall capped chimney on the messhall kitchen at the left, known as the "Darwin Rocket", poised for launch.

Don Laut and I selected a tree about two and a half feet thick and took turns at the axe. We may as well have been chopping rock. Tiny chips flew off, but there were none of those great chunks that makes chopping down a soft Canadian pine a satisfying experience. Gradually, using brute force, four or five of us signalmen-cum-lumberjacks managed, by chipping and crosscutting and hacking, in finally downing three gumwoods. It had taken an entire day to do it, but there was enough firewood in those three elongated rocks to keep the cook stoves going for many days.

There was yet a greater challenge ahead of us: helping to cast huge concrete anchor blocks for the 1CSWG radio antenna tower. This installation was the difference between a vagabond mobile army unit and one that would do what it was meant for: picking up strategic enemy messages. This job was the baby of Major Pick, a true headquarters man. Harry Wethey, himself an engineer, later said Ralph Pick was "the best theoretical and practical engineer I have ever known. He was at home with civil, electrical, electronic, and mechanical disciplines, and could plan and execute from the ground up anything from a waterworks to a giant transmitting station complete with antennae."

A diminutive, grey-haired man who seldom seemed to speak, Major Pick was not only among the oldest members of 1CSWG, he was one of its original members, having been assigned in 1943 to assess the workings and viability of Canadian signals intelligence then in existence. The creation of 1CSWG was a byproduct of his assessment.

On Major Pick's list of things for us to do in Darwin were all those mentioned above by Lieutenant-Colonel Wethey, and then some. After we'd brought in enough firewood for the time being, we were issued pick-axes and shovels and shown where we were to chisel out a shallow trench, about 300 yards long, through the rock-like ground for the lead-covered transmission cable to run to the future Intelligence Corps shack. This project also brought in bodies from Motor Transport, Intercom, and Technical Maintenance sections for the hard labour. For weeks after we had finally hacked out the trench, the cable lay alongside it, unburied and apparently abandoned. But it was live and in use, and it eventually was buried in the trench and left to the mercy of the termites.

There was a bonus for us navvies when we were joined at the end of May by what was called "the Rear Party," a group of twenty more signalmen all the way from Vimy Barracks at Royal Canadian Signals Headquarters in Kingston, Ontario. With them came twelve more Intelligence Corps men, five experienced operators from the Victoria station, another sergeant-major, and four more officers. The twenty unsuspecting signalmen were instantly pressed into service alongside "Wethey's Commandos," as we'd been tagged. Ditch digging, laying of water pipe, mixing of concrete, and the putting up of buildings were all spread among a few more hands. The snail's pace of construction ramped up to about the speed of a turtle.

Concrete for the antenna's enormous base and five-by-five-foot anchor blocks had to be mixed. For weeks we shovelled gravel, sand, and cement into huge wooden forms under a sun that seemed to set the concrete instantly. When the cement supply ran low, five of us Ops Mon Sigs were loaded onto a truck and driven over to the RAAF air base, where Major Pick had tracked down what was probably the longest and highest stack of bagged cement in the world. They were piled seven-deep and high along one wall of an enormous metal aircraft hangar built like a Quonset hut with an arching corrugated metal roof that peaked at a height of about eighty feet and touched the ground on two sides. It was at least a good city block long, having been built by the Americans to house Flying Fortress and Liberator bombers in need of repair. It seemed big enough to hold at least two B-29 Superfortresses. The Americans later turned it into a giant warehouse, stocking it with a supply of dry cement to make enough concrete to pave over half the Japanese islands. That might have been their intention for postwar Japan.

The Australians who inherited the hangar saw little use for concrete — they were happy with earthen floors in their huts. They just left the hangar open to anyone who, for some odd reason, felt they needed cement, and a lot of it. Our truck was the only vehicle and we were the only living, breathing, moving humans in that cavernous hangar. Despite the general lack of habitation, the air hung with fine cement dust disturbed from broken bags, perhaps by the two-foot-long lizards lurking among them. When we moved a bag to toss it onto the truck, great puffs of cement dust arose. Because of the dryness of the air, it never did settle down, except onto our bare skins copiously bathed in sweat, and in our lungs.

Choking on the dust, cursing the radio antenna and all the works around it, we finished the loading and rode back to camp with our truckload of cement. When we climbed down from the truck, the hoots and guffaws from everyone who saw us piled insult on top of misery. We were dead greenish-grey from head to foot — helmets, boots, shorts, and all. The cement was starting to set in the wet of our sweat. We had no idea, but much apprehension, about what cement dust might do to human lungs and skin.

And would we be turned into statues when the moist coating dried? We were the five least-amused bods in camp. But we brought great hilarity with us.

After we'd unloaded the truck, we simply turned and walked straight into the outdoor showers. We went right in, helmets and boots and shorts and all, turned on the showers, and stood there until we'd washed and scrubbed off most of the cement. For once we didn't mind that the shower water, like the drinking water, was over 100 degrees. It took off most of the cement, except for nooks and crannies here and there. We didn't dare have a speck of it left on us by the time Lieutenant-Colonel Wethey and company inspected us on parade the next morning — such dereliction of decorum would certainly draw a stretch of hard labour.

While the insect variety of airborne attacker was the bane of our existence at ground level, the dozens of Spitfires that belonged to 85 Wing of the Royal Australian Air Force were almost as bothersome as they flew over the camp at their customary altitude of about a hundred feet. The playful RAAF Spit pilots loved to zoom over the camp at treetop height, leaving the highest branches swaying in their slipstream and our teeth chattering

A Liberator bomber sits in a hangar on the Royal Australian Air Force base across the road from 1CSWG's camp. Thousands of bags of cement were stored in a similar hangar, where a team of Swiggers had to load a truck with cement for making concrete bases for the wireless antenna, becoming completely coated in cement dust in the process.

Three Swiggers perch on top of red rock outcropping on Casuarina Beach on the Arafura Sea near ICSWG's camp. Signalmen found out why the rock was heavily pockmarked when two Spitfires swooped down at high speed for firing practice but luckily spotted the men in time and sped away from the scene.

from the sudden and brief roar of their Merlins. Half a dozen might flip by in quick succession, and the squadron leader — whose Spit had a red prop spinner — liked to dive at our flagpole and come out of the dive whining along the rooftops. All of them, though, managed to avoid our towering antenna, which rose above the surrounding treetops like an exclamation mark, providing an easy mark for enemy aircraft. It was easy to forget at the time that the planes were our protectors against some Japanese suicide mission, but on reflection it was plain they certainly were.

Some of us were introduced to the Spit pilots' penchant for low-level high-speed passes when, having earned some time off, we went to Casuarina Beach, about three miles from camp. Here, in the heavily salted Arafura Sea, the swimming was excellent and the beach superb — though it was still strung with stretches of barbed wire and steel posts and the occasional pillbox cut into the red volcanic rock back from the beach. In 1942, when Darwin was being bombed daily — at first by the same task force that hit Pearl Harbor, then by land-based aircraft from Timor — these were installed to withstand or slow down any Japanese assault landing. The pillboxes were no longer manned and their guns were gone, so they now served only as havens for snakes. This was the southern edge of the Arafura, where the crystal-clear water was warm and the beach bottom stretched out underwater for hundreds of yards. You could float on the densely salted water just by stretching straight out on your back.

We half-dozen had just come out of the water and were sitting with our backs against an outcropping of porous, pockmarked rock that projected high out of the sand and looked like red Swiss cheese, to dry off. At the sound of distant engines, barely audible over the lapping of the water on the sand, we looked up and along the vast beach. Two tiny spots were visible in the sky slightly above beach level, and they were quickly getting larger. In a twinkling they became *very* large. They were Spitfires, skimming the beach at about thirty feet high and travelling about 200 miles an hour, headed straight for the rocks — and us!

Something, perhaps the fact that we'd earlier noticed empty, jettisoned .50-calibre machine-gun belts lying around in the sand here and there, caused us all to panic and dive to each side of the rocks. The movement must have been enough. The Spit pilots did not press the firing buttons of their guns. Instead, about a hundred yards from us they climbed up, screamed overhead, soared aloft, and barrel-rolled. They flattened out at high altitude, where they circled and no doubt peered down in puzzlement at whatever kind of beasts had been lolling on their private practice target, the outcropping of rock. Now we knew how it had come to be pockmarked.

One Spitfire banked and flew high over the water, then dived almost straight down and fired all its guns at the surface — or at something swimming — seeming to hang there for an instant from the backfire of the barrage. The sea churned to white foam. Then the plane swooped up and droned away along the beach. The pilot was no doubt annoyed at having his target practice foiled by a bunch of clods sunbathing on his rocks.

Two or three Spits would usually appear during later visits to the beach. They would avoid strafing the rocks while we were on the beach, choosing instead to dive at the water some distance offshore, firing at the waves or at some unfortunate giant turtle or sunbathing shark, seeming again to hang there for an instant while the sea boiled under them. Then they would fly away on other business. When we were well out from the beach they would often resume their assaults on the rocks as we watched from the water.

There were at least sixty Spitfires flying in and out of the RAAF airfield across the road from our camp. There were also about a hundred Liberator bombers, sporting rows of tiny bomb and ship silhouettes on their fuselages to indicate their bombing records. These workhorses added to the roaring noise around us with their take-offs and landings as they went off on or returned from raids on the islands, usually Timor. By July, however, these were grounded, there apparently being less need for their operations, perhaps additional testimony to Special Wireless's success in pinpointing targets that were slowly being destroyed.

If the bombers weren't being flown much, the Spitfires definitely were. I counted five flights of twelve Spits each one day as they returned from the islands at a modest altitude. They all landed at the Darwin base. Although the Aussie pilots seemed to revel in their low-level aerobatics, there was one tragic incident close to our camp one day in June. Most of our unit was attending church parade at a makeshift outdoor chapel not far from camp. As we were singing the final hymn, three Spitfires roared over the treetops at high speed — zip, zip, zip — then boom! One of them hit something, probably a tree, just a short distance away. When we passed the scene a few minutes later in our truck, there was nothing but smoking debris scattered across a clearing in the gumwoods. Needless to say, the pilot was killed.

One morning, within a week of Japan's official surrender in August, the Liberators all took off with a tremendous roar and disappeared. Over the next few days they returned — one by one, clipping the treetops as

Two 1CSWG signalmen size up the tailgun pod of a Liberator bomber, veteran of raids on the Islands. The air base near 1CSWG's camp was filled with Liberators and Spitfires which kept up harassing attacks on Japanese troops entrenched on Timor and New Guinea.

before — and landed at the airfield. It turned out that they had been sent en masse to Singapore, where the Japanese had already given up. The Libs landed on the airbase there — with Japanese troops still very much in view — and picked up Australian prisoners of war taken in 1942 during the fall of Singapore. After a medical inspection stop at Darwin, they were flown on to southern Australia for hospitalization and repatriation.

Despite all their noise and their dangerous flirtation with fate, both on their own and our behalf, the RAAF planes did keep us in touch with the reality that there was a war going on, one with no end seemingly in sight. Kamikaze suicide bombers were taking a heavy toll on U.S. warships near Okinawa. Casualties on both sides were extremely high from the fighting on Iwo Jima. Japanese wireless signal traffic was as heavy as it ever had been. Allied estimates placed the number of enemy reserve troops on the Japanese islands alone at a million or more, with considerable air support at their disposal. An attempt to invade the Japanese islands would result in hundreds of thousands, possibly millions, of Allied and Japanese casualties, far too high a cost. It seemed that, at best, there would be a few more tropical birthdays for the men of 1CSWG as the war crawled on. But another solution was ultimately found.

Chapter 12

The Pride of Harry Wethey

In the antipodal winter of 1945, much bloody fighting was going on in the jungles to the north of Australia. The Japanese, though pretty well cut off from any source of supplies except the relatively small amounts sneaked in by submarine from time to time, were still game to hold onto their illicit gains. Their show of grit was such that some holdouts lasted thirty or more years. Even into the 1970s, the odd survivor would turn up on the islands, believing that the war was still on and refusing to surrender. This fanatic refusal to give up indicated the iron-clad tenacity the Allies would encounter if they invaded the Japanese home islands.

The Japanese High Command's arrogant assumption that the Imperial forces would fight the Allies to a standstill and keep the territories they'd seized was plainly shown by aerial reconnaissance photographs. These showed their camps on the larger East Indies islands such as Java and Timor, neatly laid out and maintained like peacetime establishments. They were keeping the grass cut and had lined whitewashed boulders alongside pathways and roads. The Japanese obviously expected to stay a long time, too. After the war, it turned out that many of them were under the impression, fomented by their officers, that they were actually occupying territory deep inside Queensland and even California. These deluded souls believed they were winning or had already won the war.

To the Australians, having these unwelcome guests roosting so close to their continent's north shore was just not on. As MacArthur's forces moved farther north, the Aussies decided to do something about it. In May, helped by Special Wireless intelligence on Japanese strengths, they let loose an invasion force against Balikpapan on the big island of Borneo — one of the more westerly of the East Indies chain and one rich in oil and rubber. Attacking by land, sea, and air, the Australians annihilated the Japanese forces in savage, fanatical fighting and struck one of the most severe blows to the Co-Prosperity Sphere. They also cut off a source of the much-needed oil and rubber that the Japanese had been managing to sneak out by submarine.

No doubt with a long stay in Darwin in mind, Lieutenant-Colonel Harry Wethey seemed to be prepared to have us under his wing for years to come. He even took a personal hand in rejuvenating the tumbledown outdoor theatre by scrounging a huge canvas and pitching in to paint it himself with aluminum paint to make a presentable screen. Dozens of benches — no oilcans here — were obtained from somewhere. And someone among the officer ranks must have had connections with the movie industry, because a steady flow of Hollywood films — some of which we actually hadn't seen before — provided a reliable escape — our only one — from the daily realities of life in the 1CSWG camp. Word of this "bonzer" Canadian cinema spread quickly far and wide, and for a time the refurbished outdoor theatre became the most popular evening spot for miles around. Aussie soldiers and civilian workers alike began turning up in jeeps and trucks to see the movies, and it was getting hard to find a seat.

Despite our long, tortuous journey through strange lands and seas, Darwin was not quite the Heart of Darkness. No heads stuck on poles were visible. There was, in fact, little opportunity to do evil, although

Movie-goers, mostly Australian civilians and service personnel, sit ready to view film at ICSWG's outdoor theatre. Lieutenant.-Colonel Wethey's hand-painted movie screen saw nightly use by the Aussies, annoying the colonel. He had the camp barb-wired to keep the unauthorized out of the top-secret ICSWG camp.

Number Two Operating Section of ICSWG poses for a group portrait just before the signals group left their Darwin camp to journey to southern Australia after the end of the Pacific war.

some of the more enterprising Swiggers managed to find it. Next to the movies, the alternative source of entertainment in camp was the wet canteen. There was never a shortage of beer, although it was rationed out by ticket, three to a customer. Fortunately for the heavy-duty drinkers, there were some, like me and several others, who didn't have a taste for it. We picked up some pocket money by selling our tickets to the more dedicated drinkers.

Once in a while there was the chance to hop a truck going into the town of Darwin itself, where again there was little else to do but drink in the Aussie Army O.R.'s wet canteen. The nearest night spot was over a thousand miles away. In Darwin there were some off-limits sights to see, namely girls — nurses and AWAs — who were inaccessible to most of us. There also were the wrecks of town buildings and ships bombed out by Admiral Chuichi Nagumo's task force on its way to the Indian Ocean after its Pearl Harbor attack, and later by the land-based bombers from Timor.

The town was bombed more than sixty times. It was also a favourite bombing-practice target for the Japanese on Timor, so it was a wonder there was anything left of it. The harbour was impassable by any craft larger than a launch because its bottom was lined with the many large ships sunk in the Japanese attacks. They were still there when 1CSWG arrived.

The ordeal suffered by Darwin is worth describing here. On February 19, 1942, Nagumo's strike force of six aircraft carriers, 450 planes, two battleships, three cruisers, and nine destroyers had blasted Wake Island, Rabaul (on New Britain), and Amboina Island and taken them over. With the war only ten weeks old, Nagumo's fleet first helped capture the island of Bali, then crossed the Banda Sea and the Arafura to hammer Darwin, Australia's northernmost port. Defended by only a few P-40 Kittyhawk fighters and some scattered antiaircraft guns, Darwin had a population of about 2,500 men, women, and children. Nagumo's planes swept aside the small Kittyhawk force and devastated the town. Of the 500 civilian casualties, 250 were killed. The survivors fled south on foot, on bicycles, and in cars, garbage trucks, ice cream carts, sanitary carts, and road graders. Women and children, the aged, the infirm, and any civilian workers who could escape detection as able-bodied fled in an evacuee train of cattle trucks and flat cars.

At the time, forty-five ships — military and merchant marine — were moored in Darwin's huge harbour. Eight were sunken and others beached. On the ships, 165 were killed. Post office workers, female switchboard operators, and bank employees died as well. Darwin's extensive rail yards and wharves were destroyed. Other shore installations were bombed and strafed and Darwin was put completely out of action as a supply base for several months. Of the 188 fighters, dive bombers, and level bombers deployed by the Japanese, only five were lost. As mentioned above, over the next two years or so, Darwin would be attacked by Japanese bombers over sixty times more. Back home in Canada, we never heard about these attacks, but they dwarfed Pearl Harbor in terms of damage done.

A few months later, the departure of the remaining Kittyhawks of the U.S. Air Force's 49th Fighter Group to a base in New Guinea left Darwin protected only by about eighteen aging Wirraways of the RAAF's Number 12 Squadron, aircraft totally useless against Japan's Zekes and Zeroes. The Australians pleaded directly to Winston Churchill for better air support, and three squadrons of Spitfire Mark VC's — to be known as the Churchill Wing — were sent to Darwin. Forty-two Spits were diverted from use in North Africa just as Field Marshal Rommel's successful offensive was at its height in 1942 and were sent by ship. By fall, seventy-one Spitfires had arrived in Australia and another three hundred were on board ship and on the way.

The Churchill Wing went fully into action over Darwin in the fifty-third raid by Japanese aircraft. About forty Spitfires intercepted eighty enemy planes over Darwin harbour, shooting down seven and probably damaging seven more. Four Spits were lost due to engine trouble — probably from overheating in the tropical air, a menace that was to plague the Mark VC's. The plane flown by Squadron Leader Thorold Smith, a Spitfire ace in the European theatre, was shot down and Smith was killed. A controversy broke out in the Australian press over the Churchill Wing's effectiveness at meeting the Japanese after fourteen Spitfires were lost for numerous reasons when they tangled with a heavy force of Japanese bombers and fighters in March 1943. The Japanese land-based Zero and carrier-based Zeke fighters were more manoeuvrable than the Spitfire and could easily turn within a Spit's turn and shoot it down.

It was later shown that a variety of gremlins had combined to plague the Spitfires. Fuel ran short during the prolonged battle in March and five Spits had to make emergency landings, four of them to be recovered later on Darwin beaches. Three more had engine failures. The other six of the fourteen were shot down. The Churchill Wing claimed six Japanese aircraft destroyed, eight damaged, and four probables. Subsequently, the Spit pilots adopted new tactics to meet the Zeroes. In the eleven combat actions fought over Darwin between the Churchill Wing and Japanese air forces in 1943, the RAAF destroyed sixty-six enemy planes, probably destroyed thirteen, and damaged forty-one. The RAAF stated later that of the forty-four Spits out of action, only seventeen were shot down.

The Churchill Wing often had to rise at only half-strength to meet attacking enemy, a situation caused not only by the engine gremlins but also by a shortage of tires, which was said to have been exacerbated by strike shutdowns in Australian rubber factories. (Shades of the dock strike at Brisbane.) The rock-hard ground in the Darwin area made for some rough landing fields, so new tires were constantly in demand. It wasn't unusual for a few Spits to be grounded, without tires, when the Japanese attacked.

The Mark VC's were replaced in 1944 with the faster and more powerful Mark VIII Spits. Their greater success against the Japanese bomber and fighter squadrons would end the raids on Darwin altogether later that year. The Churchill Wing's three squadrons moved farther north after that and became part of 80 Wing of the RAAF at Morotai Island. In June 1945, Number 457 Squadron played a heavy part in the invasion of Borneo.

Burnt-out shells of buildings and bare concrete slabs where buildings had once stood were still common in Darwin when 1CSWG arrived in early 1945. The Spitfires still carried on their daily runs over the islands; the Japanese air force all gone, their new job was to photograph from the air or strafe the solidly ensconced Japanese garrisons. Many low buildings typical of a tropical port had survived or been put up since then to house Australian, British, and U.S. units headquartered in Darwin. Wrecks of the eight ships sunk by Nagumo's raiders still poked up from the harbour bottom, making navigation by any large ships impossible. Work was under way to remove enough wrecks to permit lighter shipping, but in the meantime the once-bustling port was paralyzed.

After the war, Darwin and its port were rebuilt, the harbour was cleared, and commerce resumed. The civilian population not only returned, it mushroomed into many thousands thanks to new business ventures, particularly uranium mining. Thirty years later, in 1974, the thriving city that had all but eradicated the original town was itself flattened by a monumentally violent cyclone that caused many times the damage wrought by the wartime Japanese air raids. But Darwin rose again, and went on to reclaim its prewar status as Australia's Gateway to the Orient.

Harry Wethey's showcase, the 1CSWG establishment, was already being viewed as a model of efficiency and correctness that was to serve as an example to other Allied services close enough to observe it. Actually, the inhabitants of the Australian and American camps in Arnhem Land really didn't care much for spit and polish. Many of the Aussies, both army and air force, lived in true Outback style in makeshift bamboo quarters with tin roofs and, in most cases, earthen floors. The servicemen themselves, mostly unshaven, slopped around in anything that came to hand. Tunics, when worn, were sun-bleached and bordering on the ragged. All kinds of kit hung from the low bamboo crossbeams.

When Lieutenant-Colonel Wethey got a line on some old U.S. Army huts being torn down not far off, he asked permission to claim the fly screening from them for his officers' quarters. The Aussie officer in charge of the wrecking crew couldn't fathom why Wethey wanted this stuff — *they* would never use it. He seemed to think there was something unmanly about wanting to keep out flies. For all the Aussies cared, they could buzz in and out of the huts to their little hearts' content. That wasn't good enough for Harry Wethey. His goal was to create a civilized Canadian home away from home. He got his fly screening.

The higher ranks were inclined to agree with him about making his camp more like home. Wing Commander Taylor, C.O. of the Northwest Area RAAF, and Lieutenant-Colonel Markel of the U.S. Army Air Force, came to look 1CSWG over as well as to see the Australian Army's travelling comedy/variety show, *Shells A-Poppin'*, being put on at our outdoor theatre. At another time, the Canadian military attaché to Australia, Colonel L. Moore Cosgrave, signalled from Melbourne that he'd like to inspect the unit. All of them liked what they saw.

Colonel Cosgrave was a courtly, pleasant old Canadian soldier with a sweeping white moustache and a habit of wearing his peaked officer's cap at a jaunty slant. In a way, he looked like a shorter version of General Georges P. Vanier, who would become Canada's Governor General in later years. Cosgrave inspected us in September during a stopover when he was en route to Tokyo to sign the Japanese surrender document on Canada's behalf. Aboard the battleship USS *Missouri* anchored in Tokyo Bay, with General MacArthur officiating and the newsreel cameras rolling, Colonel Cosgrave did indeed sign — but on the line meant for the Japanese. The official explanation given later was that the colonel had dispensed with his glasses for the occasion — as he indeed appears in the historic film footage.

The Australian commander-in-chief, Major-General Sir Thomas Blamey — who'd given us a going-over at Chermside while I was indisposed with dengue fever — was said to be considering a formal visit. It turned out that I wasn't to be inspected by him in Darwin, either, as he never did come and view 1CSWG's impressive new wireless intercept station. But it seemed that top brass were either coming or going much of the time. Lieutenant-Colonel A.W. Sandford and Wing Commander Roy Booth of the RAAF, two of the joint directors of the Central Bureau, checked in on their way through to Morotai and ultimately Manila on a grand inspection tour. Lower ranks from CB — Yank and Aussie — shuttled back and forth from Brisbane to Darwin, bringing secret cipher equipment and advice on how to install it. CB sent ten men to operate and give training in the radio-teletype and signals communications gadgets such as the Secrephone, a scrambling device used for top-level voice communications with CB. A captain came to coordinate intelligence duties.

Major Pick had taken on a great challenge in turning the primitive MacMillan's Road camp into an engineering showcase. That obviously didn't deter him, because it was plain that everything was going ahead at once under his direction as quickly as he could push it. We didn't often see him, but we knew he was there. Sometimes his short, grey-headed figure — always with his shirt on so that the major's crown on his epaulets showed his rank — could be seen on the fringe of a project such as the pouring of concrete for the antenna anchors, but at next glance he would be gone, no doubt to supervise another project.

While Harry Wethey's goal was to see that his orders to plant a model Canadian intercept station on Australian soil were carried out to the last digit and comma, Ralph Pick's goal seemed to be to show the Australians how their wilderness could be made tolerable by using all the means at hand to maximum advantage. There could be no hope of equalling the Americans in conveniences; despite their laconic view of camp discipline, the Yanks had an uncanny ability to bring the comforts of home with them, such as refrigerators and flush toilets. Pick may not have had these, but he did have resourcefulness and good old Canadian know-how.

For a lot of the Swiggers, the trip from Pat Bay to Darwin had really been one extended party. Even those who were saddled with shipboard fatigue duties and harassing stretches of military discipline managed to find what they were looking for in terms of entertainment. Some of them were even wildly successful — or so they said. But when we reached Darwin, reality soon set in. There were two major deficiencies to the place: beer was tightly rationed, and there was no access to women for the Other Ranks. The nurses at 107 Australian Army General Hospital in Darwin were five miles away, and the AWAs were based even farther away. The AWA camp was off-limits, and Swiggers couldn't get there anyway without stealing a vehicle — although some did. Besides, most of the nurses and AWAs outranked us. The saltpetre in the tea and coffee kept things in hand for the most part, but the leading Swig rakehells would not be deterred. They had a knack for disappearing from camp — as in San Francisco — without being missed.

The star rakehell of 1CSWG was Pierre DeMal, who regarded himself as only a temporary expatriate from Quebec. For him, life continued more or less as usual, army or no army. DeMal could handle Kana and all the rest of the training if he wanted to, but he didn't want to. (There were even hints that he might have previously been an NRMA officer who'd been knocked down to private and then volunteered for active service.) He was primarily interested in non-military pursuits, most of which involved women. Small and very Gallic — in appearance, gestures, shrugs, and accent — DeMal sported a perpetual half-grin and the savoir-faire, if not the profile, of a miniature Charles Boyer. He could jive and jitterbug, and sin was his hobby.

Upon his arrival at Pat Bay from some camp in Québec, DeMal had struck up an alliance with another fugitive from Québec whom he dubbed "Boombaw," a nickname he'd learned from Italian youths he'd known in his younger days. Boombaw was big, brawny, brainy, and loved parties. Somehow, although hardly from the same milieu as DeMal and Boombaw, Don Laut and I and a couple of others in Number Two Section became allied with these two in a fraternal way — but, thankfully, not in the escapades they managed to drum up — or most of them, at least.

For instance, we had nothing to do with the theft of the camp duty truck that shuttled from Pat Bay to Victoria and which was later found abandoned near Esquimalt one Saturday night. (The party at the navy barracks there was said to have been a good one and was not to be missed by any self-respecting rakehell.)

Neither did we have anything to do with the theft of the antique stagecoach at Victoria the night before 1CSWG was to leave for Seattle and beyond. There was, of course, that lineup-crashing incident at the movie theatre in Victoria on New Year's Eve, but that happened because the two bottles of liquor Boombaw bought from a sailor in a hotel washroom had *not* been watered down, as we thought they had, so they carried a greater punch than we had expected. Nobody could have predicted the fight with the airmen in the lineup and the way the military police would close in before anybody had a chance to cut and run.

With incidents such as this in mind, Laut and I and a few others kept clear of DeMal and Boombaw on Saturday nights. By the time we got to Brisbane they had developed social plans and followed through on them before the rest of us were clear of unloading the *Bristol Park*. This was another characteristic of the rakehell — the ability to disappear just before some sergeant came around and press-ganged "volunteers." It took a special kind of sixth sense to dodge them, and DeMal and Boombaw had it.

Our stay in Brisbane, especially after almost a month at sea, provided a timely safety valve for three hundred men under close discipline. There is probably no end to the mischief that such a bunch can get into in a seaport town as Brisbane was then. Most of the mischief and hell-raising went unrecorded, to be bragged about later in the wet canteen or in the backs of trucks bouncing along some rugged road. The rakehells did their best — or worst — to live up to their reputations. But no one would have expected them to carry on the mischief when we reached desolate Mount Isa. Against the odds, it was there, at the end of the rail line and on the edge of nowhere, that one of the biggest parties of the unit's short history took place.

It was our last stop where the beer was not rationed, and this without question led to many members trying to absorb enough of the brew to last them for our entire stay at Darwin. It didn't work, of course, but they made supreme efforts toward their goal. The whoops and Wild West hoopla ended only with the dawn, and the supply of broken bottles that surrounded the Silver City had been added to considerably. None of the fights between overloaded Canadians and Aussies caused any permanent injuries, but some of the bruises were still tender when our convoy of trucks rolled off toward Darwin.

There was one byproduct of the evening's hell-raking: booty that made it all worthwhile. One night, we were safe in our MacMillan's Road barracks huts, resigned to a world of dullness and none of the amenities of back home. Then DeMal fished out of his kit bag a treasure that none of us had expected to see the like of again until we went marching home:

phonograph records — over a dozen of them, each one a gem of jazz and swing. They bore elaborate red, purple, and green labels we'd never seen in North America — British Parlophone, His Master's Voice, English Decca — which added an exotic aura to these fragments of civilization. They were all either British or Australian pressings, but the bands recorded on them were American — Duke Ellington, Wingy Manone, Willie "the Lion" Smith, Tommy Dorsey, Benny Goodman, and others. In my career in radio in the days before I joined up, I'd played records by these bands many times — and back home in my old bedroom, my own collection was gathering dust. These prizes were as welcome as letters from home.

But how would we make these priceless time capsules produce music? Boombaw had the answer. From his own kit bag emerged a portable, wind-up gramophone. Eureka! DeMal and Boombaw, three sheets to the wind at Mount Isa, had in some devious way come into possession of the Mount Isa wet canteen's music system. They had smuggled it (though they later claimed they had bought it), along with the fragile, 78-r.p.m. records, all the way to Darwin without mishap.

Whether they'd acquired them legitimately or not wasn't really a question among us. It was soldiers' loot. Everybody agreed that we needed the canned music and its player more than those silver miners or drunken soldiers at Mount Isa did. After all, the permanent population there had all the beer they could drink, while at Darwin it was being rationed out at two quart bottles per man per night — hardly enough to quench a gnat's thirst, the Gunner maintained. So, with a lusty crank of the wind-up handle, the gramophone pealed out 1930s blues and swing from the well-worn old records.

The disks were destined to become much more worn over the months ahead, and for those in the barracks who were less receptive to swing and jazz, the squawk of the raspy recordings played for the hundredth time would prove too much. Groans and shouts to shut it off came whenever one of the dozen disks started to grind out its tune yet again.

There couldn't have been a quainter Somerset Maugham quality to this rudimentary life in the tropics: bored white men — with no women and with rationed beer — rotting in a tropic hell among shaky cots, mosquito netting, and stifling heat, in ramshackle living quarters in a heat-drenched equatorial land. Yearning for home but resigned to their fate, playing scratchy records over and over until someone cried out for deliverance from the repetitive noise. The legend of White Cargo was unconsciously played out daily. Everything was on this movie set but gin and girls like Tondaleyo. Wisely, the aboriginal girls around Darwin had long since been evacuated to even more remote parts for the war's duration — and no doubt for protection from predators other than the Japanese.

Many months later, at the end of the war — and of our sojourn in Darwin — the final, curious chapter to the saga of the phonograph records came with the question of who was going to take these prizes home. By that time they'd come to be viewed as community property. There was no thought given to simply throwing away the fragile shellac disks. Someone suggested drawing top card from a deck. Pierre DeMal was jubilant — if there was anything he excelled in, he exulted, it was cards, because he had all the luck of the natural gambler. The records were as good as his! This would be especially true as he was about to draw against the likes of me. I had never been known to touch cards — though not out of any moral or religious sanctions. I'd merely learned from the experience of watching hundreds of dollars turn over in nightly barracks poker games among the experts, of whom there were many. I'd also witnessed some sudden hot streaks among those considered not to be proficient at cards. The prospect of going into bondage over money owed to one of these card sharks was not the kind of fate I cared to envision for myself.

Pierre DeMal and I had never quite completely hit it off. So it gave me great pleasure when — after taking on and defeating all five who felt that they instead of DeMal or I should own the records — I at last faced DeMal for the final draw. Incredibly, I continued to draw the top card for each of the twelve disks, each time driving DeMal into a screeching Gallic tantrum as he failed again and again at his own game. In the end, I — who never gambled with cards — had won all the records. DeMal declaimed wildly in French. I stowed all twelve disks away in the bottom of my kit bag, grimly savouring my victory.

On our trip home, the records went with me in my kit bag — over the entire 2,885 miles by truck to Sydney; across 7,000 miles of heaving Pacific Ocean, on all modes of transport; from the docks of Vancouver to the staging camp at Chilliwack; and on the 2,000-plus mile train trip through the Rockies, across the Prairies and northern Ontario, south to Toronto and west to Brantford, my final destination. Not one record was cracked, though they barely fitted flat into the bottom of my kit bag on top of a rolled-up sweater. At this writing I still have them, over fifty-six years after they vanished from Mount Isa, some of them no doubt collectors' items.

The phonograph? As I recollect, it was used for final target practice in the bush behind the hut and became an ancient artifact awaiting discovery for the puzzlement of some future archeologist.

Snap, crackle, and pop went the corrugated steel roof over our heads every time the sun disappeared behind a cloud and came out again. The changes in temperature would send the roof into a frenzied cycle of contraction and expansion marked by a thousand violent rattling sounds, as if fistfuls of crushed stone were being flung against it.

Anyone fortunate enough to have some spare time during the day to sneak a nap in his cot soon found himself baking under the heat radiated by the corrugated steel. Even if he fled outside, he still wouldn't get relief — the only escape from the heat was at Casuarina Beach, miles away through the bush. And you could only get there without collapsing from heat stroke if you somehow wangled a ride on a truck or jeep headed that way.

There was another way to use your spare time, such as it was: laundry. In the bottom of my kit bag, my coveralls — which had become coated with grease at the San Francisco rifle-greasing session — were still covered with the stuff. There'd been no opportunity to clean them, whether at sea or at Brisbane. So I built an outdoor fire, commandeered and filled a big dixie vat with water and the caustic soap available, and boiled the coveralls until all the grease floated to the water's top. I skimmed that off, and eventually fished out the coveralls, now bone-white instead of their original khaki colour. The same fate awaited my dirty shirts, shorts, and socks. This basic laundry — which all the rest had to use, too — meant an early demise for the Canadian-issued clothing, and we had to improvise replacements with whatever Aussie, Dutch, British, and American outfits we could buy at the nearby camps. By the end of our stay in Darwin, none of the O.R.'s, and probably none of the non-coms, owned a complete Canadian uniform.

Wethey's Commandos pushed on bravely to create a model Canadian wireless intercept station that would be the envy of the South West Pacific Area. Technical personnel — Australian, Canadian, and American — shuttled back and forth between the Central Bureau in Brisbane and the Darwin camp. Top officers came and stayed for lunch with Lieutenant-Colonel Wethey. The 65th U.S. Signal Regiment down the road gave us a supply of photographic paper for the camera club that had been formed. Two top-secret Typex encoding machines were installed in the newly built (by the Commandos) Telecommunications hut. Twenty-one NCOs and men were running the teletype machines that were also in the Telecom hut, relaying intercepted messages to CB. Four seventy-foot steel masts for the antenna tower, brought all the way from Canada, were hauled into place by the wrecking truck.

Lieutenant-Colonel Wethey was very busy, too. He journeyed to Northern Territory Force Headquarters in Darwin to fill out S18 application forms to acquire the necessary materials for a boxing ring. On his first camp inspection he found the men's quarters "in a dreadful state" and ordered a full cleanup. Captain Wyman of CB flew in to coordinate Allied intelligence duties. The 1CSWG officers were beaten 32–8 in a softball game with RAAF officers. Wethey and some of his officers went kangaroo hunting with our .303 rifles — newly liberated from the Camp Stoneman grease — tramped seven miles, and saw plenty of the bouncing beasts, but didn't hit any.

The industrious Major Pick, aided by the toiling signalmen, forged on with his innovations, producing a Dutch oven of concrete and a long shed to house four giant diesel electric generators brought from Canada. Part of the shed was held up by several concrete supports, fashioned by pouring the stuff into tall forms — made from sheets of corrugated steel curved into tubes — which produced graceful, ribbed columns reminiscent of those wobbly-looking ancient Roman ones that can be seen in parts of the Vatican. They probably stood — some toppled and some possibly remaining stubbornly upright — among the remnants of the old wilderness camp for years, a collection of strange Romanesque or Greek architectural ornaments to baffle the ponderings of those who would discover them.

One of the major's greatest triumphs was the erection of a smokestack for the mess hall kitchens which, although already half-outdoors, needed something to take away the fumes created by the green firewood and the burnt, overdone foodstuffs. There being no bricks within a couple of thousand miles, the major ordered the Technical Maintenance men to cut the ends out of several forty-gallon oil drums and weld the remains end-to-end to form a thirty-five-foot tube two feet in diameter. This was hauled erect and topped with a wide conical steel cap to keep out the rain when the Wet came back. Nicknamed the Darwin Rocket, the novel but serviceable smokestack became a landmark and a source of some speculation about when the giant rocket might be fired off skyward to land across the water in New Guinea or Timor amid some startled Japanese.

These projects seemed to tell us that our guiding officers fully expected that 1CSWG was to be in this tropical paradise for a long time to come.

Chapter 13

Hot Sun and Hockey Sticks

While the rest of us set up camp, the seasoned operators of Number One Section were busy stealing Imperial Japanese communications from the airwaves, sweating under the radiated heat of the tin roofs, carrying on the work they'd done on Vancouver Island and barely missing a beat. Number One Canadian Special Wireless Group was functioning as intended, at least in producing a high volume of wireless traffic to send on to CB. Lieutenant Smith of U.S. Signals completed the hookup of a radio circuit between our Telecom hut and the Allied main communications station at San Miguel, Manila, to which two of our officers and six Intelligence Corps men were about to go to form an advance Canadian cipher section.

The closing down of the radio link between Darwin and Hollandia indicated that the Allies were making progress in moving the war northward. Until then, Hollandia had been the South West Pacific Area's main intercept-relay station. Now, 1CSWG was to become the main clearing station for signals from various points in the theatre for processing and relaying to the Central Bureau in Melbourne and San Miguel. Boombaw declared this to be "a signal honour."

Colonel Wethey, in addition to bartering the fly screen from the Aussies, got a 100-cubic-foot cooler from the U.S. Army — thanks to the application of some leverage by Colonel Sinkov, the American cipher genius and commander of CB. Our colonel also went on a two-hour bombing practice flight in RAAF Flight Lieutenant McNabb's Liberator bomber and cabled signals headquarters in Canada to send out Signalman W.G. Lawrence — whoever *he* was — who had turned nineteen and was now eligible for overseas service. Signalman Lawrence must have found some way to avoid joining 1CSWG, because he never turned up. Presumably, he became entangled in the army's own red tape and was lost in transit.

Harry Wethey wouldn't give up in his quest to make the camp a true piece of Canada in a foreign land. As his Commandos were kept hard at the tasks of construction, the Australian Work Corps bulldozed an open area for a sports field, sending little grey wallabies bouncing frantically into the refuge of the bush. Wethey planted in his private garden most of the tomato plants he got from an experimental agricultural station farther south. He didn't get the canvas for the boxing ring right away, but he did return from his trip to U.S. headquarters in Darwin with a good-sized piece of canvas to make the screen for the outdoor theatre. He would live to regret the creation of that major Darwin-area attraction.

We were down to our last member of the Australian Number 51 Special Wireless Section that had operated a smaller station near 1CSWG's site before our arrival. He was soon to follow the five who'd left after helping Number One Section to start up. That meant 1CSWG had come of age and was now on its own. Between the sessions of hard labour, we of Number Two Ops Mon Sigs were kept at "brush-up training" in one of the huts, which had been set up as a classroom. Although we could type at 75 w.p.m., take Kana at 35 w.p.m., and Morse at 23 — and thus qualified for Class B trades pay — we weren't as yet to be trusted to do the real thing. (Out of the original hundred men who'd started in the Ops Mon Sigs course at Pat Bay, only about twenty of us actually survived to pass the series of tests to qualify as full-fledged operators.)

In the meantime, the navvy work around camp still took priority. Just getting comfortable in our quarters, in their primitive state, was a major operation for every member. We signalmen had been issued flimsy, folding canvas-and-wood cots just before we left Mount Isa. Mine was defective from the beginning, but there was no returning the goods. Furthermore, the nights we spent at the many atrocious layover camps along the road to Darwin had been rough on it — over the next two weeks it became shakier and shakier, all the while threatening to give one final groan and break asunder at almost any time.

It never did get the chance to die gracefully. One steamy evening, DeMal and Ken Brewster, in an angry difference over cards, began wrestling about violently, sweating and grunting and reeling all around my cot, which they'd been using as a card table in my absence. I walked in just as the action was at its peak. The rest of the guys were ranged at a safe distance around the wrestlers, egging them on. Just about then, they both went down hard, locked fiercely together, right on top of my cot. The ruins of my sleeping accommodation made fine firewood for our next night's campfire out on the concrete slab at the back of the hut, and it heated our billycans of tea "beaut," as the Aussies would say.

I rescued my mosquito netting and the quilted paper packing I'd used as a skimpy mattress on my cot's canvas, and spent several nights with only the packing between me and the concrete floor — and the centipedes. The incident was a source of great amusement to my friendly rival DeMal, who, after settling up amicably with Brewster, put on a mock lament for the destruction of my cot. When Dalton Blackmore, who had a neighbouring cot, went into the camp hospital, I borrowed his, knowing it wasn't a permanent solution.

I wasn't alone in my bedless state. Some others were finding their cots also beginning to creak and sag ominously. The clincher came one night when, well into the small hours of the morning, the entire hut was jolted awake by tremendous crashing, splintering, ripping, and thrashing sounds from the far end of the barracks hut, where the big man from the B.C. mountains, Charlie McGraw, had established himself. In the dark it seemed certain that another wrestling match had begun, but there were agonized shouts in only one voice: McGraw's.

Then the shouts turned to screams.

Somebody finally got the lights on. Everyone was out from under his netting, gawking toward McGraw's corner. The screams stopped, but there was only feeble movement from within the heap of green mosquito netting that previously had been slung over McGraw's cot. Two or three of the nearest bods began sorting it out and calling McGraw's name. Finally, the tall, husky, black-thatched, mustachioed mountain man rose from the devastation. Clad, like the rest of us, only in undershorts, this pillar of browned muscle now sported a red slash running down one arm, and he was shaking like jelly. As much as a strong man can, he looked scared to death. He jumped out into the middle of the aisle, staring about the floor as he did.

"The snake!" he blurted out. "Where'd that bloody snake go? A great big black one… wrapped right around my leg!"

As a couple of his mates led him away, limping, to the hospital hut — and we noticed another slash on his leg from the cot's broken frame — the rest of the hut realized what the story was. McGraw had had a nightmare about a big black snake wrapped around his leg — or *was* it a nightmare? Snakes can move with great alacrity when they want to disappear. Could one have slipped away just before the lights went on — some restless beast whose seasonal alarm clock had gone off too soon? For the next half-hour or so there wasn't a man in the hut who wasn't out with a club or gun butt, poking around the of the hut by the light of the huge, brilliant, white moon, looking for any kind of snake of any size. Luckily for the snakes, we eventually gave up without finding any. We went back to bed, tucking in our mosquito nets even more securely under our paltry sleeping mats.

The McGraw affair and its destruction of yet another cot set off a chain reaction. Over the next while, one cot after another gave way and collapsed, leaving the former occupants to find some kind of padding to soften the concrete floor. Blackmore returned from hospital and I was back on the floor again myself. It was plain that the officers weren't especially concerned as long as each man kept his place in the hut in order, shone his boots, and appeared on parade in perfect form. But the time for action was at hand.

Boombaw and DeMal, perpetrators of most of the mischief that gave our section a bad name, came into the hut before lights out one night and soon passed around the news that they'd found a treasure trove of sleeping accommodation. Across and a little way down MacMillan's Road was the civilian Australian Work Corps (AWC) camp, full of huts in which all kinds of equipment was stored. One of them was jammed with iron cots, all folded, standing on end, and packed like playing cards, apparently long abandoned and unused since the last batch of U.S. troops had done with them. By all appearances, they were going to stay there until the war was over. Obviously, they needed to be liberated.

In the name of justice and decent beds, we who were cotless formed a raiding party that very night — led by Boombaw, and with DeMal as advance scout. It took only minutes for about twenty of us to pick out a cot, sling it on our backs, and tote it to Number Two Section's hut. For about ten minutes, as the brilliant tropical moon shone down, a ragged parade of signalmen, each burdened under a substantial iron cot, jogged as quickly as they could out of the AWC camp, through a hole in their fence, across MacMillan's Road, and into the 1CSWG camp. Still in the dark, we strung up mosquito netting and put paper packing over the chain-link fencing that served as "springs" for the cots. Twenty men, myself included, slept comfortably above floor level for the first time in weeks. As the rest of the men in the hut realized that the cotless now possessed much superior sleeping accommodation, the midnight raid of the AWC hut was repeated over several nights. The era of the canvas-and-wood cot was rapidly fading in the Number Two Section hut.

However, despite the tomb-like preservation of the unused iron cots in the AWC hut, one Mr. O'Dwyer, head of the AWC camp, soon noticed that some of his cots were missing. No matter that they were serving no one and that there was a greater need just across the road in the Canadian camp; there were a lot of cots missing, and "stone the crows," the bloody "larrikins" who'd taken them must be apprehended. Such was the state of the bureaucratic mind that inventory took precedence over reason. Somehow guessing accurately that the incorrigible Canadians were the culprits, Mr. O'Dwyer lodged a complaint with Lieutenant-Colonel Wethey.

One hot July morning (actually, all of them were hot), just as we were rolling out of our new beds, a party of four with brass gleaming and stripes brandishing marched into the hut without warning. Leading them was Lieutenant-Colonel H.D.W. Wethey, his peaked, brass-badged hat firmly in place, his beautifully tailored khaki shirt and shorts crisply pressed by his batman, brown boots gleaming, and puttees rolled into place just below the knee as though by some machine. The party also included Captain Ralph March, the adjutant; Company Sergeant-Major Addy; and Orderly Sergeant Jim Proctor — all equally spit and polish. CSM Addy rapped out: "Inspection! Ten hut!"

Addy, a bulky, sometimes jovial man, was decidedly not in any mood for laughs that morning. He was the spokesman for the group; the colonel remained in mid-aisle, with his captain and sergeant respectfully behind him, while Addy walked up to each man standing firmly at attention at the foot of each bed. With his long jaw jutting almost into his victim's face, he barked out, "Was that cot here when you came, Signalman?"

Of course, the only answer given was "Yes, sir!"

Lieutenant-Colonel Wethey and his party trailed behind Addy, moving methodically down the lines of rigid signalmen. None spoke, except for Addy popping the same question over and over. The quartet reached the open arch at the hut's far end, and, without a word of additional comment, they disappeared through the arch, leaving all of us still at attention, and flabbergasted. Some corporal said, "At ease." We relaxed, puzzled but elated that nobody had been singled out for reprisal. To a man we concluded that Harry Wethey must have recognized that human decency should take precedence over inhumane adherence to discipline and army red tape.

Later, Harry Wethey recorded in his daily diary that he and his party had gone through the sleeping huts and "there found over forty steel beds of various kinds." He dropped the subject, going on to note that he had also inspected the three-ton trucks and found them "quite good." From there, he recorded that he had joined Captains Hall, March, and Reid and Major Rowland on a hunting trip "to the Daly River area." Thus was carried out Lieutenant-Colonel Wethey's intensive investigation of the infamous case of the cot thefts. We slept peacefully in our commandeered cots with clear consciences and a sense of satisfaction that no blood sacrifices were made to Mr. O'Dwyer. We rose each morning refreshed and ready for the day's labour.

Most of the cots eventually ended up 2,885 miles away from Darwin after the war was over, having travelled in the backs of trucks as lounging accommodation on the long road to Sydney. We didn't bother to wonder whether Mr. O'Dwyer ever found out the fate of his blessed cots, or whether he had apoplexy as a result of his inventory shortfall.

I was just back in the barracks hut after showering away the day's sweat and grime, and was stretching out on my cot when I heard a voice behind me say, "There he is, swingin' the lead again." I turned around. Ollie Kerfoot was there in the doorway, grinning; beside him, a stocky, large-beaked, shaggy-headed man in Australian khaki shirt and shorts, with Royal Navy flashes hooked into his shirt epaulets. Before a friendly Scottish curse could escape his mouth I recognized our shipboard companion, Jimmy, the scourge of the Middle East.

I jumped up, pumped his hand, and dragged him into the hut to get riotously re-acquainted with the rest of our gang. Jimmy apparently related to me best because I, too, had been born in Scotland, and so, although I spoke only Canadian, he regarded me as a pal.

It turned out that Jimmy had been on the travel circuit again, but this time he was following orders. From Brisbane, he'd been flown with his R.N. buddies to Morotai Island, a hundred or so miles off the western tip of New Guinea and halfway between there and the Philippines. Morotai had been recaptured the previous September and was now a major Allied strongpoint in the Pacific war. It had become a base for Special Wireless monitoring by Australian and U.S. Signals intelligence units, a strategic centre for the detection of Japanese fighting ships, and a land base from which Allied bombers flew to pound Japanese seaborne supply lines.

One of the additional means for assuring that enemy ships did not make it through the maze of channels between the islands was a vicious little weapon: the midget, or two-man, submarine. Jimmy revealed as we talked on and on that he was the steersman for one of these Royal Navy midgets, the other crew member being a Royal Navy lieutenant who navigated the sub and aimed the torpedoes. Unlike the Japanese *kaitens* — the one-man subs launched from larger submarines' torpedo tubes as living missiles — the R.N. subs gave the crew a fighting chance to get home. But only a fighting chance.

Jimmy's midget sub was now operating out of Darwin. He and his boss had the assignment at that point of prowling the channels among the islands north of us, guided by Special Wireless intercepted messages, to pick off the few inter-island supply ships the Japanese had left. They also provided escort for the small, heavily armed parties of Aussies who from time to time crossed to Japanese-held territory in small landing craft to carry out harassment raids and try to assess firsthand the strength of the Japanese island garrisons to help plan later full-scale attacks.

"Did you see all them fighter planes the other day flyin' over?" Jimmy asked. I nodded. I remembered staring up at the five flights of twelve Spitfires each, all five flights massed to form an umbrella and flying over something far below on the Arafura Sea.

"Them was cover for us an' three LCTs with some sad cobbers aboard. They got away from the Japs with some flamin' code books, but they were all bein' eaten up w' jungle rot an' fever. A couple died on board and the rest are in 'ospital in Darwin. Me and the lieutenant cruised with them in the sub alongside. Them code books must have been proper bonzer!" The Aussie slang mixed in with the Scots burr made for some strange harmonies.

Nothing much had ever been said publicly about Royal Navy or Royal Australian Navy use of midget subs in the Pacific, and Jimmy was flirting with serious trouble by telling us about his line of work. We didn't have any reason not to believe him — we were used to the oddities of South West Pacific secrets and operations. Knowing how strictly we ourselves were under orders about our own top-secret line of work, Jimmy knew we weren't likely to spread the word very far, if at all. Anyway, stranded in that forsaken spot where we almost never came into contact with anybody but members of our own unit, who was there to tell?

The Japanese had used midget subs as early in the war as in the attack on Pearl Harbor, where one had been spotted and sunk in the outer reaches of the harbour itself. They continued to use *kaitens* right up until the Battle of Okinawa. Some of them were no more than torpedoes that, with a young steersman lying outstretched inside, made a direct hit almost a certainty and the steersman a willing suicide.

Jimmy's sub was one of two operating out of Darwin, he said. He wouldn't say where they'd been operating before their recent arrival in Darwin, but it was generally known that a Japanese cruiser had been sunk at its dock in Singapore by a British midget sub. That would mean a base — perhaps a floating one — closer to Singapore than Darwin, but Jimmy would neither hint that his sub or its mate had been involved nor that there was any means for them to operate from other points in the SWPA. He would only say that the midgets were at that moment hoisted out of the water for maintenance at a secret dock in Darwin.

His major diversion while this was going on, he said, was playing a gambling game he called *maja-lai* with a half-dozen Papuan natives — the real variety — who'd come over with the escaped commandos from Port Moresby, across the way in New Guinea. Apparently the stakes in this game were, on the one hand, various ornaments the Papuans wore, and on the other some beer that Jimmy had scrounged from the wet canteen. He had a few ornaments to prove it, odd little charms made of wild pigskin leather and beads.

The gambling with the primitive "fuzzy-wuzzies," as he called them, took place in the shed where the midget subs were sitting for their overhaul. These were wild sessions during which the odd blade was flashed when things weren't going well for the Papuans, but Jimmy, wisely at times, failed to try as hard with the dice as he might. The beer that changed hands was enough to put things right for a while, but it also played its part in heating Papuan tempers when the losses got too heavy. Jimmy decided that he might have pushed things a little too far with his Papuan buddies, so he had signed himself some leave papers and come to visit his old friends at 1CSWG.

We all went off to the evening's picture show at our outdoor theatre — a.k.a. the Wethey Playhouse — where *Casablanca* was playing for the umpteenth time. Jimmy had been in the real Casablanca. His morose condemnation of the place gave the movie a touch of authenticity for us. We saw Jimmy several times after that. Once he promised he'd get hold of an LCT and take a bunch of us for a cruise to some of the tiny islands that lie just outside Darwin harbour. The date was actually set and he was to give us the final word. But Jimmy never showed up at our camp again.

Officers, by nature, are perennially obsessed with the question of how fit the men are — "The Men" being the Other Ranks, or O.R.'s. This leads to the inevitable, abominable practice of ordering the O.R.'s to go on route marches. The order also requires doing daily calisthenics en masse on the parade ground. None of our officers were themselves outstanding examples of physical fitness, nor had they acquired any shining achievements in field sports. As proof: they'd been beaten too many times by Aussies at the fine old Canadian game of softball.

True to their nature, the officers of 1CSWG — or, more accurately, Lieutenant-Colonel H.D.W. Wethey — were disturbed by what they perceived as lack of formal collective exercise among the O.R.'s. Going on vigorous route marches in 100-plus-degree heat wasn't the healthiest answer. And there was no obstacle course within a couple of thousand miles, except the natural terrain around Darwin. Nor was there a vast parade ground, and certainly no officer with sufficient athletic inclination to head up a daily calisthenics program. (None of them seemed to consider that the forced labour we O.R.'s had been doing, combined with the sparse rations, had guaranteed that not a single man who'd been dragooned into Wethey's Commandos was carrying around an extra gram of fat.)

Salvation came in the form of a truckload or two of additional equipment all the way from Canada that had been in transit for about six months and finally caught up with 1CSWG in July. It was a most puzzling assortment. There were boxes of ice skates, hockey sticks, gloves, and heavy, woollen hockey sweaters. All very useful in the tropics, of course. We never learned just who had consigned this wintry gear to the sun-blackened members of 1CSWG, but there can be little doubt that he or she was simply following some desk jockey's order to ship sports equipment to all overseas Canadian troops. And, of course, the benighted bureaucrat must have decided this meant something suitable for shivery climates such as Western Europe in January. After all, wasn't Western Europe the only place in the world where Canadian troops overseas were active? Sadly, these gifts from home were put back into their boxes without further ado.

Perhaps to cover all contingencies, however, we had also been sent basketballs, tennis racquets, volleyballs, and footballs, together with the appropriate nets and other equipment. There being no smooth surfaces in our hell's half-acre on which to dribble a basketball, nor any suitable place for a tennis court or a football field, the volleyball and softball gear were the only useable items in the shipment. Nevertheless, we were glad to have these. The volleyball nets were soon hoisted on poles where the ground was reasonably even, and from then on the evening air around the huts was filled with the reddish haze of fine Arnhem Land sand and dust being kicked up as the battles of the newly formed 1CSWG volleyball league were fought out in overzealous fury. Every section of the unit had a volleyball team, and some of them even included officers and NCOs, who had to take their chances with the steel-shod boots and clenched O.R. fists flailing among the gorilla-like leaps and frenzied rushes that were the rule. The odd broken ankle might temporarily cripple a team, but the competition for first place forged on.

Despite their cellar-dwelling status in the Northern Territory Softball League, the officers were still game to keep trying to overcome the Aussies. The crate of bats, softballs, mitts, and masks was just what they needed. Gleefully, they commissioned an AWC bulldozer to flatten a big enough space for a softball playing field. In their first game against the RAAF officers, the Canadian officers won, 36–13. That was a famous victory, and a sweet one. We figured it must have been the Canadian bats and balls that tipped the balance.

Harry Wethey pushed on doggedly with his improvements to the camp. He and Major Pick jeeped off one afternoon to the bombed-out Howard Springs Hospital — which Japanese bombers had reduced to heaps of rubble — to look for gravel with which to make more concrete.

At the same time, he came upon enough wire-mesh fly screening to do every building in camp. He was even getting the camp's roads sprinkled daily by an AWC water truck. The Australians looked on in astonished incredulity. "Waterin' the flymin' roads just because of the flymin' dust? Stone the crows!" The ruddy Canucks had flipped out right and proper!

Undeterred, the colonel's scrounging continued. He prevailed upon the C.O. of the RAAF's 85 Wing to let him — read, his Commandos — tear down two abandoned buildings on MacMillan's Road for the material. He "got some very nice fir out of it." But all was not so easy. The acting quartermaster general of the Northern Territory Force put the kibosh on taking the fly screening from the hospital ruins until an okay was received from Land Head Quarters (LHQ). The ingrained Australian dismay over troops wanting to screen their huts to keep out the bloody flies had confounded the LHQ brass. Their veto seemed to Wethey to be the work of some early breed of wildlife advocates bent on preserving the little beasts.

About this time there came an urgent request from Canada to prepare for a visit from a Captain Hilmer-Smith of G3 Intelligence, who wanted to come to Australia on an important, confidential mission. He arrived in June with a sergeant in tow — a sergeant-photographer. Their mission was to take pictures and write up stories about the men of 1CSWG and send them back home for distribution to the newspapers. What about, some of us asked each other, the unit's top-secret status? Nobody could answer that.

The "G3 Intelligence" party caused a stir in official circles. The general officer commanding the Northern Territory Force asked to have pictures taken of himself at work — and his house in Darwin as well. One of our officers, Lieutenant Koehler, and Sergeant Robinson of our T.M. Section — himself an expert photographer — took Captain Hilmer-Smith and his sergeant to Bathurst Island, about a hundred miles north of Darwin and a place none of us other Canadians ever got to, to take some representative shots.

I don't recall having my picture taken to be sent back home to the Brantford *Expositor*, except as one of the faceless O.R.'s who marched by the cameras in freshly washed and pressed shirts, shorts, and pith helmets, with .303 rifles at the high port, cleansed of the black Camp Stoneman grease and shining like glass reproductions. There was even a movie of us shot for theatrical newsreels, showing these oddball Canadians at work and play in their tropical paradise. Many months later in Sydney, Laut, Boombaw, DeMal, and I saw this film in a movie theatre. Our belly laughs and guffaws disrupted the whole showing and annoyed the others in the audience. The film can still be found somewhere in the Department of National Defence archives in Ottawa, if it hasn't crumbled to dust in the can.

Chapter 14

Keeping the Computers Fed

As a result of Lieutenant-Colonel Wethey's rigid schedule to get 1CSWG into operation, we were able to hoist the Union Jack on the camp flagpole in time for Dominion Day — July 1, 1945, Canada's seventy-eighth birthday. The steel flagpole had been designed and made by Captain March and his men in Technical Maintenance. Despite all the air of permanent establishment — rather like the Japanese on Timor — the vanguard of our planned eventual move to the Philippines, two officers and five O.R.'s from the I Corps detachment we'd left at Brisbane, took off for Manila to get things under way there. There were no immediate plans to move the entire unit as yet, but as the advance upon Japan was apparently proceeding well it was plain that, when the ultimate attack on the Japanese home islands took place, all active Allied forces would be better employed closer to the target. Still, Harry Wethey was in no hurry. He and his assistants spent all of one morning hooking up his new outdoor bathtub — suitably screened off, of course — and he had his first hot bath since arriving in Australia.

Some of the finer things in life were making their way to the other officers, as well. An RAAF Squadron officer was kind enough to arrange for thirty dozen eggs — rare as platinum in our camp and far more valuable — for the officers' mess at 1CSWG. Two U.S. signals officers produced a minor feast for the officers with crackers, canned shrimp, anchovies, cheese, and horseradish to supplement a roast of beef they'd brought. There was lunch aboard HMS *Beachy Head* at Darwin, and a roast chicken dinner at the Z Special Transmitter Station south of Darwin, with a picture show afterward.

As further entertainment, Lieutenant-Colonel Wethey and four of his officers went on another hunting trip to the Daly River with four or five Aussie officers to look for kangaroos and crocodiles to shoot. Again they missed their targets. If they'd brought back a few kangaroos, even crocodiles, there might have been enough meat left over for the O.R.'s to have been granted relief from the diet of wretched "roast beef" slabs which were universally called "tarmac" in the ranks. Our diet also routinely included boiled spuds, boiled carrots, and tea. The O.R.'s did once actually receive beneficence on the part of the U.S. Signals in the form of a dollop of ice cream each; it had turned to creamy liquid in the salubrious Darwin climate by the time each man reached the dinner table with his ice cream in his mess cans.

It was this daily ordeal of unchewable meat and barely digestible, boiled-to-death vegetable matter that finally precipitated an embarrassing incident for the officers. One evening, as the tropical moon hung low and huge over the spiky pandanus trees and rendered the sky as bright as day, the O.R. wet canteen became especially active. With most of the two-quart ration of potent Aussie beer under their belts — some with five or six or more — and no more forthcoming until the following night, a mob of about fifty or sixty O.R.'s and some daring non-coms formed a roaring, weaving, jumping snake line. Their theme song, with lyrics by the eminent 1CSWG composer, Signalman Bill Gunning, was "The chickenshit is flying all around and 'round the camp" — sung to the tune of "John Brown's Body." It was repeated over and over as the giant snake line, led by Boombaw and DeMal — with your author not far from the front rank in order to record this historic event at close hand — wound through the big wet canteen hut and out into the balmy tropical night.

Around the camp roads went the snake, its tail getting longer and longer as other aggrieved signalmen caught up. The swelling chorus of the theme song must have been audible in camps for miles around. There was a switch to other infamous and beloved army ditties, such as "She's a great big fat bitch twice the size o' me" to the tune of "The Road to the Isles," and that fine old Newfoundland ballad, "Friggin' in the Riggin'," launched by none other than the Gunner. The beer had taken a good hold, but the singing rose clear as members of the snake line stumbled, recovered, wandered, and tripped, only to recover again. Strangely, no jeepload of military police put in an appearance.

Inevitably, the snake found its way to where the several huts of the officers were located. These were easily identifiable by the carefully raked gravel walkways lined with whitewashed rocks — the work of a special detail of the Commandos, which sometimes included me. This area was off-limits to O.R.'s for anything but official business. But, if anything, the bellowing of the raunchy songs increased as the snake line entered the officers' area and began to wind itself among their fly-screened huts. Officers could be seen through the lighted windows, going casually about their business, seemingly oblivious to the abominable din outside. They couldn't possibly have been unaware of what was going on, and its intended message, but they walked around, putting on shirts, taking off shirts, hanging things up, but apparently not talking to one another. Through one window we could see Lieutenant-Colonel Wethey himself, shirtless, carefully shaving his lathered face with a straight razor, in apparent serenity and with a steady hand. He seemed to be getting ready for some evening social event.

Not a move was made by any of the officers to come outside and put things right with a reading of regulations. There still was no reaction, even when every member of the snake line broke ranks long enough to grab up handfuls of gravel from the smooth walkways and hurl the stones in a hail that came down on the officers' tin roofs with a hellish roar. Wethey didn't even seem to jump, let alone cut himself.

A little subdued by this lack of reaction from what was normally a very reactive group, the snake-liners formed their line again and marched on, still shouting out the Gunner's lyrics in belligerent style, but with an underlying note of disappointed frustration. Gradually, the line wound its way back to O.R. quarters and disbanded, as the men dropped out and disappeared into their barracks huts for another dull evening, or what remained of it.

All of us waited for lightning to strike in the form of a delegation of officers and M.P.'s invading each hut. None showed up. Strangely, no one mentioned the incident the next day — or ever, during 1CSWG's stay in

Darwin or anytime afterward. The top brass evidently wanted to pretend the rowdy incident never happened. We could all have been convicted of incipient mutiny in wartime — and been given life sentences. But such an action might have left Lieutenant-Colonel Wethey with hardly anyone in his command other than his officers and senior non-coms.

In any event, the lack of official reprisal was a clever use of reverse psychology, and it worked: the O.R.'s never again put on any kind of mass demonstration, whether over atrocious food, primitive sleeping conditions, or just plain exhaustion from hard labour. And, of course, the roaring snake line didn't change a thing.

Harry Wethey's outdoor cinema was in danger of being strangled by its own success. When word spread throughout Arnhem Land that "the bleedin' Canucks has got themselves a bonzer picture screen, an' Yank movies on top," everyone who had the misfortune to be stationed in the vicinity — including Aussie troops, Yank signallers, RAAF air and ground crews, and AWC workers — flocked in trucks and Jeeps to the top-secret Canadian camp to see the shows.

Wethey complained to the head of the AWC detachment, our old friend Mr. O'Dwyer, about the civilian workers' wanton conduct in inviting themselves over, cutting through a camp that was supposed to be off-limits, and taking signalling schedule forms out of the men's mess as they did so. The colonel wasn't without an ulterior motive: O'Dwyer, by complaining about the appropriation of his iron cots, had cast doubt upon the integrity of 1CSWG — indeed, the entire Royal Canadian Signal Corps. Before that, of course, the AWC men had done very little to get the MacMillan's Road camp ready for our arrival, leaving it to us trained signalmen to do the necessary backwork. It seemed poetic justice that O'Dwyer and his men be ordered to stay away from camp.

So as not to seem unjustly discriminatory, Wethey also complained to the C.O. of 85 Wing RAAF about his officers and men coming so nonchalantly to this top-secret, restricted installation. Despite these protests to his counterparts in the upper echelon, the Aussies continued to flock from miles around. Our defences were utterly inadequate. In the end, the colonel would have to adopt some tangible defensive strategies.

One (routinely) hot morning, detachments of Wethey's Commandos were deployed around the camp perimeter. Lines of 15-cwt. trucks followed us, stopping now and then to drop bales of barbed wire. By evening, as the usual clouds of multicoloured parrots came croaking and squawking to their nightly roosts in the lofty gumwoods and squadrons of mosquitoes roared into the air for their nocturnal strikes, the boundary between the 1CSWG camp and the territory of 85 Wing RAAF was strung with barbed wire. The border with the AWC camp was secured by the next evening. Harry Wethey was showing that he meant business. As they came upon the barbed-wire fencing and the closed gate, the would-be Aussie movie-goers had to give in. The night assaults soon stopped.

Next to the movies and the wet canteen, the principal form of entertainment was mail from home. Every other week, letters would somehow find their way across the Pacific — by U.S. Army Postal Air Service to Brisbane or the occasional freighter from Canada, thence via barnstorming RAAF biplane to Darwin. Once a month a load of parcels from home containing scarves, sweaters, books, and fruitcake would come from Brisbane by truck. This link with home, partly endangered by submarines, bad weather, and labour strikes, was forever tenuous. So it was with sour resignation that we heard one day that the intrepid little biplane had done a tailspin onto the deck near Darwin. That ended our air service from Brisbane.

As if that weren't enough, word also trickled through that the *Greenhill Park,* sister ship to the *Bristol Park* which had brought our equipment, had mysteriously blown up in Vancouver harbour. That meant no mail for at least two months. At last, some burned pieces of letters, all that could be salvaged from the mail on board the *Greenhill Park,* arrived in little paper body bags. No one knew how many parcels went down with the ship.

High adventure continued. A brush with annihilation came when seven of us found ourselves on the wrong side of a tidal river that had been nothing but a trickle when we'd crossed it an hour before. We'd stopped off for a swim at Casuarina Beach after a work chore, despite the accompanying sergeant's nervousness about overstaying our time. Not at first intending to swim, I'd kept my clothes on when we walked along the beach — the others had shed theirs at the truck. Afterward, when we were swimming, the tide came in and drove us back to the beach. Hotfooting it toward the truck, we were astounded to see that the trickle had turned into a thirty-foot-wide tidal torrent speeding like an express train backward from the ocean. We were cut off from the truck.

Some of the group rolled their clothing into bundles, dived into the swirling stream, and managed to swim to the other side. The wet clothes would betray our beach stopover — which amounted to a brief AWL — to the sergeant-major back at camp. They were risking two weeks in the digger. The sergeant was getting more and more agitated as I delayed taking the plunge. Not being a strong swimmer, I lingered on my side of the tidal river with my bundle of clothes, following the bank upstream and looking for a narrower point. But the river was getting wider and more turbulent by the minute. I waded into the torrent, going in deeper and deeper, hoping I could walk across.

The roiling water got deeper with every step, and underwater rocks rolled underfoot. It was only then that an Aussie, fishing in the tidal rip from a nearby rock, took a pipe from his mouth, looked out from under his digger hat, and said to me: "I wouldn't, myte. That water's nine flymin' foot deep if it's a flymin' inch!"

I gaped at him. Here I'd been about to step out of my depth into a swirling torrent and he'd waited until I was up to my rear end in it before casually mentioning the danger. Stone the flymin' crows, indeed!

Finally Pusey, on the other side, found a skiff among the trees and paddled it across the raging river, using a tree branch for a paddle. I got aboard, and, like the sculler he'd been at school, he had us across that Styx-of-the-Outback in two minutes, my clothes still bone dry and sergeant-major-proof.

Despite these diversions, 1CSWG was beginning to shape up as a superior force in the communications network of SWPA. Communiqués from CB, acknowledging how 1CSWG's intercept work was playing a major role in Allied actions, were appearing on camp bulletin boards. The notes were terse, and there were no details, but the commendations they carried were straightforward and had some positive effects on morale.

More and more, 1CSWG was taking over signals monitoring in the entire Darwin area, developing quickly as an important arm of the Central Bureau. The unit concentrated on analysis of Japanese naval operations the length and breadth of the East Indies and the central Pacific. The chief work was to get a sense of the Japanese signal networks between Tokyo, Singapore, Rabaul, and the major Imperial Japanese stronghold of Truk in the Carolines, which had been deliberately bypassed by MacArthur in his drive north. The

1CSWG cryptanalysts of our Intelligence Corps unit pieced together the vast network systems — the routing, abnormalities in traffic, the addition of new Japanese stations, and the loss of old ones through capture.

Full texts of the daily flood of messages were radio-teletyped to CB. Traffic analyses were sent to Manila, where MacArthur was directing the Allied war drive. Captain (later Major) J. Ross Mackay, C.O. of I Corps, described the general nature of the Japanese message structure as being similar to today's telegraphic messages. They consisted of an addressee, the unit to which the message was directed, which could be anywhere in the Pacific; a sender; the location of the transmitting station; routing instructions; and often multiple addresses for the same message. This information was especially valuable to the Allied strategic operations planners.

The texts of the messages were generally sent as a series of three- or four-digit numbers which, at this stage of the coding, took the place of letters. The enemy transmitting and receiving stations in the towns, cities, or islands were usually given a four-digit number on most networks. To avoid inadvertent errors in addresses, the total of the first three digits in the number address was "sum-checked" by the last digit. For example, on the major network, Tokyo was 6635 — 6 plus 6 plus 3 equals 15; drop the 1, and you've got the fourth digit, 5. Hiroshima was 6769, Singapore 4565. If there was no number for a station, it was coded in Kana. For example, Rabaul was 9504 8727 7142 9627, which was decrypted as RA-BA-U-RU. The numbers, it may be noted, sum-check. For forward military movements, as for air force operations in New Guinea, the Japanese used a three-digit system. Wewak was U-E-WA-KU in three-digit code.

The work of the cryptanalysts — difficult at the very best of times — was made a little easier by Japanese operators' habit of indicating the start of each message in their almost continuous stream with the Kana word ATENA, meaning "beginning," and concluding it with OWARI, meaning "end." While not essential to the Japanese recipients of these messages, the lack of these clues could have caused the Allied cryptanalysts great trouble figuring out where one message ended and the other began. Place names and dates also provided clues, and the Japanese operator's "fist" was invaluable in tracking changes in the locations of communications points. Some operators were not the most expert, and appearing to be all thumbs at times; they would start to send a message, make an error, start over again, make another error, and start yet again and again. This would give the 1CSWG monitors ample opportunity to copy down the message. The

1CSWG operators even had nicknames for Japanese operators whose fists they had come to know well.

Collecting enemy wireless traffic at the rate of 80,000 groups of messages a day created a monster of a job for the cryptanalysts and traffic analysts of 1CSWG. But moving the texts and analyses from 1CSWG to CB and San Miguel, Manila, on a daily basis — and secretly — was a task of enormous proportions as well. For this phase of operations, our Telecom hut was outfitted with electric teletypes which were equipped with special attachments to perforate paper tapes. These tapes, which a keyboard operator then fed into a "Typex" encoding machine, made up a second tape, now digitally encoded. The final step was to load this second tape onto a radio-teletype machine. This sent a high-frequency radio signal — audible over the air as only a screech that was impossible for the enemy to intercept without the help of a captured Typex machine — to Brisbane and/or Manila. And they never captured one.

The Typex, the coding device which produced the digitized tape, was an advanced Allied version of the Japanese Purple and the German Enigma machines that became household words after the war. The Typex was of British origin and was in wide use in both the Japanese and the European theatres of war. Two of them had been supplied to 1CSWG when we took over the Darwin post from the Australian Army's Number Three Special Wireless Unit, which had operated there since early in the war. The Typex was also used by units of the U.S. Signals Intelligence Service in many forward areas in the Pacific, and these machines were mined with explosives to be set off by retreating personnel if Special Wireless positions were overrun and captured. The enemy's Purple machines were also mined.

After the second atomic bomb was dropped in August 1945 — and immediately after the Japanese officially agreed to surrender — I was assigned to the Telecom building to operate the Typex system along with two or three other O.R.'s, and we worked in shifts around the clock. Ops Mon Sigs operators like us had full security clearance for signals monitoring, but despite this we'd never been allowed to enter the Telecom building. Even Lieutenant-Colonel Wethey was forbidden to see the insides of this building once it had been fully equipped and begun operation.

With the war theoretically, but not actually, over, secrecy was no longer so vital. Number One Canadian Special Wireless Group became not only a collector of Japanese messages, but a distributor of Allied orders to the Japanese units scattered around the islands — instructing them on what they were to do to give up their arms and allow entry by Allied troops into their positions, or where to go to give themselves up. The messages, both from Allied headquarters and from Japanese command points, were now in cleartext English or in Kana. A tremendous flow of complex orders was being exchanged among the Japanese units, escalating the rate of message processing far beyond even the prodigious pace set when the conflict was at its peak. The Typex enciphering machines remained the single quick method for 1CSWG to transmit these messages to CB.

Typex was not such a far cry from the Enigma machine developed in strict secrecy by the Germans in the 1930s but stolen by Czechs and smuggled to Britain. The "Red" Japanese cipher machine, duplicated secretly in 1935 by U.S. Naval Intelligence, was similar in its use of electrically driven rotors for producing ever-changing messages in groups. The *97-shiki Obun Injiki,* or the famous Purple machine constructed by the Japanese in 1938 and secretly duplicated for the Allies by William Friedman's team in 1940, had the radical difference of using stepping switches instead of rotors to achieve vastly more efficient "scrambling."

Typex machines were electronic in their enciphering process, but instructions were hand-operated for each message group of seven. My new job when I was assigned to the I Corps radio shack involved "punching" an electric keyboard to produce the preliminary paper telegraphic tape with linear perforations from message copy supplied by the I Corps decrypting room. I then loaded the perforated tape roll into the Typex enciphering box attached to a radio-teletype machine. Next I selected an enciphering key of five letters, randomly and entirely at my own whim, to precede each group of seven messages. This random choice was the rogue element that enabled us to send the messages without danger of Japanese deciphering. No eavesdropper could predict it.

Compared with the instant computerized encryption techniques of today, the selection method was primitive. My choice of code was made by using a piece of board, five inches wide by about ten inches long, into which five shallow lengthwise grooves had been cut. In each groove was a long paper strip bearing the entire English alphabet, but all except for one were deliberately scrambled. Each strip could be moved in either direction so that, by sliding them one way or the other, a different combination of five letters could be read vertically at any cross-point along the board. It was up to the operator to adjust the strips and choose one of the resulting combinations.

To create a key code I would turn each of five brass rings, or rotors, in the Typex enciphering box backward or forward. Each ring bore all the letters of the alphabet in jumbled order around its edge, like the milling on a coin. I then adjusted these rotors to the same set of five letters I'd read across the board's grooves and typed the five-letter key code on the radio-teletype keyboard.

When the perforated tape was fed into the Typex machine, the information it contained was electronically encoded according to the command of the rotors as set. Then, when the encoded tape was loaded into the radio-teletype, the seven messages were transmitted at very high speed in one electronic burst. Each message group produced a printed version on the radio-teletype at the CB end bearing the enciphered information in a baffling format of mixed-up numbers, punctuation marks, and every symbol and character on the keyboard. The receiving Typex at the far end would sort it all out through the use of the five-letter code that preceded each message group. Only a Typex receiver could decipher these messages.

Simultaneously, the enciphered messages were being received in Melbourne and also being typed out on the built-in teletype in my own equipment to confirm the transmission. At the end of the transmission of each seven-message group, I would make my next choice of key code with another combination of five letters, then readjust the rotors and set the Typex into action again. For a few instants, these tiny fragments of the history of the close of the Second World War were under my control, as they were converted into electronic signals of my own choosing.

I sometimes reflected on the fact that, in the moment just before I clicked on the Typex's Send key, I was the only person in the world who controlled these top-secret messages until they arrived at CB and were deciphered. Once the messages were on their electronic way, they were beyond all human ability to decipher them, even by the operator who had chosen the random enciphering key. Should a Japanese eavesdropper actually manage to capture the messages and, perhaps using a wire recorder, play back and slow down the transmission, the randomly selected keys occurring so frequently would have taken an incredible amount of of time and trouble to decipher, if it were even possible at all.

In fact, Japanese monitors had abysmal luck trying to decode Allied messages they did pick up even from hand-operated sources. "We just couldn't break your codes," one high-ranking Japanese officer lamented after the war.

When the Japanese scattered throughout the islands north of us gave up and orders began flowing to them from Allied headquarters on how to surrender themselves and their weapons, these messages would come off our radio-teletypes, hooked up to the Allied communication network, in cleartext English. Much of them were to be relayed by 1CSWG to the targeted Japanese troops. For example, a typical message in English cleartext would order remnants of the Japanese Second Army or the Japanese Eighth Army, crammed into a pocket around Wewak, to abandon their arms and make their way to the Allied stronghold at Aitape, farther west along the north coast of New Guinea. Many a time since then I have wished that I'd kept some of the reams and reams of teletype paper carrying these texts coming off our machines. Great detail was included in these precise surrender instructions aimed directly at Japanese intercept radio units anywhere from Timor to Tokyo, and then relayed by them to the appropriate commanders in the islands. They would have been a treasure trove of research information that would have kept a military history scholar occupied for an entire sabbatical in tracing the processes of surrender by the immobilized Japanese forces in the islands and how they met their end.

I was ordered to put all of the teletype paper, containing hard copies of the English version of the messages sent out, straight into the garbage. Even after the war was officially over, surviving Special Wireless messages remained top-secret until the Official Secrets Act's mandatory thirty-year period of silence had elapsed. I'd probably have risked court-martial had I stowed some away and in my kit bag and been discovered. The army just wouldn't understand.

Throughout the latter part of the war, only the keyboard cipher machines like the Typex enabled Allied Signals Intelligence to cope with the vast and ever-rising river of Japanese message traffic that flowed into monitoring stations circling the Pacific. At the Special Wireless station at Hollandia, traffic had reached 1,000,000 message groups a day by November 1944. In Europe, traffic at the European Theatre of Operations headquarters at about the same time ran between 1,500,000 and 2,000,000 a day.

Number One Canadian Special Wireless Group's workload of 80,000 groups a day and growing promised to make it one of the most active stations in the signals intelligence chain. As the latest major installation to be constructed in the SWPA, our Canadian intercept station was capable of managing a lion's share of the Japanese traffic as well as of intercommunication between most of the Special Wireless units in the forward areas and Allied military headquarters.

Chapter 15

The Best of Tokyo Rose

The Australians were impatient. While the Japanese still occupied the islands to the north of their continent — and while the opportunity to mete out punishment and revenge still lasted — the Australians were keen to take back the stolen territories piece by piece and in face-to-face confrontation wherever possible. The prevailing feeling at SWPA command was that the Japanese armies holding the islands should be left to dry up on their own through lack of supplies. However, in one sense the Aussies were probably right in going in and dislodging them as soon as possible. The Japanese fighting men were a hard-core, die-hard group, as likely as not to stay put and keep thousands of square miles of island territory immobilized and unproductive for years to come. Only the decisive defeat of Japan would induce their surrender, and they would have to be completely convinced that this had actually happened.

Accordingly, in May 1945, the Australian I Corps, made up of the Seventh and Ninth Divisions under Lieutenant-General Sir Leslie

Moorsehead, launched an assault on the big island of Borneo. They
were armed with key information from Special Wireless stations, among
them 1CSWG. They landed at Tarakan, on the east coast of the former
Dutch Borneo; at Brunei, in the former British Borneo — the northern
third of the large island, and a region rich in the oil and rubber the
Japanese war machine desperately needed; and at Balikpapan, farther
south on the east coast.

The Japanese were taken by surprise, having expected any Allied invasion to come from the west. They had no aircraft or submarines, nor did
they have any heavily entrenched anti-invasion troops ready. General
MacArthur, who landed with the Allied troops at Brunei along with
General Moorsehead and U.S. General Kenney, praised the planning of
the campaign and the part played by Special Wireless in determining the
strength and distribution of the enemy forces on Borneo. He also said later
that rarely had such a prize been obtained at such low cost.

By the end of July the Australian forces, with, in MacArthur's words,
"skill and courage," drove inland and finished off the entire Japanese garrison throughout the island. The way was opened to allow the Australians
to forge eastward to Java, the next large land mass, and sweep back along
the East Indies island chain southeast toward New Guinea to complete the
eradication of the Japanese forces in the SWPA. MacArthur saw the
restoration of Dutch government of the East Indies as the way to bring the
return of orderly administration and law. "But," he wrote later, "for reasons I have never been able to discover, the proposed movement was summarily vetoed by Washington… This reversal soon bore fruit in the chaos
that ensued…. [I]t was a grave error and was the result of political med-
dling in what was essentially a military matter."

He was referring to the Indonesian war that broke out three years after
Japan surrendered, which culminated in the complete ouster, using abandoned Japanese armaments, of the Dutch establishment by the Republic
of Indonesia's military forces under Sukarno. MacArthur's concern seems
to have been justified many years later, when Sukarno was himself ousted
by some of his former supporters in a bloody civil war and Suharto gained
power. After many years of apparent economic success and prosperity
thanks to Indonesia's rich supplies of oil and rubber, this regime in turn
broke down in the 1990s in another civil war, and Suharto was driven
from power. Political and economic confusion, which continues at this
writing, then set in.

MacArthur summed up the results of the three years of fighting that had taken place in the South West Pacific Area: eight Japanese armies defeated or rendered powerless to conduct more than delaying actions. In the New Guinea–Solomons area, the Japanese Second, Seventeenth, and Eighteenth Armies had been crushed. In the Philippines, the Japanese Fourteenth Area and Thirty-fifth Armies, made up of about 450,000 men from twenty-three division, were annihilated in a nine-month campaign. The Allied forces were composed of seventeen divisions and, MacArthur pointed out, the defeat of the Japanese in the Philippines represented one of the rare instances in a long campaign when a ground force was entirely destroyed by a numerically inferior opponent.

In the Borneo-Celebes area, the Japanese Sixteenth, Nineteenth, and Thirty-seventh Armies were fully cut off by the Australian invasion, and these multitudes of troops were unable to make an orderly retreat back to their home territory to take part in defence of the Japanese islands. Never had such large numbers of troops been so outmanoeuvred in modern warfare, MacArthur said, separated from each other and left tactically impotent to take an active part in the final battle for their homeland.

By the last weeks of July, the Australians of Number Three Wireless Unit in Darwin who were still monitoring enemy signals were being transferred to Borneo, where the campaign was nearing its conclusion. Only thirty-five Americans were still engaged in monitoring at their own installation, and they were soon to leave for another location. That left 1CSWG as the chief signals communications link between Brisbane and Manila. As the Australian campaign swept through the East Indies, the eavesdroppers of 1CSWG were their electronic ears, identifying in advance the strengths and dispositions of the Japanese forces they were still to encounter.

Bit by bit, Harry Wethey's plans for the best little intercept station in the South West Pacific Area were coming to fruition. An elaborate water system, the pride of Major Pick, was now feeding a strong flow of water into the kitchens, the officers' quarters, the maintenance garages, the showers, and everywhere it was thought necessary — all but the O.R. quarters or the latrines. Even the problem of disposing of waste water from the mess hall kitchens was overcome by borrowing an elderly Aussie, who was an expert on growing bananas, from AWC. Under his dour direction, Wethey's Commandos hacked furrows from the rock-hard earth with hoes, heaping up the red, powdery result in long rows, like potato mounds, and planting droopy little banana plant seedlings in them. The kitchens' drain water was channelled from the rear of the mess hall by way of miniature, hand-hewn canals which then ran into little ditches between the rows in the banana patch. Within weeks the banana plants shot up to over six feet tall. We were gone by the time the bananas ripened.

Conveniences multiplied until 1CSWG was luxuriating in a lifestyle roughly equivalent to that of a lumber camp in Canada's far north, a giant leap forward from the primitive conditions that had greeted us. Technicians strung up a network of public-address speakers throughout the camp to disseminate vital announcements on behalf of the top brass. In between the bulletins, music picked up by one of 1CSWG's innumerable radio sets was piped through. We even set up a makeshift broadcasting station outdoors and ran a program of classical music, using records that belonged to Sergeant Proctor, who'd somehow hidden them amid equipment shipped from Canada. As the only experienced radio announcer in the group, it was up to me to provide between-disk commentary.

I had been around radio broadcasting since the age of seven, yet this was still a strange and novel experience. A little over a year before, I'd been announcing war bulletins, peppered with place names such as Hollandia, Darwin, and Surabaya, over CKTB in St. Catharines. Now that these places were within a few hundred miles of my microphone, here I was intoning program notes for Mozart and Beethoven symphonies two or three nights a week as if I were back on the home front. A large cluster of signals people would sit on the ground around the "studio," intrigued by the processes of "civilian" radio broadcasting.

Radio over the South West Pacific was a two-way — and in some ways a three- and four-way — street. While we and other Allied Special Wireless units diligently copied down and processed all the Japanese Imperial forces' radioed strategies, we tuned in just as attentively to Radio Tokyo, Radio Saigon, and Radio Singapore to listen to the swing and jazz music played for the "benefit" of Allied — and probably Japanese — troops throughout the Pacific theatre of war. There was a Tokyo Rose from Tokyo, a Tokyo Rose from Saigon, and a Tokyo Rose from Singapore. All three — for all we knew, the same person — obliged us with endless broadcasts of current and past repertoires of such American swing bands as Benny Goodman, Glenn Miller, Louis Armstrong, and most of the other top "orks," announced by Tokyo Rose in a very, silky-smooth delivery with a subtly mocking style and heavy use of American slang.

While she — or they — supplied us with some of the best jazz and swing programming we'd ever heard, it was accompanied by attempts — which struck us as comical — to convince Allied soldiers to give it all up and go home because the proprietors of the Co-Prosperity Sphere (read, the Japanese conquest) wished to be friends with all and desired only to keep what they had generously conquered.

Rose would follow this up by reading lists of Allied soldiers who had allegedly been killed or captured recently, giving out hometown addresses, names of alleged sweethearts, and a few other little facts designed to provide the homey touch and assure their loved ones that they were safe and sound with their Japanese friends. This information, if true, would have been obtained from dog tags and personal papers taken from bodies alive or dead. We didn't find this amusing, but we did appreciate hearing the snappy Goodman or Miller pieces played between the macabre chat.

I often wondered whether we were being entertained from Saigon and Singapore by selections from the vast jazz and swing collection formerly held by a certain Indonesian prince who, before the war, was famous in international social circles as a fan of that music. When the Japanese invaded and captured the Dutch East Indies in 1942, no more was heard of the prince or his record collection. We may well have been listening to music stolen from his collection.

In addition to Japanese military signals and Tokyo Rose, our powerful antennae could also pick up Radio Sackville in New Brunswick — the Canadian Broadcasting Corporation's overseas service outlet — and the British Broadcasting Corporation's Radio Service from London. There was also the U.S. Armed Forces Radio Service out of San Francisco, which was our alternative source for swing and jazz. All of these, including the various Tokyo Roses, were occasionally piped by wire from an otherwise-unused 1CSWG short-wave receiver into the wet and dry canteens and other points around the camp, so that we could pretty well keep up on what was going on in the outside world.

One of the events that barely affected us was the end of the war in Europe. V-E Day, May 8, 1945, was an interesting, but not terribly significant, even for us. What we wanted most to hear about was a *V-J* Day, whenever that might happen. However, that evening in the wet canteen, the regular evening drink-up was more boisterous and obstreperous than usual, and in this way the milestone in the war was, to the satisfaction of the regular patrons, suitably noted. For most, though, it was just a good excuse to dip into any extra beer rations they had. The Gunner had called dibs on mine. In the quieter quarters of the barracks hut, someone pointed out that 1CSWG was now the only Canadian army unit active in any operational theatre of war in the world.

On August 6, 1945, The Bomb was dropped. The airwaves over the Pacific were overtaken by an outpouring of voice programs in Japanese from Radio San Francisco and a few other Allied points. The outbursts were heavily sprinkled with the newly-minted words, "aa-tomik bomb-ka." These messages were beamed intensively and nonstop at the Japanese, calling upon enemy forces to surrender instantly or risk another bomb to follow the one that had just destroyed Hiroshima. Of course, at this early stage of the Atomic Age we benighted signalmen in Darwin had no idea of the horrendous nature of the first atomic bomb to be exploded in anger, so we cheered the phenomenon.

One signalman, who'd been a chemist before the army got him, refused to believe that such a thing as an atomic bomb could be built, and declared that the radio reports must be wrong in calling it "atomic." Nevertheless, the news of the Hiroshima bomb brought jubilation to 1CSWG. Our sensitivities had long before been numbed by reports of far greater casualties, on both sides of the war, caused by massive thousand-pound bombings, so the Hiroshima toll made little impression on us. All it meant, we thought in our innocence, was that we'd be going home soon.

Strangely, one of the phonograph records DeMal and Boombaw had smuggled from Mount Isa was a 1936 Louis Prima recording of "Nagasaki." On August 9, the second atomic bomb was dropped on the Japanese city of Nagasaki, all the Allied radio broadcasters' pleas and exhortations to surrender having been ignored by the Imperial Japanese military leaders. The end of the war seemed near, and we played "Nagasaki" on the wind-up gramophone over and over in anticipation of an early return home. The former possibility did come early. The latter would not be reality for another five and a half months.

Besides the unending stream of Allied broadcasts delivering the message to Japan over every available radio circuit that a third "aa-tomik-bomb-ka" would fall unless the Imperial government admitted defeat, we noticed another pronounced difference in our radio listening. Tokyo Rose, all three of her, had vanished. Never again were we to hear the fluid, throaty voices of these three intrepid Oriental ladies — or was she just one on some budding Japanese radio network? — invite us to give up and go home. Nor would Benny Goodman or Glenn Miller's music ever again float across the ether to us from Radio Tokyo, Radio Saigon, or Radio Singapore. (After the war, one of the announcers, an American-born Nisei by the name of Iva Toguri, returned to the U.S., only to be convicted of treason. She was released in 1956 and was pardoned by Gerald Ford in 1977.) In the Atomic Age, Radio Everything became boring. Even U.S. Armed Forces Radio was too busy exhorting the Japanese to surrender to play any more jazz or swing.

The Japanese military wireless circuits continued at pretty much full capacity during this time, as if the war was still business as usual. The feedback from I Corps, which was translating the traffic, was that the messages were of a holding-pattern nature, neither ordering the far-flung Japanese Imperial units to prepare for new action nor giving direct orders to be ready for surrender. From 1CSWG's reading of Japanese military communications, one would have thought that there had been no such thing as an atomic bomb, nor any other kind of bomb, dropped on Japan. There was no sign of concern among Imperial military circles in Tokyo that a good part of the Japanese population stood to be wiped out if things continued as usual. Japan's warlords evidently didn't think annihilation was too high a price to pay.

During the five days after the dropping of the second atomic bomb, things were actually in a feverish state in Tokyo. The outside world, including 1CSWG, knew only of an implacable, fanatical enemy stubbornly continuing a war it couldn't win. But within Japan there was turmoil between the military factions and even the Emperor himself, who wanted to sue for peace. Despite the Allies' declared intention to destroy one Japanese city after another, and despite a separate approach through diplomatic channels by Allied atomic scientists to pre-war colleagues in Japan who would understand the devastating implications of atomic bombing, there was strong pressure within Japan to continue the war.

The Japanese Supreme War Council met in an underground chamber of the Imperial Palace, with Emperor Hirohito present, right after news of the Nagasaki bomb was received. Their conference went on far into the next morning. Of all people, the notorious Foreign Minister Tojo argued that the time had come to end the war if the Emperor's constitutional position could be preserved. But War Minister Anami argued that resistance should go on, asserting that Japan's war strength was far from exhausted and that, if the enemy invaded the home islands, the Imperial forces could still strike a damaging blow that would oblige the Allies to end the war on terms more favourable than those offered by the Potsdam Declaration.

Bravely going against the military's urgings, and thinking of the fate that would be suffered by the Japanese people if the war continued, the Emperor himself ultimately made the decision to surrender, to "endure the unendurable and suffer what is insufferable." A note was sent to the Allies early on August 10 with the rider that the Emperor was to remain sovereign ruler of Japan. Meanwhile, the Japanese Board of Information issued an ambiguous announcement to the Japanese people that left the impression that the government meant to continue the war with the utmost determination.

The War Ministry also issued a statement full of bravado about fighting to the end of everybody. It claimed that by fighting with determination, "there will be a way found out of our difficulty." Actually, the ministry meant that everybody in Japan would "find life in death." The War Ministry had previously argued with the Supreme Council that a reply be made to the Allies only on the grounds that there be no Allied occupation of the home islands.

The Allied reply to the Japanese cabinet's response was to make a further stipulation that there could only be unconditional surrender. This brought about another crisis for the Supreme Council. The Emperor indicated again that surrender was the only way. War Minister Anami is said to have grovelled in tears at the foot of the conference table and begged the Emperor — who was regarded by the Japanese as a supernatural being — to change his decision. Other cabinet members also wept. But the Emperor said he would go on the radio to announce the news of surrender to the people. An announcement was approved by the cabinet, and the Emperor's voice was recorded on a phonograph disk for broadcast the next day.

The militarists were far from ready to give up without a last-ditch, suicidal battle against any invading force and, like most minority groups, were anxious to make this decision allegedly on behalf of the people if the people didn't make it for themselves. This caught the War Minister in a difficult position, torn between his Emperor and his armed forces. The next day, after Hirohito's final decision, War Minister Anami solved his personal dilemma by committing suicide at his official residence. He was said to have been considering a coup d'état to take over and continue the war.

From the Imperial army itself came handbills passed out in the streets that urged the overthrow of the cabinet. A group of general staff officers plotted to seize control of the government and demand that the Emperor continue the war. Though they had failed to get support from the war minister, the vice-minister, or the chief of the general staff, on August 15 a group of army plotters drove to the palace headquarters of Lieutenant-General Takeshi Mori, chief of the Imperial Guard Division, and demanded that he co-operate. When Mori refused, he was shot dead instantly.

All staff officers of the guard division were herded into one room. Forging an order and using General Mori's seal, they directed the guards at each palace gate to deny entry to the grounds by any armed group. General Shigeru Hasnuma, chief aide-de-camp to the Emperor, and other palace officials were taken into custody, but the Imperial Household Minister and the Keeper of the Privy Seal couldn't be found. All communication with the outside was cut off.

The rebels' prime objective was to find and destroy the recording of the Emperor's public announcement, which was to be broadcast the next day. One palace official after another was brought forward and interrogated about the recording's location, but none could give it. A search, lit by flashlight, was made through the darkened rooms of the palace — blacked out because of air-raid alerts — but they never found the recording. It remained in a safe in the headquarters of Imperial Household Minister Tokugawa. The next day it was played over Radio Tokyo. For the first time in their country's history, the people of Japan heard the voice of their sacred Emperor.

The beginnings of an insurrection continued. The Tokyo homes of Prime Minister Suzuki and of one of his ministers were burned. A Major Hatanaka and thirty rebel Imperial guards took over the Japan Broadcasting Corporation building and forced forty employees to assemble in a single room. Hatanaka demanded permission to broadcast at gunpoint, but the insurrectionists were told that an air-raid alert was in effect and broadcasts were forbidden unless Eastern Army Corps headquarters permitted. Hatanaka phoned the corps headquarters but failed to get the required permission. In an air-raid alert, he was told, no broadcasts were allowed, as the approaching U.S. bombers could use the Tokyo frequency to fly directly to the heart of the city more accurately. (The Japanese bomber fleet that attacked Pearl Harbor employed the same tactic, using a Honolulu radio station's broadcast as a navigational fix.)

Word of the rebellion reached General Tanaka, head of the Eastern Army Corps. He ordered the insurrection called off, saying it was in direct conflict with the Emperor's desire. Four rebel officers instantly committed suicide, and Major Hatanaka killed himself later the same day near the palace. General Tanaka, who had once been Tojo's right-hand man and who might have been more likely to have led a rebellion himself, committed suicide nine days later. Before the end of August, more than a thousand officers and professional soldiers killed themselves rather than agree to surrender to the Allies.

Those militants who remained continued to oppose surrender. Special Imperial Navy Attack Corps planes flew over the capital several times and dropped leaflets urging that the war go on, saying that the Emperor's order was false. Another revolt, by troops stationed near the centre of Tokyo, took place. High-ranking officers persuaded these rebels to give up. All the rebels killed themselves with hand grenades, while all their young officers committed *hara-kiri*.

Suicides by those who felt guilt or responsibility for Japan's defeat were happening daily. Even Admiral Onishi, head of the elite kamikaze suicide corps known as the Special Attack Corps, took his own life. So did the former army chief of staff, Marshal Sugiyama, and his wife, who carried out the traditional *hara-kiri* ritual in white robes and wielding short swords. Others of the Special Attack Corps attempted to organize resistance, but their efforts were suppressed by the strong spiritual force of the Emperor's wishes. Japanese Air Force planes continued to intercept, and sometimes shoot down, American planes even though a ceasefire had been declared. The Japanese government appealed to the Allies to send no planes over the home islands until surrender could be completed, but despite this, U.S. planes often appeared overhead.

Charles Bateson, in his book *The War with Japan*, analyzes the question of whether the Allies were justified in using the atomic bomb to end the Pacific war. He suggests that if the Allies had created face-saving conditions earlier in the war, it might have made possible a surrender before the bombings of Hiroshima and Nagasaki were deemed necessary. He asserts that no attempt was made to induce Japan's surrender — such as guaranteeing the Emperor's sanctity and exemption from trial as a war criminal.

However, Bateson and others had the benefit of hindsight, as well as access to official wartime Japanese papers and documents which Allied leaders did not have in 1945. Before the surrender, insights into the attitudes of Japan's leaders and its official levels could only be gained through signals intelligence monitoring and the miniscule amount of on-site spying that was possible. So far as is known, there was no Japanese attempt to convey those conditions until after the second bomb was dropped.

Bateson does point out that invasion of Japan's home islands would have ultimately ended the war, but only at a frightening cost in lives to the Allies and the Japanese themselves because of the fanaticism of the Japanese home forces, which were far larger even than the numbers of troops Japan had sent abroad to the South West Pacific and the Asian continent. A combination of blockade and orthodox bombing, he adds, would also have ultimately ended the war. This, however, would have been prolonged and would have probably brought suffering upon the Japanese civilian population. He observes that heavier casualties, through starvation and disease, would have been caused than the use of the atomic bomb could ever have done.

Chapter 16

After the Bomb

"Today, Japan officially surrendered." The words came from Clement Attlee, the prime minister of Great Britain, and they boomed over 1CSWG's public-address system at 8:30 a.m. on August 15, 1945. I was sitting at one of the rough-hewn tables in the wet canteen, waiting for the sergeant-major to come and give me a job in my role as one of the Number Two Section's hard labourers for the day. To pass the time, I was prepared to sit there and listen to the BBC once more say that an announcement could be expected "very soon" on the Japanese surrender question — as we'd all been doing for the past five days and nights.

Since August 10, after the second atom bomb was dropped, diplomatic channels were saying that Japan would consider giving up, and we'd clustered around our radio — tuned to public frequencies — hoping for the word that the war was over. When it actually came, it was hard to believe. To be soon free of army discipline, to see an end to the never-ceasing casualty lists, to direct your own affairs and live your own life, to wear whatever you liked — it hadn't seemed possible that the day would ever come. Army life, for the O.R.'s, was lived in an atmosphere of fear and yearning for freedom from captivity that later generations who opposed The Bomb on principle would never understand.

From my vantage point in the wet canteen I could see that men were running out of the huts, still buttoning up their shorts, to get close to a radio speaker and hear the good news. Almost as welcome as the end of the war was the news that the rest of the day and the next were declared holidays. Thus my day at hard labour was abolished the same day as the war in the Pacific. Later in the day, 1CSWG's troops climbed onto trucks and went over to the RAAF base to take part in a joint thanksgiving church parade.

The surrender announcement was somewhat of an anticlimax. Because of our steady monitoring of Japanese messages, it had become plain well before August 15 that something was happening to the enemy's war effort. Signals that indicated offensive movements in the islands had begun to wane, and most now had to do with housekeeping chores. At 1CSWG, we'd actually begun to assume that the war was over the day after the Nagasaki bomb was dropped. From a strictly military point of view, which was how we were obliged to see it, the Japanese had already lost. On August 11, still four days before the official surrender, a historic and unheard-of invitation was given by the officers to the sergeants and other NCOs — but not to the O.R.'s — to come to a party at the officer's mess.

The camp orchestra was there and it played far into the next morning. There was also much jubilant drunkenness in the O.R. canteen, of course, but the party at the officers' mess yielded a spectacle that we few modest or non-drinkers had never thought we'd know: virtually the entire corps of officers and senior NCOs, gloriously and riotously drunk — and the war was still officially on. Between them, the fifty or so commissioned and non-commissioned stalwarts emptied 103 bottles of various kinds, mostly hard liquor. The noise from the officers' mess and the O.R. wet canteen was incredible. Nobody slept that night.

Some of the members of the signalmen's sections, with Number Two Section in the vanguard, made a brave attempt to set right an injustice that was evident to everyone: the beer was still being rationed at the rate of two quarts per evening per man — hardly enough to close out a war on. They moved on two fronts. While the sergeants were over at the officers' mess drinking up the officers' liquor, a task force led by the Gunner left the wet canteen, broke into the sergeants' mess, and made a break for the beer supply. However, Sergeant-Major Addy, a teetotaller who'd declined the invitation to the officers' party, caught them in the act.

They were dealt with two or three days later by Lieutenant-Colonel Wethey, who personally travelled into Darwin to obtain authority from the Northern Territory Force to try the culprits summarily under Australian Army Section 18, Paragraph 4. He gave them seven days' detention for their reprehensible drunken behaviour. One of the three was among the nine of us who went AWL in San Francisco, and this additional skylark of pinching the sergeants' beer while they were drinking up at the officers' party made him 1CSWG's most notorious offender — or, at any rate, the most notorious of those caught. The Gunner, on the other hand, had been in the army since early 1940 and in five happily drunken years this was the first time he had ever been caught red-handed at anything. After all this time, he would spend the war's-end celebrations in an Australian digger.

The second front of the attack on the camp's beer supply, from another point, was carried out by my friendly rival Pierre DeMal and one Corporal Silver, a universally liked junior NCO who was a raging firebrand when drunk. These two were caught before they actually succeeded in breaking into the camp's basic beer supply. They were brought up on charges before the colonel, and although their cases were suspended, Corporal Silver was demoted to the rank of signalman. DeMal couldn't be demoted any further down from signalman, which was the bottom of the heap. Clearly, attempted theft of beer was a very serious military offence — even more serious than being AWL at embarkation for overseas, and even when everybody knew the war and its airtight discipline were done with.

Silver's demotion meant he would suffer a considerable loss of money when he was finally demobilized and his re-establishment credits were totalled up. For an ex-soldier thrown on the civilian job market after the war, it would be a serious matter to be deprived of the pittance that would have come to him for his NCO service. He put up a brave front, however. On the other hand, DeMal, who seemed to have no money worries either as soldier or civilian, laughed loud and long at his tap on the wrist and continued with the roguish life he'd led throughout his association with 1CSWG.

In his diary, Lieutenant-Colonel Wethey wrote that the day after the pre-victory party was a very quiet day, even for a Sunday. This was understandable, considering the hangovers that must have raged through both the officers', NCOs', and O.R.s' barracks. But on Monday the colonel was hard at work trying to sort out a list of promotions being given to the NCOs and men before the war was over, to meet some official regulation or other.

Despite the surrender, the Japanese message circuits after August 15 were again functioning at almost the pre-surrender rate, but the subject matter was shifting, carrying orders to the outlying units in the islands and the Malay Peninsula to move to surrender points. The Central Bureau ordered all Special Wireless units to carry on as usual until further advice was given, and Harry Wethey was only too willing to do just that. After all, he was a permanent force soldier, and he would continue serving the army wherever he was assigned, war or no war.

He gathered the unit together and told us that it might take some time to get us all home, although Colonel Cosgrave, the Canadian military attaché to Australia who had been visiting Darwin, said he would try to get a ship into Darwin harbour to take us back to Canada. Lieutenant-Colonel Wethey's private opinion was that this was being a little too optimistic. He was right: we still had almost another six months to go.

As a career soldier, the colonel was not one to let things fall apart just because a war was over, so he gave the camp a thorough inspection a few days after the official surrender. Not unexpectedly, he found that "things had slipped badly." Once more the orders were up to get things into shape. After all, shoals of high-ranking folks from the Australian Army, the RAAF, the British Army, and even the Royal Navy and U.S. Army were still floating through the camp on their way to and from Brisbane and Manila. On top of this, there was to be an inspection by His Royal Highness, the Duke of Gloucester — which, for some reason, never did come off.

Lieutenant-Colonel Wethey found the wireless intercept room extremely untidy and ordered instant remedial action. A work gang was put to building an incinerator behind the men's mess — as though we were still expecting long-term residence. Plans for a laundry for the O.R.'s were going ahead. A U.S. Army lieutenant dropped by to talk about passing radio-teletype traffic to Manila, an apparently difficult problem that required two or three of our officers to put their heads together over it. The intercept operators were still banging out Japanese messages on their typewriters, though the traffic was flagging a little more each day. Even Manila Radioteletype — our side — wasn't taking the work too seriously any more.

The Central Bureau was still formulating plans, however, and even Lieutenant-Colonel Wethey was surprised to receive Amendment #3 to 1CSWG's establishment, which was meant to add "20 Ops, Keyboard (including one sergeant, two corporals, full, and four corporals, lance), one sanitary corporal, and four sappers, Royal Canadian Engineers, for power plant duty." There was no indication that there ever would be any such bodies, except, for some mysterious purpose known only to the army, on paper.

While a far cry from the hundreds of thousands of message groups per day that had been the rule just weeks before, messages were still pouring into the Radioteletype Building in Manila, by way of plain-English teletype, from both Allied headquarters and the commands of Japanese army and naval units scattered throughout the islands. These messages were aimed at sorting everybody out so that we could all go home — to Canada, the United States, Britain, Japan, China, the Malay Peninsula, Indo-China, India, the Netherlands, Germany, Australia, New Zealand, and everywhere else that the war-weary and peed-off were longing to return to.

The weather was getting hotter and more humid as the early-warning signs of the Wet began to make themselves known. The flies were becoming a plagued nuisance — they actually seemed to love the DDT that we sprayed all over the camp. As a diversion, the colonel and Major Corbett from the Z Special Transmitter went up for a flip around the area in Flight Lieutenant Murphy's Liberator. They took aerial pictures of the camps around Darwin and then went to a party at Fortress Signals' mess in Darwin.

Prayers for salvation from the war now being a thing of the past, only seven bodies turned up for the next Sunday's church parade. (Wethey would order compulsory attendance for the one after that.) The officers spent that Sunday afternoon at Casuarina Beach, tossing around a medicine ball while a photojournalist took their pictures for publicity purposes. Some of the monotony was relieved by taking an inventory of the unit's goods and chattels; this was carried out under the supervision of the Quartermaster, Captain Hall. It turned out that there was a long list of "deficiencies," or things missing, including forty-three items of tools. It was thought that most of these might have been legitimately "borrowed," but there was no question that one missing item that we'd never heard used — a fire siren — had definitely been stolen. For what purpose, nobody knew.

The message traffic having mainly switched away from radiotelegraph signals sent out by Japanese operators to radio-teletype plain language, there was a need in the Telecom building for more bodies to handle the flow of surrender communications. That was when I was detached from Ops Mon Sigs to Ops TT Sigs, mainly on the strength of my newly acquired typing talent (I was qualified at 75 w.p.m. clean), to help encode messages for headquarters and send them out via the Typex machine.

The unit was actually starting to break up. National Defence Headquarters back in Ottawa requested the immediate return of Captain Mackay, the veteran (at the age of twenty-nine) code expert of the Intelligence Corps who had directed all the decoding operations of our unit. Captain Mackay set out by civil aircraft to fly the 1,500 miles or so over the Great Australian Desert to Melbourne on the first leg of the long journey home. Another I Corps officer, Captain K.C. Woodworth, and three of his non-coms, all Japanese-speaking, were later shuffled off to Japan to carry on their work there.

Though it was now officially illegal for Allied and Japanese troops to shoot at each other, full mutual trust had not yet been achieved. In this respect we were frozen in the geographical state of hostilities that had existed before Tokyo threw in the towel: several hundred thousand tough Japanese fighting men, albeit down to their last rations and ammo, were holed up in positions of strength throughout the hundreds of SWPA islands, while every possible escape avenue was tightly nailed down by powerful Allied air, sea, and land forces.

A few months of determined offensives by the Allies would have undoubtedly rooted them all out, but many lives could have been lost — if not to enemy resistance then to the accidents, fevers, and odds and ends of calamities that take their toll whenever and wherever wars are fought. During those weeks after the official surrender, men on the winning side were becoming less and less anxious with each day that passed to risk their lives by probing in person those hearts of darkness in the South West Pacific jungles.

Not being the sort to put instant trust in an enemy so recently dedicated to annihilating them and all their associates, intelligence officers assessed the lull in the shooting — as they saw it — as a chance to throw their opposite numbers further off-balance in case the shooting started again.

Even before the official signing of the surrender aboard the U.S. battleship *Missouri* in Tokyo Bay on September 2, a couple of high-ranking G3 officers came to see Lieutenant-Colonel Wethey about contacting the Japanese on the big island of Timor, 300 miles north of us, on the subject of formal surrender. What G3 was really most interested in was to obtain from the Japanese base at Koepang all the secret information that could be found regarding their ever-changing signals codes. You never knew just when such information might be useful, they reasoned. And they obviously weren't quite ready to believe that the Japanese had actually caved in and completely surrendered. There could still come a day when those codes might be re-activated.

The upshot of this was that Lieutenant John W. Holmes, from Hull, Québec, a member of the 1CSWG I Corps, was delegated to board an RAAF Liberator from the Darwin base and be flown to Koepang to pick up all the code books he could find at the Japanese transmitter. This was no small challenge, considering that Koepang was one of the stronger Japanese bases in the SWPA. (It was so strong, in fact, that the Allies had bypassed it — as well as the massive island fortress of Truk, not far away — and gone on instead to seize Borneo farther west, irrevocably cutting off any further supplies or reinforcements from Japan or Asia.) The Japanese had maintained their well-trained garrison as if they fully expected that it would be one part of the Co-Prosperity Sphere that they wouldn't have to give up. No one really knew how pleased — or displeased — they might be to receive a visitor from Hull, Québec, in a Canadian Army uniform (to them, British) this early in peacetime.

Holmes was fluent in Japanese, being one of those I Corps members who had spent his boyhood in Japan before the war. Tall and blond, about twenty-five years old and as far from Japanese in appearance as might be possible, he would be a novelty for the heretofore enemy to view as a sample of what they had been fighting the last four years. As it was, the Liberator arrived over Koepang on schedule after firmly worded messages had been exchanged between the Darwin Allied headquarters, through 1CSWG, and the Japanese base commander on the details of this ice-breaking visit. A cover of about a dozen armed Spitfires from Darwin zoomed about as the Lib touched down on the Koepang air base runway, from which Japanese air force bombers had taken off so many times to bomb Darwin.

What struck Holmes, he said later, was the general appearance of the base. This was not a deep jungle stronghold. As I noted earlier, barracks huts were in neat rows, pathways were lined with whitewashed rocks, green lawns and hedges were as precisely trimmed as they would be at any peacetime garrison in Canada. Antiaircraft batteries were sited in regulation defensive style but apparently unmanned and unarmed. As the Lib taxied toward the buildings it was evident that the whole garrison force was on parade for Holmes's benefit. The Rising Sun flag was high on its pole. Stone-faced Japanese troops by the hundreds were formed up in perfect military formation with rifles at "present arms," their gleaming bayonets fixed — of course, only for ceremonial purposes.

As Holmes descended from the plane, the Koepang commander and his aides came forward, saluted, and stood at attention. Ominous silence prevailed, except for the snap and flutter of the flag in the light wind. Very few words were exchanged. No smiles were flashed. Anything could have happened at this point despite all the correctness. As it didn't look as if there were going to be cocktails and a hospitality luncheon, Holmes took a firm grip on his authority as an Allied officer assuming temporary command of Koepang, and told the commander to remain where he was — and to keep his men there, too. Holmes then strode off as quickly as he could without appearing to be in an inordinate hurry and found his way to the signals transmitting station. There, as Japanese operators snapped to attention at his presence, he went straight to the library of code books, ran through them quickly to find those that contained yet-uncracked codes, and left the station with a bundle of them under one arm, quickly and with authority.

Maintaining his pace, he strode back to the Liberator, where the base commander and his group were still standing at attention and the troops were still lined up, nothing moving but the cloth sun flaps on the backs of their caps, disturbed by the light breeze. Holmes stopped in front of the commanding officer, who snapped up a smart salute, which he returned and said a few words of goodbye. He wheeled about in correct military style and climbed aboard the Liberator. The engines roared, the plane took off, and when Holmes last saw the Koepang garrison they were still in place and at attention, without question a bewildered, defeated, disappointed group of former fighting men, puzzled by the actions of this lone blond Canadian (or was that British?) officer who had stepped off an enemy aircraft, helped himself to their property, and left without a word about what they were supposed to do next in this new game of surrender.

For Holmes, getting airborne again was the greatest relief he'd felt to date in his young life. From the moment that he stepped down to the tarmac of the landing strip, he fully expected that some indignant Japanese soldier, boiling over at the sight of the "British" uniform, might decide that the war wasn't over yet and let fly with whatever weapon he had in hand. I don't know whether Lieutenant Holmes ever received a decoration for his daring, but he should have. (Although it would probably have been impossible: any recognition would have required a public acknowledgement that Canadians had taken part in a top-secret facet of the war against Japan.)

Back at Number One Canadian Special Wireless Group's camp another challenge was developing: how to get more than three hundred men and many tons of equipment out of Northern Territory before the Wet moved in and turned all access roads leading to the Bitumen into pudding. If the Wet won, we would have to settle in for another six or seven months before mass movement was again possible. The only other way out would have been by ship from Darwin harbour — which was not a practical option because the harbour was full of wrecks. Besides, we would have needed *two* ships — one for the equipment and the other for the men. That would have been a logistical problem that even Lieutenant-Colonel H.D.W. Wethey's firm hand would have had trouble keeping in check. Thus the colonel and his advisors determined that things would have to get going before the end of October — that is, if the Central Bureau decided that the war was really over and it was safe to put 1CSWG out of business.

The colonel decided that a personal reconnaissance by road from Darwin to Brisbane would be informative, if not necessary. This trip would involve a journey over the same paved route we'd taken by truck convoy between Darwin and Mount Isa, then eastbound from Mount Isa to Brisbane largely by way of a primitive bush track — for a total distance of over 2,000 miles!

The undaunted colonel, the dour Major Pick, and the dashing Lieutenant Legere set out early on the morning of September 14 in the colonel's 1942 Chevy staff car, with the lieutenant behind the wheel. They hurtled due south down the Bitumen, the road that cut through the sun-blasted khaki-coloured wasteland. The temperature rose above 100 degrees and the air became dryer and dryer as they penetrated progressively inland. They rolled into the stopover camp of Larrimah in time for lunch, a sprint of 300 miles from Darwin at an average speed of 83 miles an hour over a completely empty highway.

Larrimah wasn't a place to linger for pleasure, being nothing more than a collection of a few mulga trees and some huts populated by a few Aussie quartermaster bods and millions of flies. The three Canadian officers sped off in their trusty Chevy as soon as they could. They made about seventy miles more before one of the tires, succumbing to hot air, high speed, hot asphalt, and general fatigue, blew out. Fortunately they had got as far as the next camp, Banka Banka, which rivalled Larrimah as an oasis unspoiled by civilization — or by any civilized place to lay one's head down. But they did get the blowout replaced. The Chevy's trunk lock refused to budge, probably also a victim of the heat. The ever-resourceful Major Pick pried out the rear seat, got the panel behind it loose, and dragged out the spare tire.

Next day they streaked another 300 miles by lunch, arriving in the small town of Camooweal on the border between Northern Territory and Queensland. Camooweal was large enough to have a hotel, and the owner treated the daring Canucks to free beer. They pressed on, reaching Mount Isa, the Silver City, by 1500 hours, or three p.m. They'd covered a satisfactory thousand miles since leaving Darwin the previous morning.

Taking turns driving, they hit the bumpy, rocky bush track that ran between Mount Isa and Queensland's eastern seaboard, a distance of over 900 miles which the unit had previously traversed in the other direction by narrow-gauge railway. Between the little hamlets of Cloncurry and Winton, the Chev had to crawl along a rocky track where occasional small creeks had to be crossed by bumping down shale ledges, then crawling up shale ledges on the other side. Something punctured the gas tank — Major Pick plugged the hole with chewing gum. They "raced" the twelve miles back to Cloncurry, where a mechanic fixed the tank. On track once again, they took the wrong fork in the road near Kynuna and ended up by dark at Julia Creek, literally nowhere. They slept in the car that night.

After retracing their steps to Kynuna the next day, they were almost as far as Winton when, with Harry Wethey driving, they bumped down a rocky ledge and again speared the gas tank. This time, out of chewing gum, with gasoline trickling along the trail behind them and with their fate riding on the hope that the Chevy's overhung rear wouldn't strike sparks from a rock and blow them all into the next world, they made it to Winton, where the tank was patched once more. Starting out the next morning from Winton for Longreach, the Chevy blew another tire. They got out the original tire, which had been patched at Cloncurry, substituted it for the flat, forged on, and twelve miles from Longreach blew yet another tire. A passing sheep farmer supplied the stranded Canadian contingent with tube patches, and they finally made it to Longreach that evening.

The garage in Longreach had no spare tires that would fit the Chevy, so the colonel decided enough was enough. He telephoned Darwin to fly some tires by plane — civil or military — posthaste, or on the double. Then the 1CSWG safari settled down for a couple of days' rest and rehabilitation.

With the luck that always follows officers, they had landed in Longreach just as the Diggers Cup Race Meet was about to begin. The fifty-bed hotel was jammed with two hundred guests in town for the major event of the year. The three Canadians eventually bunked in cots set up in what had been the hotel's ballroom — shades of the *Monterey*! But, as the festivities were wide open, all formalities were abandoned as only Australians can abandon them, and the wait for the spare tires was, in Harry Wethey's words, "grand." Unrationed beer flowed freely as wine. Friday and Saturday were the days of the races and the colonel, betting five shillings at a time, came out ahead by one pound, nineteen shillings when the contests were over.

What had become an Outback adventure suddenly dimmed for the trio. Lieutenant Reid phoned from Darwin with bad news. Lieutenant Jack Miller had died of acute encephalitis the previous Sunday night at the 107 Australian Army General Hospital. Stunned, they cut short their socializing and deliberated on what to do. The colonel ought to be at the funeral. But Lieutenant Miller had already been buried — it had to be done quickly in the Torrid Zone. There was no use in the trio going back to Darwin. When the Qantas plane arrived at Longreach with the new tires, Lieutenant-Colonel Wethey boarded the aircraft and flew on to Brisbane to save time, leaving Pick and Legere to get the Chevy the rest of the way. They arrived in Brisbane twenty-four hours later in the battered, dust-choked staff car without any more misadventures.

Monday, September 17, 1945, was one of the hottest days of our months in Northern Territory. That was the day we buried Jack Miller. About a dozen of us were singled out as the lieutenant's burial party. The nearest military cemetery was about forty miles south of Darwin, in real Outback country. Three trucks were wheeled out for the funeral cortege down the Bitumen, the honour guard was turned out in full kit — steel helmets, rifles, packs and all — the coffin was loaded onto another truck with the Union Jack draped over it, and off we went. A steel helmet under a tropical sun is not the most comfortable sunshade. The sun's heat pressed down on us, hardly brightening our gloomy assignment. As we moved farther and farther away from the sea coast, the superheated air swirled dust around the back of the truck, where it mixed with our sweat to form thin mud packs on our skins.

There was no breeze at the cemetery to swirl the dust around. The ground seemed to have a bonfire burning under it, fuelled by the sun. We did get a chance to slosh some water from a hand pump over our heads and arms and sluice off some of the dust while the pallbearers slid the coffin off the truck. We of the honour guard then fell into place behind them as they shouldered the coffin. There were plenty of grave markers. Rows of crosses stretched across a stony plain where an attempt had been made to sow coarse grass and create a respectable final resting place for the hundreds of Australian military dead brought back from battles in the islands, as well as for most of the 250 people killed in the first Japanese bombing of Darwin.

We marched behind the coffin as well as we could up a rocky trail on a barren hillside overlooking the stony plain. Beyond it lay a vast, flat desert of mulga tree scrub and tan-coloured rocky earth. We trudged silently behind the coffin, each of us lost in our own thoughts. Lieutenant Miller, no doubt dedicated to his duty, had not been a beloved figure among us. A strict disciplinarian to the point of obsession, he had few friends among the Other Ranks. It was he who had drilled us unmercifully in and around the Vancouver Island camp, shouting threats and admonitions at any of us who failed to meet his exacting demands. For what purpose? We were being trained as signals intelligence operators, not parade ground precision marchers, but the drilling and grilling had gone on — and on — just the same.

A small, red-faced man of unimposing stature whose uniform never seemed to fit, Lieutenant Miller did have the presence to enforce commands and get some grudging, but not friendly, respect from the men. Still, it was unfair that he would serve almost from the outbreak of war, live to see its successful end, and then, within a little more than a month, be struck down by a tropical virus and be buried amid the heat and dust of a remote Australian Outback cemetery, ten thousand miles from home.

The march to the graveside, carried out without the precision that Lieutenant Miller would have demanded, was one of the most unpleasant trips of my life. Morbid tissue decays quickly in such torrid heat, and although the task was worst for the pallbearers, the stench of decay was almost overwhelming for the whole party. At the burial site, the coffin was lowered into the grave. We of the honour guard lined up on both sides and fired three volleys from our rifles over the grave in traditional military style.

I was then pulled summarily from the ranks by the sergeant-major, who took my rifle, marched me a short distance off, handed me a camera, and told me to take pictures of the site and the rest of the ceremony for Lieutenant Miller's family. The last rites finished, we got into the trucks on more than the double and went back to Darwin. It was one time we were glad to see the MacMillan's Road camp. The showers were our first target after we dumped our kit. Warm as they were, they were welcome enough to banish the last traces of a sad and unpleasant duty.

In 1999, an article on the discovery of Lieutenant Miller's grave and a photograph of the site were published in the *Ottawa Sun* and later in the *Kingston Whig-Standard*. When I saw the picture, the site looked quite different from what I remembered. It showed a level, grassy area, with a grove of trees in the background — not the barren hillside I recalled. I could only guess that Lieutenant Miller's remains must have been removed, along with others in the desert cemetery, to this sylvan setting after the war — and not back to Canada.

One would naturally assume that the government of Canada in 1945 would have been informed of Lieutenant Miller's death and would have made arrangements to bring this single Canadian body home for burial in a Canadian military cemetery. But it was only after an extensive search of the Department of National Defence's records that the fact was unearthed that a Royal Canadian Signal Corps officer had been buried in wartime in Northern Australia. Had these particular records been deliberately consigned to obscure archives, along with the story of the brief life of 1CSWG? It seems possible that, even years after the end of the war, the Canadian government still wanted there to be no mention of the very existence of 1CSWG that would have forced it to explain how a Canadian officer's body happened to be buried in this remote part of the world in wartime.

There was neither celebration nor ceremony at 0730 hours on October 11, 1945, when Number One Canadian Special Wireless Station switched off for the first and last time with a ...——., or *dit-dit-dit-daw-dit,* spelling "Vic Eddy," the signal operator's traditional sign for "end of message."

That and the silence that followed spread the word from Manila to Brisbane that Canadian Special Wireless had finished its job in the South West Pacific Area. For 1CSWG, the war was finally over.

Book Two:

The Long Journey Home

Chapter 1

Rolling Down the Bitumen

The rest of the story deals with the journey home to Canada, and it's a Chaucerian tale in itself. The war with Japan now over, thousands of Americans and Britons who had fought the more visible battles were wasting no time in making their way home, taking every available ship or plane that could be commandeered. Almost on the day of the official Japanese surrender, the two hundred or so RAAF Liberator bombers tied down in the field across the road had vanished west. They were dispatched to Singapore to fly home thousands of Australians who'd spent over four hellish years in the gigantic Japanese prisoner-of-war camp there.

Over the next couple of days, the Libs zoomed overhead on their way south to hospitals in Sydney and Melbourne, carrying full loads of Aussie diggers who had been severely weakened by malnutrition and mistreatment. The Dutch passenger ship *Oranje* somehow made it through the sunken hulks that littered Darwin harbour to drop off a shipload of ex-POWs who were in slightly better shape. A half-dozen of us went down to the Darwin docks to say hello and welcome them (home) to Australia, an odd role for a group of expatriate Canadians. They were ticketed for examination and treatment at the 107 Australian Army General Hospital. Unfortunately for us, this did *not* then make the ship available to 1CSWG personnel to go aboard and get out of Darwin. Instead, the *Oranje* pulled out and headed back to Singapore for another load of POWs, which, we lamely admitted to ourselves, was only right and proper. After all, they'd had to wait longer to get home than we had.

The higher authorities, such as Major-General Blamey, the Australian commander-in-chief, and Colonel Cosgrave, our own military attaché (recently returned from mis-signing the Japanese surrender document) were still making reassuring sounds to Lieutenant-Colonel Wethey, who was by this time visiting Brisbane and Melbourne, about getting a ship into Darwin harbour. Somehow the brass at 1CSWG weren't convinced that would ever happen. They thought it would make more sense to cross the continent by land and try to find a ship in Sydney, with its great harbour.

While our fate was being decided, Captain Wardrop and the quartermaster, Captain Hall, went to work totting up the weight of our equipment to see how many trucks would be needed. It came to about 89 tons. Wardrop and Hall calculated that it would take 36 three-ton trucks just to carry the gear. We would also need enough vehicles to accommodate us human bods who had to be shipped out as well.

Captain March, Lieutenant Rutherglen, and two fitters went down the Bitumen to Number 3 Australian Ordnance Depot at Twenty-Four Mile Camp and picked over the roughly forty Aussie trucks there, choosing fifteen that they believed might last the trip. Eventually they scrounged up thirty trucks from points near and far around Darwin. Most were far from in top shape. One of them just made it into our camp before a front wheel fell off. Flat tires were also common. It was up to our Motor Transport Section to get the fleet into shape for the 2,885-mile trip to Sydney. In the midst of all this, Major Pick and Lieutenant Legere — who was now Captain Legere, having been promoted during the trip south — arrived back from Brisbane in the beaten-up staff car along with a Royal Signals major they'd picked up somewhere.

Major Pick instantly took command of getting the trucks shipshape and loaded up with 1CSWG's equipment. Special care was taken with the still-top-secret Typex machines and associated gear. A dependable truck, carrying a load of 336 pounds of Typex machines, cipher equipment, and decoding document, set out with one of our jeeps as escort for Melbourne, over 2,000 miles away, to turn it all over to Australian H.Q. for disposal.

The indomitable Pick wasn't chancing anything. He arranged to borrow two 950-gallon petrol trucks and a water tanker from the Aussies to take with us in our vehicle convoy. He also borrowed twenty Australian drivers from the Northern Territory Force. These were added to the volunteers from all sections of 1CSWG who'd signed up for what would be probably the strangest and most taxing job of highway driving they would ever face.

Meanwhile, Lieutenant-Colonel Wethey had arrived from Adelaide, 1,600 miles to the south, aboard an RAAF Liberator. He'd been busy. After reaching in Brisbane in the Qantas plane that had brought the tires to Longreach, he'd spent his first evening there, hearing Colonel Cosgrave tell about his trip to Tokyo Bay for the surrender ceremonies. The next day, Wethey had ordered the Intelligence Corps members at CB off to Darwin by air, then hopped on a courier plane at Brisbane's Archer Field to fly to Sydney. The luck he'd had on the road to Longreach followed him onto the plane. The aircraft took off, immediately developed engine trouble, and landed again. He went back to Brisbane, where he ran into Pick and Legere, who'd just rolled in with the staff car. He later returned to Archer Field. The plane took off after lunch, circled the field, and once again landed with engine trouble. Exasperated at this outrageous inefficiency, Wethey went back once more to Brisbane, met Pick and Legere again, and spent the night at the Officers' Club.

The next day they finally made it off Archer Field in a Dutch C-57 and reached Sydney. Pick and Legere went on by plane to Melbourne, while Wethey went around to the Sydney printing firm that was to print the 1CSWG souvenir booklet. The printers were all on strike. No chance of printing the booklet there.

He took off again by plane for Melbourne, muttering to his diary about the slap-happy way in which service aircraft were run ("not at all well organized militarily"). In Melbourne he stayed at the Army, Navy and Air Force Club ("very nice"), had dinner with Pick and Legere at Scott's, the hotel where they were staying, and in the evening went to see *The Voice of the Turtle*, playing at a theatre in town. The Australians had a very well developed tradition of theatre, with performances by actors of the highest professional level, at a time when Canada could barely boast a single outstanding actor braving it out at home.

Now in Australian Army Headquarters territory, Wethey went to see the senior officer in command, Major-General Simpson, about getting our little band of Canadians back where we belonged. Simpson spoke to Blamey at the next officers' conference, and the word came back that Blamey thought we should be taken out of Darwin by sea. Everyone else said it was impossible: no ships about, too many half-sunken wrecks in the harbour, bad show all round.

To kill time while they waited for an official decision on our departure plans, Wethey and his companions did a few odd chores. Legere was sent to 115 Army General Hospital Heidelberg to visit one of our signalmen who'd been flown south with a jaw infection some time before. Wethey and Pick had a "nice drive and tea" with the Canadian trade commissioner and his lady at the Peninsula Golf Club. Word reached him that in Darwin the weather was getting hotter and more humid and rain showers were happening more frequently.

Wethey sent Captain Legere off to another printer to get the souvenir booklet underway (there being no strike at that particular moment in Melbourne). Meanwhile, he and Pick lobbied additional senior Aussie officers about getting 1CSWG out of the North before the rains came and the mud locked us in for another season. (There had not yet been any official recommendation from Major-General Blamey that we go out by sea, and when Wethey finally saw the commander-in-chief's memo on the subject there was indeed no mention of this route.) A transport colonel suggested quietly that Wethey plan on bringing us all south via the Bitumen. The Wet hadn't struck yet and the access roads were still firm enough to carry us to the asphalt highway.

Pick and Legere set out for Brisbane on service aircraft. Wethey talked once again with Colonel Cosgrave by phone and learned that the military attaché was leaving for Canada on October 24 — which, it turned out, was to be the very day that 1CSWG left Darwin. (It also was my twentieth birthday, although that fact had very little bearing on either decision.) Lieutenant-Colonel Wethey, after having his talk with the man most experienced in dealing with the Aussie high command, let Major-General Simpson know that the overland route would be okay, if it had to be that way. The general was happy with that, and no doubt promptly forgot all about those flymin' bleedin' pests from Canada. It was an odd turn of events. We'd been earnestly invited to come to Australia and had been welcomed with thanks for volunteering. Now that the war was over, it was up to us to find a way home across 7,000 miles of ocean. Good on ye, myte! Wack-ow!

Wethey had lunch with the British trade commissioner, had his picture taken for the souvenir booklet at the printer's, and enjoyed himself that evening at the Senior Officer Commanding's party. Ever dedicated, though, he was up at 0300 hours (three o'clock in the morning) to fly back to Darwin in one of those slap-happy Liberators.

The Wet was starting. The very day the station signed off, thunder, lightning, and a tropical downpour drenched the Darwin district. Almost as soon as it stopped, the sun came out and everything was quickly dry as a bone again. Signs that we were soon to be on the move were everywhere. Our telephone exchange was closed down and the next day the teletype link with Manila was also given the Vic Eddy. Officers from Northwest Territory Command and RAAF officers from across the road scouted the camp to find some peacetime use for it — or perhaps just to find things to scavenge when we were gone.

One grand gesture by Harry Wethey was the breaking out and distribution to everybody who smoked of 35,680 cigarettes sent out by the National Committee of the Royal Canadian Signals Auxiliary and Number Three Special Wireless Station at Victoria, British Columbia. Evidently, the theft of the old Victoria stagecoach on the eve of 1CSWG's departure from Vancouver Island had been forgiven. The colonel also found that there was a cash surplus of £249, one shilling, tuppence when the O.R.'s wet canteen was closed.

Slowly all the recreational diversions were disappearing. The volleyball nets were taken down. Even the swimming at Casuarina Beach was finished for the season: sharks and Portuguese men-of-war, a stinging jellyfish that could knock a man cold with its venom, were coming in to shore to spawn in the increasingly warm waters where we usually swam. Some of us went to observe them while the tide was out, stepping gingerly among the quivering little fornicating masses with our bare feet, getting some vicarious excitement out of the proximity to danger. But swimming was out of the question. When the tide was in, the Portuguese men-of-war floated around in the water, like stinging mines waiting to brush against some tender human skin to devastating effect. And somewhere, we knew, the sharks lurked.

The weather was actually getting cloudy and cooler. We could even wear shirts without smothering our pores. The nights were more comfortable for sleeping — when it didn't thunder and flash — and we were beginning to feel human again. The loading of the trucks went ahead, yet somehow the former Wethey's Commandos were escaping the work of heaving around the same wooden boxes we'd manhandled from Brisbane so many months before. Captain Hall, the quartermaster, and Captain March, the adjutant, seemed to have found themselves a different crew, and we former W.C.'s thought it was high time.

While all this was going on, the colonel and his surplus officers who now had nothing to do, plus the mysterious Major Bittlestone of Royal Signals (he had arrived in the back seat of the staff car with Pick and Legere), amused themselves with picnics to Berry Springs, a waterhole oasis several miles down the Bitumen, and Casuarina Beach for sunbaths. Even we lowly O.R.'s got to go to Berry Springs for a one-time outing. The officers' final farewell party brought in droves of brother officers from every imaginable establishment around Darwin: the RAAF, the RAF, the Royal Australian Navy, the Royal Navy, the Australian Army (men and women), and even a scattering of Netherlands Army and one or two U.S. Signals stragglers still around. This event officially and emphatically closed down the officers' mess once and for all.

The lightning bolt that jarred us all out of our iron beds early on the morning of October 24 also dramatically cancelled Number One Canadian Special Wireless Group's receiving/transmitting station forever. It sent the tall main antenna tower crashing as though to ensure that no military memo could reverse the closure order and put 1CSWG back into business again. The head-splitting crack of the giant electric spark gave us an early start for the trek to the far south. By dawn we had the huts stripped of our gear and our packs packed. I carefully stored my records, wrapped in a sweater, in the bottom of my kit bag.

The day had an extra special magic: it rained heavily for almost the first time in seven months. We'd had a spattering of raindrops before, but it poured on this day. I remember it particularly because, as observed above, it was my twentieth birthday. Finally starting out on the long road home was enough of a birthday present for me.

By the time of our departure, we'd lined up and breakfasted for the last time in the mess hut of the MacMillan's Road camp. The sun came out just as fiercely again and sucked dry every last bit of moisture that had fallen. Then we lined up to board our "first-class" transportation, which consisted of a string of three-ton Australian Army trucks whose backs were enclosed by one-inch-square wire mesh. Rolled-up tarpaulins provided a canopy to keep out the sun and — an unlikely occurrence — the rain. They certainly didn't keep out the dust.

At high noon on October 24, 1945, the unit's officers, non-coms, and ordinary ranks climbed aboard ninety-six vehicles of various types and started the trip of 2,885 miles by road and rail, down through the hot, bone-dry heart of the Australian continent on the first leg of the long journey back to Canada. In a manoeuvre typical of the army, we had to go south to go north. There wasn't a tear in the eye for the Darwin camp among any of the gang who piled into the trucks and jeeps that would roll down the single paved road across the desert to Alice Springs.

Once there, the trucks, jeeps, and troops were to board the flat cars and rickety coaches of The Ghan, a little narrow-gauge nineteenth-century train that would trolley us over hundreds of miles of desert to Adelaide, on the south coast. Upon our arrival in the South Australian capital, we would become a grand parade of trucks and jeeps through the cities, towns, and villages of the states of Victoria and New South Wales. All along the way, we were to be gracious but surprised at being greeted warmly and hailed wildly as victorious returning troops! In our wake, we were sure to leave a trail of puzzled Australians. They — like everyone else to whom I would ever mention my service in Australia — would not be able to fathom just why this crowd of sun-blackened northerners, clad in a hodgepodge of worn-out Canadian, American, Australian, Dutch, and British uniforms, should be rolling along the shores of the Great Australian Bight in nearly a hundred Australian and Canadian trucks and Jeeps. After all, didn't we belong on the opposite side of the earth?

Altogether, the mixed convoy rolled out of the camp, bound for Sydney by way of the Great Australian Desert which made up most of the continent. About a third of the men in our convoy had vowed to stay drunk the whole way. This, of course, we believed impossible, because no one could carry enough liquor with them. But sometimes the impossible can be overcome by those who are sufficiently enterprising and determined.

In our truck, Number 85 in the convoy, Tom McInniny took a solemn oath that he'd do it, and made a £25 bet with his crony Art Kenwood to boot. Somehow, somewhere, he'd laid in a supply of four bottles of Scotch with which he proposed to carry out the job. These, he calculated, would

Part of the ninety-six vehicle convoy taking Number One Special Wireless Group on its 2,885 mile journey south from Darwin to Sydney, two months after the war ended.

last him until we reached some civilized point where a fresh supply could be had. Where he'd got the Scotch remained a mystery. Only the officers' mess had liquor in stock. And so, part of our entertainment was to watch Tom McInniny guzzle down his Scotch, bellow every bawdy army ballad he could recall, and eat dust for hours between meal stops.

We went down the Bitumen at a good clip, the convoy alternately stretching out and closing up like an enormous accordion as the inexperienced Canadian drivers strove to keep up the pace. It was a strange and ludicrous mixture: battered Aussie trucks that probably had seen service in the deserts of North Africa in 1941, now loaded with hot, bored, dust-covered Canadian signalmen; 15-cwt. Canadian Ford trucks bearing boxes and crates of now-obsolete signals equipment, once worth a million dollars; a couple of dozen jeeps carrying officers and sergeants; a dozen or so CZ13 radio vans whose steel boxes were big enough to move half the furniture in an average house and which were crammed with technical junk; more 15-cwt. trucks bearing assortments of rifles and Bren guns that we never did use for anything but drill — except for the colonel's hunting trips; the two petrol trucks scrounged by Major Pick; two or three Aussie trucks carrying the cooks and their cooking gear; a water tank truck; two

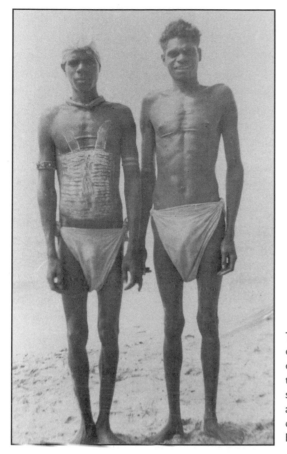

Two aborigines from a tribe on Bathurst Island just north of Darwin pose for their picture. Note the horizontal stripes on the left-hand man's abdomen, reminiscent of the cording on eighteeth-century British military uniforms.

tow trucks; and two Australian Comforts Fund "lollywater" or soft drink vans. Heading up this motley procession was Lieutenant-Colonel H.D.W. Wethey, joined by three or four of his officers, in the beaten-up staff car. It must have been the very last military convoy of any notable size to leave Darwin and travel the Bitumen back to civilization.

Despite tire blowouts that stopped the whole convoy a couple of times, we made 215 miles the first day to Katherine — one of the camps we'd stopped at overnight on the way north from Mount Isa to Darwin. The quarters were as primitive as ever, but at least we could get ourselves showered and stabilized after the all-day tossing, bouncing, and dust-eating on the road. All, that is, but the sad sacks like Tom McInniny — almost upstaged by the Gunner, who claimed greater capability for the marathon drunk and was already proving it admirably. It was believed that the Gunner got his booze from the colonel's own stock, and it was further rumoured that he, a lowly signalman, had somehow crashed the officers' farewell party at Darwin and even navigated the colonel back to his quarters after the rigours of the night's celebrations. This brief friendship hadn't prevented the colonel from confining the Gunner to the Adelaide River digger for being involved in the looting of the sergeants' beer supply. But somehow the Gunner, with his long years of army service behind him, had the knack of coming out on top. At Adelaide River jail, for instance, he'd had the benefit of fresh fruit, tomatoes, lettuce, and other greens in his meals — things we honest troops hadn't seen in months — because the jail was also the site of an experimental Australian "garden-in-the-desert" operation. One questions whether crime might pay after all.

On the second day we made 246 miles, all the way to Banka Banka, the worst of the stopover camps we'd encountered on the way north. At least it was dry this time, the Wet not yet having reached it yet. During our previous stay it had been a mud hole. At any rate, we were too battered and exhausted to notice. On a positive note, we'd been issued new folding camp cots just before leaving Darwin and they seemed positively luxurious to us now as we rolled into them. Not even the frog-sized spiders or the six-inch centipedes occupying the camp's hovels kept our eyes from closing in thankful sleep.

We covered another 180 miles the following day, as far as Barrow Creek. We were growing bored with the incredible sameness of the dried-out desert that was truly the Waste Land of T.S. Eliot. The little mulga trees that somehow survived their environment among the cactus and pulverized rock were grouped here and there like petrified, fossilized, miniaturized apple orchards that never bore edible fruit. On the eastern and southern horizons lurked the ancient, flat-topped mountains of the Murchison Range, while to the west rolled the Sahara-like furrowed sands of the Tanami Desert. The sight of the strange, round boulders known as the Devil's Marbles was so arresting that the convoy was ordered to stop so that we could get down from the trucks and stare at these incredible, enormous, perfect stone spheres, sitting incongruously on top of each other, which the elements had shaped over millions of years.

The food was good at Barrow Creek and the huts were surprisingly clean. On top of that, it rained during the night. The moisture freshened the air, tempering the furnace-like heat of the past few days, but only temporarily. In the morning we trucked out again, and by late afternoon we'd covered the 194 miles to the place that was later to become a character — as well a favourite tourist haunt — through Nevil Shute's book, *A Town Like Alice*.

Chapter 2

Alice and The Ghan

Truck Number 85 was among the last of the ninety-six-vehicle parade to wheel into the camp at Alice Springs. There'd been a startling change of temperature during the trip from Barrow Creek. From the 100-degree heat we'd known all the way from Darwin, we were suddenly plunged into the relative chill of the higher altitude at which "The Alice" sits. Having become so accustomed to the torrid, desert climate, to us the 50-degree drop in temperature came as a considerable shock. By the time we reached the Alice, we'd dug out our heavy winter battledress, which we hadn't worn in nearly a year, from our kits.

Alice Springs, celebrated in books and films as a "gateway" to the North and its mineral riches (much like Whitehorse in Canada's Yukon Territory), was not terribly impressive to the dusty, chilled, and hungry Canadians whose open trucks filed into the adjacent staging camp on that October afternoon of 1945. We'd seen so much strange country that it had the opposite effect upon us from what it apparently had upon those tourists who arrived there later from the other direction, from the lush greenery of the south. Although about a thousand people were living there at that point, the Alice seemed to us like a ghost town. Not one human being could be found in the streets.

There were rows of small, neat bungalows that showed every sign of being inhabited and kept in good repair. Most striking to us refugees from the barren North were the little green patches of lawn in front of every house, almost glowing in the late afternoon light. We had not seen anything like them in so long that their colour, their grooming, and their geometric precision were to be stared at in incredulous wonder. There were tiny flower beds, too, filled with the blooms of desert plants cultivated to bring out their best. But no people. We found out later that the word had gone ahead of us that over three hundred sex-starved, probably drunken — and in some cases they were largely right — foreign soldiers were about to descend on the Alice. The townsfolk had, quite wisely, locked themselves and their daughters safely inside those neat little bungalows.

As an oasis in the desert, Alice Springs did have some unique features. Situated a thousand miles from any other town, the Alice is almost at the dead centre of the Australian continent, one of the oldest lands in the world geologically. The dry plain upon which the Alice sits — underlain by a vast water table within drillable reach — is almost surrounded by the ancient MacDonnell Ranges. These mountains are so ground down by time, sandstorms, and the weather that they show no sharp edges or peaks. Instead, they appear either perfectly flat for long stretches or rounded or ribbed as they crouch on the horizon like carcasses of gigantic prehistoric beasts.

Most startling about them are their colours, which range from crimson to terra cotta to delicate mauve as the sunlight shifts and plays across their backs over the course of the day. On the plain, the light from the setting sun comes from high above in such a way that the sunset goes on for over half an hour. The twilight is filled with a yellow glow that seems to come from directly overhead and magically tints the mountains' bare rocks in colours ranging from red to gold, fading gradually into great masses of green and mauve, and finally to a dark blue before becoming mere black humps against a star-speckled, velvety backdrop of night sky.

The stalwarts of 1CSWG didn't pay much attention to these phenomena when they clambered down from the trucks. The initial objective was to get a hot shower and some hot food and fan out into the town to look for beer and blondes. But a town like Alice, — at that time, anyway

— wasn't prepared for an influx of more than three hundred tourists, military or otherwise, who would want instant entertainment. At any rate, the locals had probably had it with transient foreign troops.

We of Truck 85 bolted for the showers with alacrity, but about two hundred or so of our fellow travellers had been there ahead of us. When we raced into the corrugated iron shed where the showers were running constantly, we suffered one of the most violent shocks we had on the entire trip: *the showers were ice cold!* Our predecessors had quickly used up the small supply of hot water, which was heated in a tiny boiler by a wood fire that was tended by two aborigines, who seemed to have suddenly abandoned their post and departed on a walkabout. To a man, we let out bloodcurdling shrieks upon dousing ourselves with the frigid water. It was the only time in my life when I saw men actually turn blue with cold — and I was one of them.

Almost as bad was the effect that the combination of soap and alkaline water had on our hair: when the combination was rubbed in, our hair immediately stuck straight out from our heads like spikes and stayed that way for hours, despite innumerable rinsings. The effect would be considered "cool" among youths forty to fifty years later, but not for us hardened signalmen.

For Truck 85, there was one distinct benefit of the icy showers: they drove Tom McInniny cold sober and broke his resolve to remain drunk the whole trip. It was a desperate struggle for him to get back into his former condition after that.

Once more in battledress, we were better able to withstand the rigours of an Australian desert evening. Some old sweat who'd served in the Mediterranean theatre observed that Alice Springs at this time of year was pretty much like northwestern Africa, where the days were sunny and mild but the nights were dark and frigid. We saw no moon, but the Southern Cross hung low over us, sparkling like ice chips.

The would-be revellers among us found the night life cold, too. With all the girls locked up and the beer still rationed to two quarts apiece, even in the Alice there was very little to warm us, nor anything to thicken the blood. It seemed we'd come to Alice Springs too late for the big party that had in earlier times continued as long as armies passed through on their way to the northern battlefields. On the other hand, we were too early for the armies of postwar tourists who were later to surge north to see the sights denied them during the war.

The stopover in Alice was only thirty-eight hours — long enough for two cold nights' sleep, as each of us carried with him only two army blankets. Most of us slept in our battledress uniforms and on the splintery wooden floors of the barracks sheds. This helped us beat the cold and made it a quicker job to get up in the mornings and get to the mess hall for a cup or two of hot tea. We rose just as the sun was getting up, too, and reversing the colour spectacle of the previous night's sunset, this time playing its optical tricks on the rocky hills and mountains to the west. The early-morning sunlight seemed strangely cold.

Lieutenant-Colonel Wethey and his staff had been busy with plans for the next stage of the move south even as they lingered over the fine dinner held in their honour the previous evening by the Area Headquarters commander. Alice Springs was the point where the Bitumen ended and the railway to South Australia began — or, depending on which way you were bound between Adelaide and Darwin, this was where the railway from South Australia ended and the Bitumen began.

The route that joined these two centres more than 1,500 miles apart was almost identical to that taken by the nineteenth-century explorer, John McDouall Stuart, who in 1838 set out to be the first white man to penetrate the unexplored interior of Australia. After four attempts, he made it as far as about the present site of Alice Springs, but, after planting the Union Jack on a mountaintop, was chased back south by angry aborigines. Later, on his sixth try, he and a party of twelve men and forty-nine horses actually made it from Adelaide to near where Darwin is today, in a four-month journey that almost killed them all through thirst, heat, and generally hellish conditions.

As far as we were concerned, things hadn't progressed much in the hundred years since. Conditions were still hellish, but we could move a little faster. It had taken us four days to get from Darwin to Alice Springs by truck on our first and only try, and the aborigines were friendly, if only curious. Now we were about to put the trucks aboard two trains, and ourselves aboard another, and zip south to Adelaide within three and a half more days.

All day Monday, Harry Wethey and his officers busied themselves with planning the train trip south. The colonel was triumphant in his victory over the local military transport officer who had guessed it would take three and a half trains to move 1CSWG farther south. Wethey had worked it so we needed only three. The bods would go on the first train, and the vehicles, with six officers and thirty-four O.R.'s in charge, would be loaded onto the other two. Boxcars which served as mess kitchens were part of each train. The trains would stop at will whenever necessary; there being no others anywhere along the 800-mile rail line, there was no danger of collision.

This primitive railway was a wonder of the world. It was of the variety seen in remote parts of India, Asia, or Africa in some earlier colonial time. Normally, two trains travelled in the same direction between Terowie, — near Adelaide on the southern coast — and Alice Springs, perhaps once a week, maybe more often, maybe less. The leading train was known as "The Ghan" and the second was "The Chaser." Ordinarily, human passengers travelled on The Ghan, while vehicles and livestock, if any, went on The Chaser, which lagged behind at some distance.

The Ghan and The Chaser were introduced to the Australian Outback in 1929, but judging by appearances it might just as well have been some time in the 1880s or '90s. The track, like the one over which we'd travelled across Queensland, was narrow gauge. The passenger coaches on The Ghan were about the size and width of an old Toronto streetcar. They were also like streetcars of the 1920s and '30s on the inside; a hard, leather-covered bench ran the length of the car along each wall. They rattled and swayed just as streetcars would if they were linked together and pulled along a track whose rails were rippled and wobbled by the intense heat of the Outback sun.

The Ghan is said to have got its name from the Afghan camel drivers imported to provide transportation across the same desert before the railway came. These camel caravans travelled the same desert track over which the rails were later laid — and which had first been traversed by Stuart. No doubt The Ghan was a vast improvement for travellers over those bad-tempered beasts of burden. But the accommodations weren't luxurious to a bunch of Canadians spoiled after riding in the backs of trucks.

Once more in full pack, we were loaded onto The Ghan at 0700 hours, about twenty or twenty-five bodies to a coach. Somehow we lost track of Tom McInniny and even The Gunner, but we assumed they had gotten into another coach. It would be someone else's misfortune to have to look after them and make sure they didn't fall off the train.

The Ghan gave a gigantic spasm, lurched once or twice, stopped, then started again and began its bumping, bouncing progress out of the Alice Springs rail yard. There was no one around to bid us goodbye, except for one or two aborigines who raised sinewy black arms. Also being left behind were a few of our officers who were going to ride The Chaser, and they didn't bother to acknowledge our departure.

Each of us heaved off our packs and dropped them and our kits on the floor of the coach because there was nowhere else to put them. We then found we had little or nothing to do but try to stay on the hard benches while the coach rocked and rolled and lurched, or to stare out the windows across the way at the khaki-coloured desert rocks.

The sun had climbed high now and the frigidity of the previous days became a memory. We found ourselves perspiring mightily as the temperature in the coach returned to the boiling point we were accustomed to. We didn't try to open the windows because of the engine's soft-coal smoke rolling by. The Ghan was beginning to snake through a gap in the MacDonnell Range and descend to a lower, warmer altitude. It wasn't long before we'd peeled off our battledress and were back once more into shorts and boots — but this time with shirts on, at least for the moment.

Barrelling along at its top speed of 25 miles per hour, The Ghan gave its passengers an experience that might rival a ride inside a cement mixer. The train ground on, with a lurch here, a yank there, and a bounce and a shake — repeated endlessly in random order. Not surprisingly, a few of the lads got violently "trainsick." Men who'd spent almost a month at sea aboard the *Monterey* and *Shawnee* without once showing any ill effects were turning green around the gills.

At this point, a bird's-eye view of the Outback south of the Alice might have been more in keeping with the late 1920s — or, in many places, the 1880s. The scene was one of an outspreading, empty land blending from rocky, sandy desert into dry, sun-baked plains marked only by a thin, almost perfectly straight double line that was The Ghan's steel track. If the bird were flying high enough, it might have observed, spaced out several miles apart, the three trains in our convoy: The Ghan, of course; The Chaser, its flatcars loaded with trucks, vans, and Jeeps; and The Chaser's second section, carrying more vehicles as well as first-class coaches that housed most of 1CSWG's officers. All three trains would be rolling along at cruising speed, with full steam up but almost no smoke visible at their stacks.

A look at the trains would reveal numerous objects on the roofs of The Ghan's coaches, which would prove upon closer examination to be Canadian soldiers, many of whom clutched quart-sized green or brown bottles. When the bottles were empty they tossed them with great glee at the millions of rocks alongside the track. The head of other Canadian soldiers also poked out of the train's windows, through which the occasional bottle would also fly and explode on a rock.

It was clear that we Canadians weren't the only rowdies to engage in this pastime. The entire length of The Ghan's route, from the Alice to the railway terminus at Terowie, was littered on both sides with shards of broken bottles. It was apparently a tradition for all red-blooded vagabonds who ever rode The Ghan to fire their empties at the railside rocks.

Three days on The Ghan was like a month at sea. The blank landscape, upon which a single tree might stand out like a beacon, combined with the unrelenting sunlight and the never-ending jerking and bouncing of the coach had a hypnotic effect, one which provoked this odd behaviour among the passengers. By all accounts, the same was true of civilian travellers riding this line both before and after the war. The glittering pieces of glass strewn along the length of the rail line were evidence of their passing through. Some energetic sociologists would have their work cut out for them if they tried to document the significance of this phenomenon.

The bottles, incidentally, had been obtained full at one of The Ghan's first stops many miles south of the Alice, at a place called Marree. There is some cause to question whether Marree was actually "a place." It consisted of one small corrugated-iron building that had been erected — in the distant past — about a hundred yards from the track under two or three ghost gum trees. These white-barked trees formed a lonely grouping on a broad, sandy plain that stretched westward from the railway track. There were a couple of other ghost gums slightly to the south, and under these were tethered three camels. Their driver was nowhere to be seen, but he was undoubtedly inside the iron shack, as there was no other reason for anyone to visit Marree.

Even though there was no station, The Ghan lurched and groaned to a halt at this point on the track as if it were a regular stop. We soon found out why. This shack under the ghost gums was the first place south of Alice Springs where the beer was not rationed. The word spread throughout the train like a lit dynamite fuse. The little doors along the sides of the coaches flew open and the Canadians charged out in a scene that resembled nothing more than the start of the Boston Marathon. The pristine sands were instantly pockmarked by the churning feet of a couple of hundred soldiers bent on reaching the little building that would probably accommodate about twenty bodies besides the proprietor's.

The dash was successful, if not slightly disappointing, for most. Men emerged from the shack, each with a wooden case — some with two — on their shoulders. But it wasn't beer they carried. The only stock on hand at the only emporium in Marree was — stout. The Swiggers, driven almost mad by thirst — as is often said in G.A. Henty novels — didn't care. Our water bottles held the only other drink available to us. The boys took all the stout they could procure at the exorbitant price that the delighted owner demanded. The Ghan's crew were most accommodating. They held up the train for as long the Canadians needed to load the entire stock of the Marree pub into the coaches.

Some of us who were not especially keen on stout wandered off to bother the camels. The beasts stood haughtily in the sparse shade of the gum trees, eyeing us warily, then shying a little and grunting menacingly as we got near. They were saddled and harnessed and some bore packs. Their mangy hides gave them the appearance of being half worn-out.

So much like Afghanistan or North Africa was this part of Australia that somebody got the idea in the nineteenth century that camels would be right at home. After all, Australia already had some of the strangest beasties on earth, so what harm could be done? The camels were import-ed from Afghanistan along with native drivers and became for many years the most reliable form of transport in the Australian desert. Not long after they were displaced by the fleet trains of The Ghan system, the Afghan camels' descendants came to be used only for local conveyance. Still, in a land where it almost never rained and where water was worth more than gold, camels were a reliable backup form of transport.

While The Ghan locomotive chuffed contentedly in its place, we took turns trying to climb up into the camels' saddles. The challenge was formi-dable. The camels stood half again as tall as any of us, and besides they did-n't take kindly to these nervy intruders trying to mount them. In our igno-rance we didn't know that the camels must kneel first if you want to climb aboard, and we certainly didn't know the magic word that would make them assume this position. And so the skittish creatures, their heads held aloof and their large lips curled in contempt, kept backing away each time we tried to hoist a leg up high enough to get a foot into some part of the harness.

Louis Rousseau was the only one of the five of us to succeed. But as soon as he managed to get up into the saddle, the camel decided to go down on its knees and belly. Down it went on its front knees, nearly throwing Louis over its head, and then down went the rear set. Rousseau's

Two coaches of The Ghan, a relic of Australian desert travel, stop for a break at Marree in mid-desert. The narrow-gauge railway was more like an old-fashioned streetcar line, with coaches smaller and narrower than old-time street trams. Troops sweltered by day and were chilled by night as they slept on stout-soaked floors between the hard seats.

camel was content to stay where it was. It didn't matter how many times he dug into the beast's mangy sides with his steel-shod boot heels, it was determined to remain folded down into an unmoving lump. The last thing it was going to do was give Louis or any of the rest of us a free ride. They seemed to think that if we'd arrived on The Ghan, we could damn' well leave on The Ghan.

We did just that. Once the engineers were satisfied that every available drop of stout had been taken on, The Ghan gave a big blast from its steam whistle and the train lurched back into motion. We could imagine the camel driver in the corrugated shack gleefully counting up the pounds and shillings he'd reaped from these strange-talking characters from somewhere. We suspected that he would later settle up with the train crew, making good on whatever financial arrangements had been made to get The Ghan to make this pit stop on behalf of the thirsty — and gullible — travellers of Number One Canadian Special Wireless Group.

The trip south grew far more convivial after the stop at Marree. As bottle after bottle of stout was emptied, so were the coaches. The revellers somehow found their way onto the coach roofs without falling off the train, and there they took up the pastime of pitching empties at the rocks. Down below, bottles that were set down on the floor half-empty would tip over with the train's inevitable wobbling and lurching. The floors were soon awash in stout and littered with rolling bottles, making navigation exceptionally hazardous. But it seemed to matter little to the revellers. Tom McInniny had been outdone in his campaign by a couple of hundred others with the same idea in mind. In one way they couldn't be blamed, given the monotony, the jerking and wobbling of the train, and the lack of anything other than the deadly desert to look upon if you were sober, which a few of us were.

Along the way, there were actually a few notable sights for those of us still in a condition to notice. Every now and then we could see a little corrugated-iron igloo that was the home of a tiny family of aborigines who apparently lived on some part off the largesse thrown from The Ghan on its trips past.

Some of the more generous — or more drunken — would fling shillings and florins in their direction, laughing as they scrambled among the rocks to retrieve them. The young vagabond soldiers rolling by hardly owned any more that the aborigines outside. Their generosity was prompted in some part by the stout, but they were also drunk with exuberance in the knowledge that they were on their way home.

Twice a day, when mealtime came, the train would stop wherever it happened to be. These pauses were announced by the whole train suddenly jerking to a stop, toppling any bottles of stout that had been opened and left on the floor since the last meal. Everyone would pile off the train, mess tins in hand, and shamble alongside the track to a boxcar that doubled as a kitchen. Down came the food from an opening in the side of the boxcar, on long ladles or simply at the end of the long arms of the cooks. There would be bully beef, rice cooked and loaded with curry until was like bright yellow swamp glop, a slab of bread, and a pint of corrosive black tea so hot that it steamed even in the 90-degree air. Sometimes we'd have curried stew, also a bright yellow from the curry that was liberally dumped in to cover the smell of bad meat.

There being no place to sit down on the flat, pebbly desert where the train crew chose to stop, you would clasp the handles of your two mess tins in one hand, the burning handle of the tin tea mug in the other, and somehow, with a fork slipped in between a thumb and the mug handle, shovel food into your mouth. This might not seem to differ much from the average Canadian cookout, when a third hand would be valuable, but in this case a *fourth* hand was a necessity, to brush — and not *wave* — off the great clouds of maddeningly persistent desert flies that rendezvoused with our train precisely at mealtime. These creatures knew no fear of man. They settled onto us and instantly began to explore every possible body orifice. They seemed especially fond of clustering on the face of anyone who might have cut himself shaving that morning and sampling the still-fresh blood. They would try to force their way into eyes squeezed nearly shut and attempt to ride into mouths aboard forkfuls of bully beef. Nobody knew how many got into the curried rice.

Thanks to the flies, mealtimes saw more than three hundred Canadians take part in a kind of St. Vitus's dance as we tried gamely to feed ourselves while at the same time swatting or brushing energetically at our tormentors, wriggling to dislodge them from under our collars, and violently shaking our heads to get them off our faces. We ate in near-blindness as we squinted and squeezed our eyes shut to keep the insects out.

The most astounding sight in all this was the coolness displayed by a group of about a dozen almost-naked aborigines who appeared almost magically out of the apparent emptiness that surrounded us. These magnificent men, carrying hunting spears and boomerangs and with white paint streaked over face and body, gathered about to watch us. We must have seemed odd to them, as we consumed our strange diet with our unusual implements. More baffling to them must have been our attempts to do battle with the flies. The aborigines stood almost dead still, making no effort to disperse the flies which harassed them as much as they did us. True, they kept their mouths closed and their eyes squinted almost to slits, but they never once raised a finger to brush the insects away. I have since read an account by some of the first British sailors to visit Australia in the eighteenth century, long before white settlement began, in which an officer noted exactly the same characteristic among the aborigines they encountered. In actual fact, ignoring the little pests was the only way to handle them because it was plain they were not going to go away on account of the brief passing of a few decadent tenderfeet.

Although the chance to talk to the natives, a link to the dawn of man's existence, was tempting, none of us could stand the incessant plague of flies for longer than it took to wolf down our food, rinse out our mess tins

in a nearby artesian hot-water spring, run behind a rock to perform necessary kidney relief, and dash back on board our train. The windows still
being closed, and with no bodies or food present, the flies hadn't bothered
to invade our home base. Despite the floors swimming in stout, the rock-
hard seats, and the hot, dusty interior air, we were only too glad to be back
on the lurching, yanking Ghan as it pulled away. The aborigines, to whom
the cooks had passed out billycans of curried rice and bully beef before
sliding the boxcar doors shut, waved curiously as we rolled by. We
returned the favour but kept the windows shut tight.

Getting a night's sleep on The Ghan took a fair bit of ingenuity as well
as the ability to sleep through anything. There were, of course, no Pullman
cars, and the seating was only suitable for sitting bolt upright. That left the
floor, which reeked of stale stout. The thinkers among us saw instantly
that the only solution was to fill the space on the floor between the facing
seats by randomly piling up all of our packs and assorted gear. This created a level surface flush with the seats. We could spread ourselves out on
top of the packs, if not in comfort then at least somewhat insulated from
the bouncing, lurching, stout-stained floor.

I remembered Corbett's trick on the little train from Brisbane to
Mount Isa, and rigged one of my blankets as a hammock, hitched at each
end to the tiny ornate iron luggage racks near the ceiling with web straps.
I slept peacefully all night, the hammock swinging back and forth gently
to the rocking and lurching of the train as it hurtled at full throttle at 25
m.p.h. through the chilly Outback night.

The second day on The Ghan was the dullest of the three. After
extracting myself from the hammock and getting my back and legs free of
the kinks caused by the half-moon supine position I'd had to maintain, I
was ready to dash with the rest the hundred feet or so away to the boxcar
for another sumptuous breakfast.

There is something epic about the sight of nearly three hundred soldiers charging in a solid phalanx, stopping to form a single line without
any shouted command, and then urinating into the desert sands in unison. It is truly one of nature's most poignant scenes. Our kidneys shared a
common response to the night's lurchings and joltings aboard The Ghan
— and its lack of sanitary facilities.

But who needed man-made conveniences when the sands and
pebbles of the Outback had been waiting patiently for millennia for all
things to pass? This land, still within the Northern Territory, was a dry

land. It felt moisture only every few years and any contribution was probably an asset.

As soon as our fly-ridden breakfast was over, we hastened back into our train coaches and once more were rolling southward toward civilization. That night was Halloween, but we could see no pumpkins in the desert to make into jack-o'-lanterns.

By our third and last full day on rails The Ghan had crossed into the state of South Australia. The terrain was changing to one of greener plains where rain fell more frequently. In fact, it had rained the night before, and as The Ghan snaked through hilly, foliage-covered country we noticed a distinct absence of the dust we'd been eating almost all the way from Darwin. So it came as a surprise to encounter Lake Eyre and, farther south, Lake Torrens. We had expected our first glimpse of the blue water of an inland freshwater lake, but these turned out to be vast expanses of white — lakes of sun-dried salt.

The Ghan forged onward through this arid country toward the greenery of the real south. It rolled on past Woomera, an Outback village that would become known in the 1960s as Australia's rocket testing range. It stopped for a while at Quorn, a tiny place along the railside where we were served our first civilized meal since going north — not by our square-handed cooks but by the ladies of the Country Women's Association. And, at some establishment out of sight of the ladies, most of the boys re-stocked their beverage supplies — this time with real — and unrationed — beer as well as a modest supply of liquor to tide them over the rest of the way to Adelaide.

We found out that Quorn was our changeover point from the Commonwealth Railways to the South Australian Railways system. It didn't make any difference, as far as we were concerned — it was still The Ghan. At dusk, having crossed the Flinders Range, we came upon a fairly large town called Peterborough, which raised some cheers from those of us who were from Ontario, where there is a city of the same name. It was dark when the desert chariots of Number One Canadian Special Wireless Group at last clanked and clattered into the yards of the southern railhead at Terowie — the end of the line, 800 miles south of Alice Springs and 1,600 dusty miles from Darwin.

Chapter 3

Trucking Through the South

Another perilously cold 50-degree night ended with the sun beginning to peek over the rail yard into an azure sky. Sleeping in the raunchy, stout-tainted air of The Ghan's coaches — with the windows shut tight to preserve as much heat rising from the prostrate bodies as possible — had seemed bad enough when the train was rolling and swaying along. But now, standing still in the Terowie rail yard, with no hypnotic, sleep-inducing motion to induce sleep, The Ghan was farther than ever from being a luxury hotel.

We climbed stiffly down from the train for the morning ablutions and breakfast, with pinched faces and pink noses from the unaccustomed cold. The stark, crude, unheated latrines and washrooms echoed to plaintive curses and bitter jibes heaped upon the primitivism of our host country. The morning sun brought the temperature up to about 60 degrees, but it felt more like a frosty morning in February back home. It must have been unusual for the district, too, for there was no sign of any kind of heating device in the cavernous railway shed where we stood in a long, shivering line to get breakfast. The number of hangovers among those in line rendered the sight of us even sorrier.

All three trains of our Commonwealth Railways convoy had pulled into Terowie the previous night. By the time we had hauled our kit and gear out of the coaches, most of our fleet of vehicles had been driven off The Chaser's flatcars and were lined up, ready for us to swing aboard for the next leg of the epic journey. The target was now Adelaide — or more precisely, Woodside Camp, north of the city. On the way, the countryside grew startlingly greener, and even towns and villages appeared.

Before we came anywhere close to Woodside Camp we encountered the first instances of a phenomenon that was to bemuse and surprise us all along the remaining thousand miles or so to Sydney: the inhabitants of the towns and villages turning out *en masse* to cheer and wave and shout greetings to these conquering Canadians who had so bravely, they apparently believed, played their part alongside the Aussies to bring an end to the war. No one could have been more astonished than we were by the semi-delirious welcomes we received in town after town. The crowds would be jam-packed along both sides of the routes into each town, right from the outskirts to the town hall where, in most cases, the lord mayor was waiting to call Lieutenant-Colonel H.D.W. Wethey to his side for a welcoming address in the crowded square. There could have been no more dramatic demonstration of Australian relief and gratitude over the defeat of Japan.

At first we thought the townspeople must be mistaking us for some legitimate group of battle-weary veterans of the jungles. We had no inkling of the lingering hysteria over the end of the war. Back in Darwin, the booze-up on V-J Day hadn't been much different from most nights in the wet canteen. The impromptu celebrations and outpourings of jubilation at the sight of *any* troops who were on the right side of the victory was totally unexpected. The unseen work of the Australian Army's public relations corps in spreading the advance word of our homeward trek was just as likely to be responsible.

Between Terowie and Woodside Camp, our immediate destination, there were several of these spontaneous outbursts, at places with names like Burra, Marabel, Kapunda, and Gepps-Cross, not to mention Gawler. There was an unexpected civic welcome at Burra, marked by frantic waving and cheering by schoolchildren and townspeople of all ages. At our lunch stop, a Major MacArthur, commanding officer of the South

Australia Line of Commununications, paid a congratulatory visit with two newsmen in tow. At Gawler we were met by the provost, or police chief, with a police escort.

At Gepps-Cross the police commissioner brought us jovially to a halt in the middle of town, so that Lieutenant-Colonel Wethey could be conducted to the city hall steps. There he was placed beside the lord mayor while the rest of us climbed down from the trucks to mingle with the crowd and be greeted with an enthusiasm that was almost embarrassing. None of us felt we deserved these wild welcomes. Bells pealed, a band played loudly, the lord mayor made an expansive speech praising the brotherhood of Australia and Canada, and the crowd cheered.

Afterward, as the trucks began pulling out, I almost was left behind while I raced frantically among the nearby pubs looking for Tom McInniny, who'd vanished almost immediately after our arrival. I made it back to Truck 85 just in the nick of time. As it began to move off, there was Tom lolling amid the kit in the back of the truck with the other bods, in the glorious state to which he had dedicated himself in Darwin.

We at last got to Woodside Camp at 2000 hours that night. The contrast between Woodside and our former Darwin home could be measured only in words. We'd gone from the dusty red and khaki of the parched Outback to the damp verdant green of Mount Lofty, four hundred feet above the picture-book city of Adelaide. We had left behind the open-sided, tin-roofed shacks and mosquito netting of the MacMillan's Road camp and the studied ruggedness of Woodside's carefully built lodges took their place. The buildings resembled those of a high-class hunting or ski resort in northern Ontario or British Columbia.

Over the course of one Australian winter, we had also gone from the arid blasting heat of Darwin to the damp chill of Mount Lofty. There was no heat at Woodside Camp; each of the handsome barracks "lodges" had a tiny coal stove of the sort you might find in an ice-fishing hut on Lake Simcoe, and this was meant to warm a building that held more than a hundred cots and with enough headroom above the open rafters to put two more storeys among the beams. The stove was useless to anyone more than a foot away.

In the magnificent lounge of the chalet-like central lodge there was a fireplace big enough to park a jeep in, which we filled with logs and lit. The heat went straight up the beautiful fieldstone chimney, leaving us huddled around the fireplace mouth trying to soak up some of the heat before it vanished. For all they'd prepared for our stay, the Aussies in charge of the camp must have assumed that we Canadians, being from the Arctic Circle, would be quite comfortable in a 40-degree environment.

To this point the hard-partying members of 1CSWG had — at least since their first departure for Darwin — carried on their carousing in the style of a Canadian lumber or mining camp. Now that we had returned to civilization in Adelaide, more sophisticated behaviour would be in order. And we rose to the occasion. We could afford to; those who hadn't already gambled it all away had plenty of money for the simple reason that there'd been nowhere to spend it in Darwin except at the wet canteen or at craps. Most of us had arranged for the paymaster to defer payment and let our grand sum of $60 a month accumulate on his books, drawing only a little at a time for refreshments and sundries as we needed them. On the first payday after our arrival at Camp Woodside, the paymaster's books were suddenly and quickly put right. All at once, three hundred officers and men were inundated with currency.

Next came the ultimate prize that the army could bestow upon a lowly signalman: a seventy-two-hour pass. This meant three days of gracious living for some, boredom for others, but a riot for most. The Tom McInninys who'd vowed to drink their way back home could now honour their oath to the utmost.

Adelaide was no Paris, but it had its bright side. Most importantly, it had girls. And the Australian girls were for the most part free-spirited. Having been all but sequestered for the past eight months, the combination of money, girls, and an unfettered seventy-two hours in civilization threatened to be an explosive one. Two hundred Canadians invaded Adelaide in the first wave, with over a hundred more to follow as soon all the unit's possessions were safely stored at Woodside. The city of Adelaide declared the Monday of our first appearance a public holiday, a grand gesture toward a fellow member of the British Commonwealth and ally in war, we all felt. There was even a band on hand to welcome us at the city hall.

Wethey and half a dozen of his officers were guests of the lord mayor of Adelaide at a reception given for the United States consul, a Mr. Hutchison, who was going home. Wethey and some others of his officer corps had already spent a day at Scottsburn, the estate of a prominent personage. They went on to further gracious entertainments while the Other Ranks, characteristically, fanned out in search of the less grandiose, and more earthy.

Adelaide was a charming place, encircled by an enormous greenbelt. Laid out by a military man, the city was a study in precise squares full of brilliant flowering plants and fine buildings, with streets lined with palm trees and full of what to Canadians was a quasi-English quaintness over-lain by rugged Australian individualism. As a counterpoint to the raw frontierism of Darwin and the Outback, it gave us a wholly different insight into this subequatorial British nation.

After renewing acquaintance with civilization, 1CSWG was ready to move on, following the coastal route around the Great Australian Bight with Melbourne as a stopover and Sydney as the ultimate goal. The way was sprinkled with a succession of places such as Bordertown and Ararat. Once we spotted the local racetrack or fairgrounds on the way into any of these towns, we knew where we would be sleeping that night.

Impromptu dance extravaganzas, free milkshakes, and freedom of cities, towns, and villages were the rule as 1CSWG progressed toward Sydney. Ballarat was another point of celebration where the citizens dropped everything they were doing and extended welcoming words to the conquering Canadians.

In fact, in most of these places, some of the Canadians made undreamed-of conquests. Some would fail to appear for roll call, then return for duty with likely excuses for their absence. One or two actually disappeared at one point on the route and mysteriously — even to them-selves — rejoined the convoy farther along at some town or village, none too sure of how they got there. Stories like this were reminiscent of the Middle Eastern adventures of Jimmy, our Royal Navy pal, and his serendip-itous return to his ship at Haifa. There was a certain breed of serviceman who had this ability to land on both feet and escape penalties.

Along the way, the colonel was in demand for press and radio interviews. The colonel described, with typical Wethey reticence, only the public part of the role of the Canadians in the late Pacific war.

Our six-day stay in the great metropolis of Melbourne was a landmark of our journey. Leaves were extended for almost the entire six days. Now well versed in exploiting all the advantages of the triumphant transient, and led by DeMal and Boombaw, we of Number Two Section sought out the best hotels in which to squander our back pay. The sophisticated city lived up to an almost Continental standard, one to which we were completely unaccustomed. The effects of the sybaritic life were beginning to be show on not only the McInninys but also the main body of 1CSWG. Real soldiering was forgotten in this new peacetime, even by the officers. Discipline faded, and the rakehell prevailed.

We'd survived the near-arctic conditions at Woodside, and found that the Watsonia Camp at Melbourne was just as cold — its "shelter" was atrocious. We ordinary ranks slept outdoors on collapsible cots — which may not have been bad in Darwin in the Dry, but here in the green, dampish state of Victoria, winter outdoor slumber was something else again. If it hadn't been so cold — by our recently acquired standard — it might not have been so bad; if it hadn't rained, it mightn't have been so bad, either. And the food was like an afterthought, resembling nothing more than the product of a mess hall where the best had already been thrown in the garbage. Some of our numbers swore they'd seen the Watsonia cooks actually reclaim tidbits out of the trash cans behind the mess hall, but this, like much of what 1CSWG latrinograms conveyed, was probably trash itself.

Perhaps the Aussie army cooks were exasperated by the arrival of these tardy foreigners. After all, the bleedin' war was kaput for months, eh, myte? To make matters worse, as usual it wasn't easy to convince our Australian service brethren that we were not, on the one hand, Yanks in cast-off British uniforms, or, on the other, British pommies who talked like Yanks. Perhaps it was a sign that our welcome was beginning to wear, at least among the Aussie cobbers who were impatient to return to civvy life and were jumpy over the continued presence of foreign troops.

Even though we carried Canada flashes in our shoulder epaulets, our uniforms were by now a puzzling amalgam of Canadian, Yankee, Dutch, and Aussie shirts, shorts, and boots, with a few Royal Canadian Navy touches thrown in. Our original Canadian Army clothing issues were long since worn to shreds in the hard labour at Darwin and the constant boiling in caustic soapy water to get them clean. We felt like some Lost Brigade wandering the desert.

Another source of confusion was our changeover to brown leather boots from the regulation black Canadian Army footwear. Our quartermaster had neglected to stock fresh boots for us before we left Canada, so as our black boots wore out on the hard, volcanic ground in Darwin, Lieutenant-Colonel Wethey obtained a supply of the brown Australian boots that were standard issue for Aussie O.R.'s. Under the eagle eye of Sergeant-Major Addy, we kept these brown boots as highly polished as we had our blacks.

A fact that didn't bother us much in Australia was that, in the Canadian Army, only officers were allowed to wear brown boots. But when we got back to Canada, our exotic footwear would cause some of us O.R.'s to get an earful from some outraged officers.

The rude reception from the Aussie cooks and the awful conditions at Watsonia didn't spoil our impressions of Melbourne. The people of the city were anxious to welcome us. The lord mayor gave a civic reception and dance, at which the colonel and his officers would be, of course, the official guests of honour. About forty of the better-behaved O.R.'s were hand-picked to go along. None of us who were known to associate with Boombaw, DeMal, or the Gunner were even considered. The brass needn't have been so choosey. The O.R.'s who did attend managed to enjoy themselves a little too much and had to be asked to leave once it was all over. The rest of us didn't mind being excluded, however, as we had all been granted additional seventy-two-hour passes. Not only were we spared the drudgery of having to be on our best behaviour, but we also avoided the drizzle and cold of Watsonia Camp. For three days, some of Melbourne's best hotels had to persevere through the tumultuous stay of three hundred Canadians unleashed from the Outback.

The free time offered the chance to go on cruises down the palm-lined Yarra River or strolls through the Botanic Gardens with newfound girl-friends. But for many of the 1CSWG complement these might as well not have existed. Their world consisted of pubs, taxis, dance halls, service hostels, homes of the girls they met, and, for a few, the red-light districts and all the strange haunts and pastimes that certain individuals manage to find by some arcane instinct no matter where in the world they are.

Putting the pleasures of Melbourne behind us, we marshalled our convoy again and left the lovely Watsonia Camp with no regrets. Our next objective was Sydney, the port which we hoped to exit from for home as soon as possible. Anxious though we were to get home, the charms of this city with its beautiful harbour and the striking structure that spanned it — "'ave yer seen the 'Ahbuh Bridge, myte?" — were to captivate us more than any other on the island continent. And as it turned out, we would have two more months in which to remain captivated.

Along the road to Sydney, the temperature fluctuated wildly between about 40 and 90 degrees. We alternately peeled down to shorts and boots then went back to winter battledress.

Despite the fact that most of Australia's population of about seven million was concentrated in the four or five major cities, the southern highway seemed to be dotted with flourishing little centres that appeared all at once and disappeared behind the truck convoy just as quickly. Towns and villages nestled in the pretty countryside of Victoria and New South Wales fell one after another to our rolling assaults. Cheering schoolchildren and massed citizenry lined the approaches to all the towns, and we were kept busy returning the greetings with as much enthusiasm as we could muster, although the almost-continuous succession of well-wishers was exhausting. And no matter where we were along the route, there were many in the unit who were suffering the after-effects of the previous night's merriment for whom it was hard to show much gusto.

For example, we had just put one of these little places behind us and the convoy was cruising along through beautiful forested country where, thanks to the nibblings of flocks of sheep, open stretches of green hills bore a close resemblance to parkland. The highway was winding through these hills at about 2,300 feet above sea level when Tom McInniny roused himself from his sodden sleep and mumbled that he was in need of a latrine. There being none on board, and there being no chance of the convoy stopping just for the sake of Tom's kidneys, he was passed from hand to hand along the dozen or so close-packed bodies back to the truck's tailgate. A couple of mates supported his slumping, wobbling body in a semi-standing position at the tailgate, and shouted instructions on how to handle what was, for him, a monumental task. Meanwhile, the driver and co-pilot in the cab of the truck behind shook their fists angrily and slowed their vehicle, dropping farther and farther back in the interests of self-preservation. Now rising well to the occasion, Tom doffed his beret and waved it benignly at them, breaking out into a huge grin, while a meandering dark line traced itself on the asphalt in the gap between the trucks. Great guffaws and cheers roared out of our truck.

As the truck took one of those tight bends in the road into another village, what had been a quiet, deserted country road was suddenly lined by cheering schoolchildren, their teachers, and their mothers — and perhaps their aunts and grandmothers, too. Tom's reaction time was slow and the thin, dark wiggling line on the pavement continued to be traced even as the crowd's cheers filled the air. His closest mates managed to call out and grab him back from the tailgate before we actually rolled past the official welcoming party.

Where Tom's performance had so recently riled up the pair in the following truck, the whole episode was now vastly entertaining to them — we could see them practically rolling around in the cab seat at Tom's sudden public exposure. Fortunately for us, neither of them was an officer or a non-com, or we might have been in even worse trouble than we'd been in at San Francisco.

The six-day tour across the bottom of the continent took us through a series of places with such colourful names as Camp Pukka Punyal, Bonegilla, Wangaratta, Albury on the Murray River, and Tumbarumba. We passed "the dog that sits on the tucker box, nine miles from Gundagai," as immortalized by Rudyard Kipling in a poem he wrote after travelling the same route some decades before us. Incidentally, the dog, carved in wood, sat just as Kipling described him on top of a wooden tucker box. He was a landmark, and it was indeed nine miles east of Gundagai, a little town on the Murrumbidgee River, in what was then open country. If the dog still sits on the tucker box today, he has no doubt been all but swallowed up by urban sprawl.

As spied by our sharp-eyed lookouts, there was a show ground at Gundagai, and this was, of course, to be our overnight quarters. A Captain Fraser of the Australian Army Service Corps brought over some Italian prisoners-of-war from his camp farther up the river at Wagga Wagga, and they rigged up showers and other temporary facilities for us on the spot. We O.R.'s were mystified, if not miffed, at the permission given a 1CSWG corporal and a lance-corporal to take one of the jeeps on a jaunt to Cootamundra, about thirty miles north and off our route, on some mysterious excuse. We had our satisfaction, however, when the corporal reported to the colonel the next day that the jeep had been stolen while they were in Cootamundra on their mission and the police had had to get it back. This unfortunately delayed the corporal's return until morning. In this case, unlike in San Francisco, it an AWL inquiry wasn't deemed necessary.

When we left Gundagai on November 23, we left behind one of the gasoline truck drivers, an RAAF leading airman, whose malaria had come back on him. However, we replenished our numbers with Mr. Alfred Pick, secretary to the Canadian high commissioner's office and a cousin of our indomitable Major Ralph Pick. Alfred Pick had come over from the capital of Canberra, which we were going to bypass. In what was presumably a symbolic gesture of Canadian support, Mr. Pick rode with the colonel in his staff car as far as Goulburn, our next stop, where there was another show ground for our overnight use. After the requisite welcoming speech by the mayor, the convoy spread out across the grounds, where the preparations for our arrival were practically nil. Either the Australian Army had lost interest in us or the army public relations office had found another toy.

Next day, cold and stiff once more in the chilly morning, we pulled out of Goulburn to make the final 108-mile dash to Sydney. By mid-morning we were peeling down to our shorts again as the sun and the temperature climbed higher. By mid-afternoon the men of 1CSWG steered the ninety-six-vehicle convoy into Ingleburn Camp, about twenty miles north of Sydney. We were now 2,885 miles by road from our old Darwin home, and about 10,000 miles from our real ones in Canada. We didn't know it, but instead of being home for Christmas 1945, we'd still be Down Under, if not down-and-out, well into February 1946.

Chapter 4

The Capture of Sydney

Our "capture" of the port city of Sydney, which sprawled around its deep harbour spanned by a magnificent bridge, was not nearly as spectacular as our town by-town conquests along the road from Darwin. Two million people would hardly notice the addition of three-hundred-odd military bods, no matter where they came from. Sydney had seen thousands of foreign troops pour on and off of ships throughout the war, been shelled by a Japanese submarine or two from inside the harbour, and had limped through wartime shortages of food and goods. And, like most seaports, it was accustomed to having the unusual pass through its portals.

Tucked away as we were in a camp twenty miles off, 1CSWG wasn't likely to make all that much of a splash in this sophisticated city. For us, though, there were undoubtedly plenty of diversions waiting. No sooner had the unit deposited its gear at Ingleburn Camp than its members were grabbing up the suddenly-available seventy-two-hour passes, shaving, shining, and sprinting for the electric railway that ran directly into the heart of

Sydney. From there, the conquerors dispersed to seek out whatever mischief, high jinks, cultural activities, and general hellery they could find. My own gang of eight or nine cronies made the expensive but civilized Claridge's Hotel our headquarters. Boombaw and DeMal instantly organized unending rounds of parties that moved from Claridge's to the notorious King's Cross district on Rushcutters Bay. Even the respectable homes of young ladies with whom they struck up more than passing friendships became 1CSWG party haunts. In a few cases, marriages resulted.

Sydney had legitimate theatres, ballrooms, coffeehouses, ritzy cocktail bars, and restaurants of a kind unknown in Canada in the 1930s and 1940s. We newly minted connoisseurs of wines, liqueurs, whiskies, and beers were in our glory in this sunny land of vineyards and distilleries. For a while, until our money ran out, Swiggers imitated the hedonistic expatriates of the 1920s who haunted the fleshpots of Paris. And all of this by the time most of us had barely turned twenty.

After a few weeks of high living we were scraping the bottom of the barrel as the pay that had piled up over many months was exhausted. Claridge's, now beyond our means, faded into memory. King's Cross was too risky a base; its pubs and streets were full of carousing sailors off the warships in Sydney Harbour, battle-hardened American and British soldiers living it up until troopships took them home, and the polyglot crowds of the kind that hang out in most of world's seaports. The place looked more like a set for one of those Clark Gable movies about Shanghai or the Barbary Coast. Still, there were some Canadians who, should some atabrin-yellowed Aussie commando fresh from the New Britain jungles insist on calling them "bloody pommies" or "flymin' Yankee dingoes," weren't averse to indulging in a knock-'em-down session in the pubs.

In spite of all these attractions, we'd toured everything there was to see in Sydney and most of us didn't even have rail fare anymore. Then, soon after we arrived in Sydney, the coal miners went on strike. It took us back almost to the conditions we'd left behind in Darwin — perhaps even worse, because now the city's coal-fired electricity generators were shut down. Lighting, trams, movies, refrigeration, restaurant air-conditioning (such as it was), radio stations, and all things run electrically dried up. Belligerent strikers were being denounced by belligerent citizens. The spirit of pulling together in the all-too-recent war was forgotten. The only really pleasing atmosphere was in the candlelit coffeehouses. And on the beaches.

Somehow the city kept functioning, if at a low level. The water

pumps, probably driven by diesel- or oil-powered generators, kept pump-
ing and bathrooms kept operating. Taxis did a roaring business in the
absence of trams — at least until even the gasoline supply faltered.
Everybody seemed to be on strike. For us it recalled Brisbane, where we'd
had to do the striking dockworkers' jobs just to keep our part in the war
effort going. Now labour unrest threatened to prevent 1CSWG from ever
leaving Australia. Instead of being home by Christmas, we found ourselves
— when we could get into town — looking through shop windows at the
stuffed, jolly, red-suited Santas, the artificial pine trees, the imitation rein-
deer, and the simulated snow, while the sweat ran down our backs in the
daily 105-degree heat.

Ten Sydney residents died of the heat — at virtually the same time
that people in North America were dying of the cold. We tried to beat the
heat by standing under cold showers and drying off by evaporation. The
heat would peak, and then there would be rain, followed by a 10-degree
drop in temperature. As we crawled into our heavy woollen battledress
uniforms to keep warm, we never ceased to marvel at the extremes of this
incredible country.

A couple of weeks before Christmas, the miners finally condescended
to go back to work, ensuring that there would indeed be a Christmas in
Sydney after all. What caused the union to make peace was that the power
blackout had started to close the breweries, and the frightening spectre of
a beer drought loomed. But the brewery workers did get a further sixteen-
day holiday with pay while the power plants got going again.

With the electricity back on, the theatres reopened and we were able
to see ourselves in a newsreel from the film shot in Darwin. It was by turns
hilarious, contemptible, and outrageous, as it depicted what could easily
have been a summer camp where volleyball, baseball, and medicine-ball
tossing on Casuarina Beach were the main activities. Once more we had
been done in by the top-secret nature of the real work of monitoring
Japanese signals and pointing an electronic finger at some of the enemy's
most threatening military thrusts. We were denied our chance at individual immortality on film; the camera panned down to our putteed legs and
boots, showing no faces as we marched into the big parade sequence.

With almost nothing to do, we were finding the wait for a ship to take
us home getting weightier and weightier. Our recreational and cultural
options were now limited by our regular $60-per-month pay, half of which
was assigned by most of us to our families back home. In a ludicrous turn

of events, the officers were trying to talk the O.R.'s into taking leaves of absence of as long as twenty-one days! A few weeks before, we could barely get a twenty-four hour pass unless it was to be checked into a hospital.

Some of the Swiggers had been lucky enough at craps or cards to finance further adventures in Sydney, leaving the losers resigned to camp life. Others actually found civilian jobs, getting work permits through the officers, who were only too glad to get as many of the O.R.'s out of their hair as possible. Some even moved in with girlfriends and took up the domestic life. Staying in camp could leave one vulnerable to the pitfalls of make-work duty — which included such jobs as spraying DDT around the officers' quarters to tease the bush fly population.

With loads of time and no money for fun-seeking, a handful of us camp-bound O.R.'s had only one choice: find diversion in Ingleburn Camp wherever we could. Then somebody discovered the tennis equipment. Among the hockey sticks and ice skates sent by those well-meaning souls back home were several sets of tennis racquets, nets, and balls. The officers had already gotten hold of these and a group of them were playing a few sets each morning before the day became unbearably hot, at which point they drove off in 1CSWG's Jeeps for the pleasures of the cricket clubs and fashionable cocktail lounges in Sydney.

Their workouts took place on some clay courts hidden behind their quarters that we hadn't noticed until a couple of us were assigned to sweep and clean them up. Don Laut, Dave Corbett, Bert Pusey, and I saw an opportunity; we moved in and claimed the courts. Corbett was a formidable player, as was Laut. Pusey and I had played a little tennis in pre-army days, but we were rank amateurs, sitting ducks for the other two — at first. For the next two months, despite of the savagely hot sun, we hammered the ball back and forth most afternoons. Some other accomplished players, who, like us were probably also broke, were recruited. Before long, Pusey and I were blistering the ball net-high at our former masters and gradually raising ourselves to a high level of play.

It got to the point where even some officers spending the day in camp joined in as our advanced form was recognized. We organized an amateur tennis league and were soon competing against a nearby camp of Royal Australian Air Force bods — and doing very well against these officer diggers who'd literally grown up with tennis racquets in their fists year-round.

We'd pulled ourselves up by our sneakers and were almost ready to take on the Aussie pros, so mighty did we feel. Strangely, once back in Canada, work got in the way and I hardly played tennis again.

Harry Wethey was not having a good time of it. With his social calendar full, he was cajoling and applying subtle pressure on high-level Australian authorities, both military and civilian, to get us on a ship back to Canada. But restrictions were many and sea transport was nowhere to be found. Almost all available shipping had been appropriated by the U.S. military to rush home their thousands of personnel from Australia, the islands, and even from Japan. That old luxury liner, the *Monterey*, which had brought us from San Francisco to New Guinea, put in at Sydney, but she was already spoken for. Still in troopship grey, the *Aquitania*, last of the four-stacker liners, had just brought a load of Aussies back from the Middle East. We stared longingly at her docked at Woolloomoolloo but she was due to go to England in five weeks' time with another load of troops.

More Australians arrived home from the islands aboard the aircraft carrier HMS *Implacable*. There was another British carrier in port: HMS *Magnificent*, or the "Maggie." Years later, she was acquired by the Royal Canadian Navy, renamed the *Bonaventure*, and her renovation became the subject of great controversy and scandal. On a rare visit to Sydney, Pusey and I chummed up with two English sub-lieutenants from the Royal Navy Fleet Air Arm who crewed an *Implacable* dive bomber flying off the *Maggie*. It was uncommon for officers to mix with O.R.'s. Together we did the rounds of Kings Cross, Sydney's roughhouse dock area. Unlike one or two of our fellow Swiggers, we didn't get into any fistfights with sailors.

Those warships bringing Aussies home from the Middle East and the islands often made the scrapyard near the Captain Cook graving docks their next stop. The famous "KG Five" battleship, HMS *King George V*, was in for repairs. We watched as HMS *Puncher*, an escort carrier, made her last trip. The Canadian auxiliary cruiser HMCS *Prince Robert*, paid off her crew and followed the *Puncher*. How fitting, we thought, if the *Prince Robert* or one of the other ships could have made one more trip and taken 1CSWG home. But even the scrapyard took priority over us.

For a few days there was a chance we might get on the only other active Royal Canadian Navy ship that came our way, the cruiser HMCS *Uganda*. But there had been trouble among the *Uganda's* crew, who'd

demanded the ship head for home the minute the war ended. Things had
turned ugly. So, ironically, Number One Canadian Special Wireless Group
was not invited aboard this sole Canadian warship in Sydney's harbour.

Don Laut and I ran across half a dozen sailors from the USS
Birmingham as we viewed from the dock this veteran cruiser that had figured in so many Pacific sea battles. They invited us aboard for Christmas
dinner, but we didn't go — we were relishing the thought of being served
Christmas dinner at Chermside camp by our own officers, an old army
tradition which offered us the unique chance to give *them* the orders for a
change. So that was our choice.

Carriers and cruisers kept arriving, departing, or navigating into the
scrapyard. British ships set out for Singapore or Hong Kong, the Middle East,
Gibraltar — or even for Britain to be scrapped. American ships went back to
the Philippines, Guam, or Japan to pick up homebound G.I.'s. In these vast
oceans of human cargoes, a handful of Canadians represented hardly a drop,
and we could envision our Australian stay stretching out even longer than
planned. We truly seemed to be stuck at the far end of the universe.

By now, seven-day passes were actually being pressed on us by the officers. So we would go to Bondi and Manly beaches, where the bikini was
just starting to make its debut. We crossed Botany Bay to see where
Captain Cook and La Perouse first set foot on Australian soil. We took in
the Taronga Park Zoo, on the other side of the harbour; the motorcycle
races; and the Flemington Race Course, where all good Sydneysiders went
on Saturdays. Alec McDougall and I took a memorable minibus tour to
Katoomba in the Blue Mountains and its spectacular Jenolan Caves, and
dropped in at the museum honouring Ned Kelly, the legendary and much-
revered bank robber who wore a homemade knight's helmet in his celebrated robberies. The helmet had a bullet hole in it.

Don Laut and I spent an adventurous weekend at the home of a
Sydney family, the St. Clairs, a short ferryboat ride up the harbour to
Longueville. We later paddled around the harbour in our hosts' two-man
kayak, riding the wakes of mountainous ocean liners and battleships and
trying not to show our fear of these giants. On our second day, we were
flabbergasted at the arrival of the two Royal Navy dive bomber sub-lieutenants with whom we'd made our foray into Kings Cross. They had come
for a short stay and they were eager for a sail of the harbour. We joined
them as ballast in a borrowed thirty-foot sailing yacht; we charged about
the harbour and they happily pretended they were about to ram us against

the stone cliffs bordering the bay, laying-to just in time to avoid a crash. As ballast, Laut and I dared catastrophe, leaning way out from the gunwales to counter the yacht's wild heeling-over as the sails took the wind full-on. Once or twice I came close to going right over the side.

At dinner that evening, Mrs. St. Clair asked how we'd enjoyed our days in the kayak and the yacht. We responded with enthusiasm, and I related how I'd almost gone for a swim from the kayak in the harbour to cool off in the fierce heat. As she went about serving the potatoes and vegetables, Mrs. St. Clair casually remarked that it was lucky I hadn't; the newspapers were reporting that there were more sharks in the harbour that day than had ever before been sighted. On hearing that, the hair on my neck stood up. We hadn't even considered the possibility that there might be sharks in those waters.

It turned out that the harbour was filled with these monsters, which could be up to twelve feet long. In the paper the next day there was a story about a shark that had seized a young girl in four feet of water just off her family's dock on the harbour edge — not far from the St. Clairs's. Her father jumped in, beat the shark on the head with his fists, and drove it away, but the girl lost a leg. She died later. Aircraft flying over the Sydney beaches on shark patrol reported seeing more sharks in the water than they could count. Shark nets that had protected the beaches before the war had collapsed or been destroyed by Japanese submarines. So far, the frenzied surfing and swimming of the thousands at the beaches was keeping the beasts at bay. Between the giant surf and the prowling of the sharks, we Canadians found it best to indulge in tamer pursuits, such as lying on the beach and admiring the bikini-clad girls.

Harry Wethey was having about as much trouble with the Australians in charge of controlling troop movements as the shark patrol was with the sharks. The phone system from Ingleburn to Sydney kept breaking down, a galling situation for a unit whose business was signalling. At one point, the colonel called us all together to read a letter from the Canadian high commissioner at Canberra saying we would probably be in Sydney for some time yet. And attempts to communicate with the brass at National Defence Headquarters in Ottawa were also fruitless.

He was getting fidgety over the lack of things to keep his men occupied. There had already been riots among Canadian troops stuck in

Aldershot, England, and Wethey was determined that his record would not show that he'd allowed things to turn sour like that. The memory of the snake line back at Darwin and the pebble shower on the roof may have been still fresh in his mind.

Therefore, he and his officers invented some make-work projects for the O.R.'s to carry out, such as ripping out and rebuilding the bar in the officers' mess. But few of the projects came to pass, possibly because the officers and non-coms were losing interest in discipline for discipline's sake. After all, this was now peacetime. There was a possibility that some of them might find themselves in a civilian job where they were taking direction from some of these lowly O.R.'s. So, for the most part, we went on resting, playing tennis, escaping to Sydney when we had a few shillings, and pursuing the army private's traditional pastime of bitching about everything.

One of Wethey's highest priorities was to get rid of the radio trucks, lorries, shortwave wireless sets, and the rest of the million dollars' worth of equipment we'd been hauling around all year — and all over the eastern half of Australia. It was to be easier said than done. When the colonel finally did get through to Ottawa, somebody there suggested he make them a gift to the Australians, who would undoubtedly be grateful for the goods. Wethey could have almost cried when he heard that suggestion. All over the continent, work crews were dumping leftover war materiel into the surrounding seas and oceans, everything from Spitfires to typewriters to cannons. Naturally, they turned down our generous gifts, and they didn't offer to dump our junk for us, either. Nor was it an option just to leave the equipment at Ingleburn. Had we authorized that, Wethey would risk a charge of insubordination from the Aussie military. *Sic transit gloria.* As far as the Australian officers were concerned, Number One Canadian Special Wireless Group was no longer the welcome guest of a grateful nation. There was no choice but to tote the stuff back across the Pacific — *if* Wethey could ever find a ship to accommodate it and us as well.

By now, over a month after our arrival in Sydney, everyone in the unit, from top officers through non-coms and down to lowly signalmen, was pretty well coming and going in and out of camp at will, with or without passes. And we'd seen everything there was to see and spent our pay. Laut, Pusey, and I were strolling through Hyde Park in downtown Sydney one day, having observed the hookers at the St. James railway station (known for this reason as "the meat market"), and counting the numbers of servicemen, in uniforms of all kinds, who were curled about on the park's grass with their girlfriends and openly exercising their libidos. We heard a shout and looked around.

A Royal Navy sailor in full bell-bottomed and round-capped regulation uniform came charging toward us at full throttle. We didn't need to hear the rasping Scottish burr that mangled the Aussie slang to know instantly that it was Jimmy, whom we had last seen in Darwin. After all the backslapping and hoo-hawing, we learned that Jimmy was in literally the same boat as we were — trying to swing a passage home. He did have a chance that night to get on board a floating navy machine-shop called the *Flamborough Head*, bound for Liverpool through the Red Sea and the Mediterranean, his old stomping grounds.

What had happened to him at Darwin? Oh, the bastards transferred him to Morotai, where he and his boss operated their little sub for the rest of the war, then ditched it at sea.

We shook hands in goodbye, sure we'd never see him again. But there was yet one more time. Years later, in Toronto, a policeman called me to our apartment door, where he was holding a dejected-looking Scot who'd been reported by neighbours as a prowler. My wife and I took him in for a visit. He'd come to Canada to find work, possibly learn a trade. That was the last I ever saw of Jimmy.

Commander Knight of the Australian Sea Transport Division told Lieutenant-Colonel Wethey that we might have to go home by way of the United Kingdom, thereby completing a circumnavigation of the globe. (Our mail had been going that way ever since the *Greenhill Park* blew up in Vancouver harbour.) But the U.K. trip fell through and we were again in the doldrums. Then, Lieutenant-Colonel Osborn of Sea Transport said he had a line on a small freighter, the SS *Socotra*, a British-owned tramp out of Bombay that could be fixed up well enough to get us to Canada. If Canada's National Defence Headquarters would foot the bill, *Socotra* could be fitted out with living quarters for 350 bodies. There was one hitch: the Australian admiralty hadn't yet agreed to surrender the *Socotra* to Sea Transport. Despite this, Wethey read out Move 3581 to all of us at Christmas dinner, our second since we'd been in 1CSWG. The howl of jubilation that went up was deafening. Maybe by the new year…

Nothing could stand in the way of our marking the mountain of green equipment boxes that began to grow right after Christmas. The order to board ship might come any day, we thought, and off we'd go. A latrino-gram circulated the news that Commander Knight was thinking again that we'd have to go home by way of Britain whenever a ship came available, or just stay Down Under indefinitely. We shrugged that off and began to feel more relaxed as the temperature sank down to the mid-eighties. Even the flies and mosquitoes became bearable for a while.

We marvelled at the way the flies could plague the middle of a city the size of Sydney. Sunset was their best time. Waiting for a bus, you might find yourself continually swatting or brushing flies off your face and neck as if it were the Outback. The difference was that, unlike the desert abo-rigines, the city people couldn't stand them any more than we could. What really mystified us was the location of their breeding ground.

On the first day of 1946, Lieutenant-Colonel Wethey and Major Pick were called on to visit Pier 20 and have a look at the *Socotra*. To Wethey's disgust, the ship was nothing more than a dirty little tramp steamer a few hundred feet long, badly in need of a cleanup and paint job. It had proba-bly crawled about the islands and the Indian Ocean for years, hauling very dirty cargoes. The colonel was invited to take it or leave it. After a quick conference in the master's cabin, Wethey decided to leave it. Lieutenant-Colonel Osborn agreed, and recommended to Sea Transport in Melbourne that 1CSWG be put aboard SS *Athlone Castle* bound for Liverpool. He got no answer.

Wethey concluded that we must take *Socotra* home or take out Australian citizenship. The truckloads of 1CSWG equipment, most of which we'd brought with us from Canada, began migrating to Pier 20 on January 9. Despite the prospects of finally starting for home, vast numbers of O.R.'s were suddenly lining up for sick parade when bodies were need-ed for loading duty. Wethey had to invoke Paragraph 967 of the King's Regulations (Canada), which required claimants of the sickness to be con-fined to barracks to convalesce. The malingerers recovered quickly.

The work ethic wasn't much better on the docks. Our officers chafed at the tortoise-like efforts of the truculent dock workers, who were no doubt still fondly remembering their many hours of leisure during the coal miners' strike. Even with men of 1CSWG pitching in, it took days for the assorted wartime junk to be readied for loading into *Socotra's* holds.

There was a further delay when Colonel Wethey, unsatisfied that the little ship was properly prepared for a trip that could last three weeks or more, wheedled some time out of Sea Transport to have *Socotra* spruced up to a more military standard. Major Pick and Captain March went aboard on January 15 to sail the rusty old tub to Adelaide for a refitting. They originally expected the ship to return within fourteen days. From Adelaide, Pick reported that the refitters had estimated it would take more like twenty-one days, plus travel time back to Sydney.

Two weeks later, Wethey asked a colonel at Movement Control when *Socotra* would be back, and he was told it was none of his business! Wethey thought this a strange reaction, since it was on his head to get over three hundred men, plus tons of equipment nobody wanted, back to Canada — at Canadian expense, and in his name. "The only miserable bastard we met in Australia!" was his uncharacteristic comment.

On top of getting lading orders for the ship signed and laying in food and other supplies for the voyage, the colonel had other administrative problems. Some of the men were asking for the colonel's permission to get married. At least half a dozen were super-anxious to tie the knot before *Socotra* cast off. A mere lance-corporal had somehow met a daughter of a wine-making family rich on the commerce of huge tracts of vineyard in New South Wales. (He married her.) One or two of the others not only wanted to marry, they wanted to stay on in Sydney! Eventually, Dave Corbett did just that, returning to Australia about a year later, marrying the girl he'd met in Sydney, and becoming a professor at the University of Canberra, where he remained forever after.

As a result, Wethey and his officers were fighting the battle against red tape on two fronts. On the one hand, there was a bureaucratic fuss over the per-ton rate for the unwanted cargo, which Wethey struggled to get defined more cheaply as "return cargo" but lost. On the other hand, there was the unexpected entanglement with police magistrates over approvals for quickie weddings. (Even Alfred, Major Pick's brother, and secretary to the Canadian high commissioner, was getting married and being re-posted to South Africa.) At their wits' end, Wethey and Captains Hall and Reid took off and went surfing at Bondi Beach.

A minor source of consolation came in the form of a letter Wethey received from Major-General C.H. Simpson, Australian Signals officer-in-chief, wishing us bon voyage and expressing his and his service's gratitude for the "invaluable assistance" given Australia by Number One Canadian Special Wireless Group. At the time, he wrote, "the Australian Corps of Signals was fully extended in providing … essential communications throughout the vast areas of the South West Pacific theatre…. (W)ithout the assistance of your unit, the communication service urgently required by Allied Forces … could not have been provided.

"I feel that the results of the work performed by your unit in no small measure contributed towards achieving final victory…. Your unit must be complimented on the high standard of its work … I trust that your short stay in our country, despite the emergency of the times, has been as pleasant to you as it has been to we of the Australian Corps of Signals…"

The weather turned stinking hot again as January turned to February. The *Socotra* was on its way back from Adelaide, but Wethey couldn't extract the date of 1CSWG's departure out of Sea Transport. He also failed in his attempts to get some movies to show on board. And, at the last minute he learned he would be responsible for more passengers: three wives and several children of the men who'd weathered the war on tiny Fanning Island, halfway along our 7,000-mile transpacific route to Vancouver.

Adding insult to injury, Sea Transport slipped seven more individuals onto the *Socotra*'s passenger manifest: a lieutenant-commander from the Royal Australian Naval Volunteer Reserve; a Royal Australian Air Force wing commander; a flight-lieutenant and a flying officer; a Royal Navy able seaman and two Royal Canadian Navy midshipmen, wherever *they'd* come from and wherever they were going! The extra officers added to 1CSWG's own complement posed a number of problems for Lieutenant-Colonel Wethey, not the least of which was that, with the stores already loaded, there wouldn't be enough rationed butter to go around.

The situation sparked Wethey's first run-in with the ship's crusty master, Captain West, who steadfastly refused to issue cabin-class tickets over Wethey's signature to allow all of the officers to dine in the saloon. Wethey, frustrated to his limit, fired off a cable to National Defence Headquarters in Ottawa, but no reply came back.

At last, a year and a month after shipping out from Victoria — and two months after arriving in Sydney — Number One Canadian Special Wireless Group climbed aboard five City of Sydney double-decker buses and were whisked to Pier 20 just before dusk on February 6, 1946. As darkness fell on that sweltering hot day the Swiggers filed aboard the *Socotra*. We were finally beginning the long voyage home.

The powers that controlled our fate had decreed that about four hundred souls were to travel 7,000 miles aboard a tramp freighter (who knew how old?) that was 495 feet long and of 7,980 tons. Flat out, it might be capable of 16 knots, or 25 m.p.h. In a way it was comparable to The Ghan. Still, the Adelaide outfitters had done a remarkable fix-up job on the old tub. We were reasonably comfortable among conditions light years ahead of those on the *Monterey* and the S*hawnee* — and in all those abominable Australian army camps we'd inhabited.

The first hold, one deck down, had new lighting and sparkled with new white paint. On each side of a wide aisle, carpeted with sisal matting, was a long row of double bunks with high wooden sides — and, of all things, spring mattresses! Down the carpeted aisle were picnic-type tables for eating or playing cards.

We could hardly believe it when we found that the washrooms on the rear outdoor main deck had flush toilets, and washbasins that flipped up to reveal laundry tubs underneath — without question a Pick innovation. Commander Knight had snorted at Harry Wethey that these quarters were altogether *too* luxurious for "a twenty-one day cruise." But the war was over, in case he hadn't heard, and the Swiggers would soon be voting civilians again. Who knew but when we got to Vancouver the army might even be providing us with sheets on our bunks!

Our actual departure from Sydney harbour was quiet but dramatic in its own way. There were certainly no throngs of cheering crowds flinging bunting, nor any brass band or ladies' auxiliary to serve us farewell cookies. We hung over the taffrail to watch the dock activity twenty feet below, and all we saw were a few officers chatting with their Australian counterparts and some girlfriends and new wives waving to their men on the *Socotra*.

I felt something bump my elbow where it rested on the rail and looked up. One of the ship's crew — a lascar, as most of them turned out to be — was walking patiently, with perfect balance, along the four-inch-wide flat taffrail with a rope in one hand. He gently nudged the elbow of each man on the rail with a big brown bare toe as he made his way like a tightrope walker. It was our introduction to these agile men from Bombay whose feet were as dexterous as a second set of hands. And to say they were busy doesn't do them justice: by the time the voyage was over they would have chipped off all the old paint and applied a completely new coat to the ship's entire hull and superstructure.

A dramatic moment came as the *Socotra* cruised across the harbour in the moonless dark of the hot night. Many of us were staring back at the lights of the great city that surrounded us as the ship ploughed slowly toward the Sydney Heads, the two massive rock protrusions that form a narrow channel through which ships pass on their way to and from the ocean beyond. Just inside the Heads, the ship came to a full stop. A heavy, choppy swell churned the waters as the ocean swept in through the narrow channel and out again with the flow of the Paramatta River that empties into the harbour. The *Socotra* heaved and rolled alarmingly.

We had stopped because the harbour pilot who'd taken us out this far needed to get off the ship before we passed between the Heads. The *Captain Cook*, a pilot boat — no more than a tug, really — drew up about 200 feet off our starboard. It was also rolling and heaving like a cork. At times, the dark, roaring, rolling waters lifted the tug above us before dropping it below. Crewmen on both craft lowered shaded lamps over the sides of their ships and we could see that a smaller boat, about 15 feet long, was being lowered from the tug with two men in it. This smaller boat touched the water just in time to meet a violently rising swell. The two men began rowing furiously toward us through the swirling, leaping water.

The scene in the glare of the lights was starkly unreal. On the heaving water, the boat always seemed on the verge of dumping its occupants — a horrifying prospect as it was certain they'd vanish in the whirlpools. The scene became more horrendous when a long, underwater streak of foaming light-green bubbles came curving slowly out of the regions of dark water, into the light, and directly under the small boat. It was unmistakably the wake of a shark at least 10 feet long which had been attracted by the lights. Everyone hanging over the rail yelled and pointed at the dim shape, which moved like a torpedo streaking toard the *Socotra*'s hull. Then, as quickly as it had appeared, it just vanished in the dark. There could be little doubt, however, that the monster, and perhaps some companions, were still waiting around somewhere nearby for dinner.

Little by little the small boat came closer, tossed up and down all the way, until it was right below us. One of the seamen caught a line thrown from the *Socotra* and pulled the boat tight against the hull. Down a rope ladder went the pilot. He timed his leap with a rising wave and dropped into the boat amidships. A great cheer went up from the *Socotra*'s passengers. The rowers hauled on their oars, the line to the *Socotra* was cast off, and the boat bounded over the heaving sea back to the *Captain Cook* without supplying an evening snack for the sharks.

The trio climbed aboard the pilot ship and waved at us as though the whole exercise was just routine. The *Captain Cook* blasted its whistle, the lights were extinguished, the *Socotra's* whistle answered, and the two ships went their separate ways. The tug headed back to the docks and the *Socotra*, with its strange cargo of cheering landlubber-soldiers and assorted guests eased between the Sydney Heads and thrust its way out into the dark South Pacific. The last we could see of Australia were the coastal lights rapidly dimming into the dark of the land.

Chapter 5

All Aboard Socotra

When I came out on deck the next morning I enjoyed one of the best moments of my short history in 1CSWG. The sun shone bright but not hot, a light breeze blew, and the deep blue sea was calm and slipping past smoothly under a powder-blue sky. The salt air was fresh and free of the muggy oppression of Sydney, now 400 miles behind us. We weren't to enjoy a warm, sunny cruise for long. In the first half of the trip, long before we reached Fanning Island, there would be fog and heavy rain, with temperatures much lower than what we'd been used to for so many months.

The *Socotra* kept a steady cruising speed of around fourteen and a half knots, covering an average of 350 miles a day. Almost the first day out from Sydney the lascar crewmen began their job of chipping the thick paint off every part of the ship above the water line with little hammers until they'd removed it all and had repainted the exposed steel as they went. The tap-tap of the little hammers all over the ship was a continuous background to the growing boredom of the long trip.

We really seemed to be standing still in the vast, featureless ocean, a cork bobbing up and down and going nowhere. On the island-dotted map of the South Pacific it looks as though a ship could hardly navigate between the maze of the Loyalties, the New Hebrides, the Fijis, the Western Samoas, the Tokelaus, and the Phoenix groups of islands without winding up on a reef. In fact, the only land we spied in the 3,500-mile stretch from Sydney to Fanning Island was the far-off, towering grey southern cliff of New Caledonia, the French island more than a thousand miles from Australia. Although the *Socotra* crawled past within fifteen miles of Walpole Island — a little more than a hundred miles north of Suva on Fiji — it was too misty or dark to glimpse any land.

For us it was excitement enough to watch a school of dolphins cavorting alongside the ship, or an albatross or frigate bird flying lazily beside us. A wooden life raft, weather-beaten and empty and adrift for who knows from what sinking and for how many years, floated along-side until even the turtle's pace of the *Socotra* left it behind to fade away into the sunlit mist. For the entire trip a cloud of seabirds, probably renewed daily from islands over the horizon, hovered just behind the ship awaiting the daily jettison of galley garbage.

Scattered about the circular horizon, rain squalls slanted down from some distant cloud here and there to the dividing line between sea and sky, often clues to the location of unseen islands. Sometimes the *Socotra* would plough directly into one of these squalls beating straight down on the ocean. These would prompt most of the troops to skip out on deck naked to be washed clean in the rain — a rare treat on a ship whose washroom showers gushed forth only salt water. The squall would pass soon enough, and with the southern sun again beaming, the decks would once more be covered by men lying all about in khaki shorts, smoking cigarettes, and reading books. At these times the voyage was very much like Commander Knight's "twenty-one-day cruise." Still, there were some highly unpleasant and un-cruise-like moments to come.

These were the waters so ably charted by Captain James Cook on his voyages of discovery in the eighteenth century. The more learned among us speculated as to when we might cross the navigation line followed by Captain William Bligh. In 1789, he and his eighteen loyal crewmen were set adrift in an open boat by Fletcher Christian and his mutineers. They successfully sailed the 4,000 miles from near Tahiti to our old neighbour, Timor, setting a historic record for navigation by dead-reckoning.

Our lolling on the decks and hatch covers of the *Socotra* in 1946 led to a surprising scene one day that did smack of the Mutiny on the Bounty, in the very stretch of ocean crossed by that ship and those mutineers two hundred years before. Was there something in these latitudes that provoked high drama?

More likely it was the apparent lack of concern for safety among the Swiggers that prompted Captain West to turn into a twentieth-century version of Captain Bligh. The ship's four hatch covers were well battened down and covered with heavy sailcloth to shed sea water slopping over the rails. They were more attractive for the troops to lounge on than the sizzling-hot steel plates of the deck. After a few days at sea, several small burn marks began to appear on these canvases. The obvious cause was the innumerable cigarettes consumed by the members of 1CSWG.

One sunny day, when the Canadians were thick on the hatch covers, basking in the sun and reading, Captain West suddenly appeared on

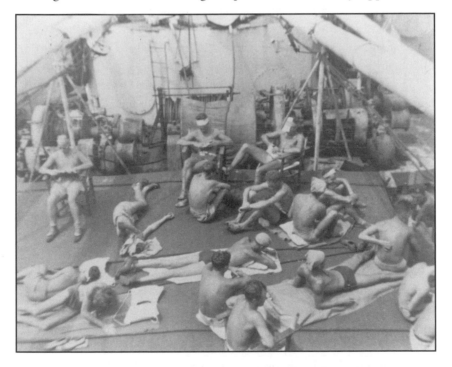

On the long postwar voyage home, the troops of 1CSWG lolled in unaccustomed luxury on the hatch covers of the S.S. *Socotra*. However, the smokers of the group got a stern lecture about fire hazards from the ship's captain, who threatened to clap them in irons.

Number One hatch cover. A bald, stocky, round, apoplectic figure — who rather resembled Captain Bligh — clad in white shirt, black shorts, white knee socks, and sneakers, Captain West was of the old school in that he didn't need a public-address system to be heard. The message came through loud and clear as the captain bellowed, "There will no more of smokin' on the hatches!" The Swiggers just as suddenly sat bolt upright.

The sailcloth covers were already ruined, he pointed out, and he would be billing Canada for them. One of the Swiggers, hidden among his mates, grumbled mutinously that there weren't any no-smoking signs up. Outraged by this landlubberly remark, Captain West went into a tirade on the laws of the sea that made him supreme commander of all on board, and that anybody who defied him would be "clapped in irons for the rest of the trip." Yes, he actually did say clapped in irons, a threat that carried all the quaint redolence of an Errol Flynn movie — or the menace of Charles Laughton's Hollywood version of Captain Bligh. But Captain West of the *Socotra* meant what he said. For a moment or two, the roar of the ship sloshing through the water was the only sound. Then there was a flurry of cigarette stubs through the air and over the side, as this latter-day Bligh got his unchallenged recognition.

It was only later on that word filtered through that the *Socotra* was carrying, besides us and our equipment, twenty thousand bales of greasy Australian wool in Number One hold. Had a smouldering cigarette accidentally slipped down into this potent mess of a floating fire hazard could easily have put a smoky, fiery end to the voyage of the *Socotra,* not to mention to a lot of Canadian signalmen and assorted fellow passengers in these shark-infested waters. After Captain West's performance, smokers were usually seen drooped over the taffrail as they smoked, letting their ashes and stubs descend into the blue Pacific waters.

The knowledge about the cargo of wool told us a lot about why we'd finally got our transportation home. Were it not for this shipment, 1CSWG would not have been allowed to have *Socotra* as a means of getting home. Somehow this too was reminiscent of the tale of Captain Bligh and his crew, who had been sent far from Britain into the South Pacific to deliver breadfruit plants.

It was only about two days out from Sydney before boredom set in, followed by a great scourge of seasickness. The North Tasman Sea stretches south from the Coral Sea between Australia and New Caledonia, down past New Zealand to the east and Tasmania to the southwest. The two seas come together, with results not unlike the inside of an enormous, churning washing machine, at just about the point where the *Socotra* was cutting its way eastward. Inevitably, rough seas developed, and for the next five days the *Socotra* bobbed, rolled, and bucked in the maelstrom, never seeming to make way.

During those five days, the decks were dotted with men crawling across to the rail, not to smoke but to upchuck. Some, including me, were so weak we couldn't raise ourselves to the rail. Instead, we stuck our heads through hawserholes to seek relief. It may have been fortunate that we couldn't get any higher, for the victims of the world's worst stomach condition might well have thrown themselves overboard — a death wish does accompany the *mal de mer*, from which there is neither escape nor respite. Everyone on board, including even some of the seasoned crew, fell ill to varying degrees at one time or another. Naturally, we blamed the food.

To a victim of seasickness, there is no humour at all to the condition. The unceasing heaving of the ship from stem to stern, then the alarming side-to-side rolling, made existence a hell worse than the captain's threat to clap us in irons might have been, in the minds of those so stricken. Between paraplegic trips to the rail, one could easily lie prone in one's bunk and pray for the release that death would bring.

As the *Socotra* kept up its relentless plunging and rolling across the Tasman Sea, some of us wondered whether Lieutenant-Colonel Wethey had made the right decision in accepting this old tub for a lengthy trip across the Pacific Ocean. Would her ancient plates hold together in these conditions the whole way? The view through an open door from a seat in the aft latrines alternated from sky at one moment, as the ship's prow drove deep into the water, to a direct stare into the raging water itself as the prow rose high and the stern dropped low. Each time the stern heaved up out of the water, the ship's twin screws would roar and the whole ship would shudder as the screws lost the resistance of the water. Then came another rise in the prow and the screws went under again, stopping the shudder.

At that stage of our "twenty-one day cruise," one could be convinced that hell was not made up of fire and sulphur but blue, foaming, roaring, thrashing ocean and the sensation of being forever flung from side to side, up and down, and forward and back. One mathematically minded Swigger calculated that, every minute for over three days, we were violently yanked up and then dropped the equivalent of four storeys, as if we were on some crazed, out-of-control skyscraper elevator.

Once we were well east of New Caledonia the sea calmed, the ship stopped pitching and yawing, colour returned to Canadian cheeks, eyes sparkled again, and the *mal de mer* was forgotten. There was only monotony to contend with now. Plenty of books had come aboard with us to counter this, and some Swiggers I'd never seen crack the spine of one had their noses buried in them.

Among the "guest" officers was a pleasant black lieutenant from Trinidad, a Royal Canadian Signals member who had apparently joined us at Sydney. He spoke Spanish and English, and volunteered to teach the rudiments of Spanish to any of us who wished to learn. Coincidentally, I'd always fancied learning that language; I had even bought a "Teach Yourself Spanish" book in Sydney (the dozen or so of us who took up the officer on his offer used it as a textbook). It helped kill the monotony, and I found later that I'd learned the equivalent of Grade 12 Spanish on our trip from Sydney to Vancouver.

Fanning Island seemed hardly real. It looked so much like what Gauguin had painted in Tahiti, or a visual version of what Somerset Maugham and Joseph Conrad had written about the South Seas, that it seemed more like a mirage than a real coral atoll. Fanning popped up so quickly and vividly out of an azure sea under an azure sky that it recalled to mind the cliché of the hallucinating Argonauts, those victims of their own overheated brains who were confronted by visions out of their own imaginations.

At about eleven o'clock on the morning of February 16, we spotted a low mark on the horizon. Less than an hour later the *Socotra* was tied to a floating buoy in a little bay some distance from one of the atoll's curving, outstretched arms. There was no harbour or dock. The water beneath us was so clear that every detail of the ship's submerged hull could be seen by leaning out over the taffrail. For the first time we could see the ship's screws, startlingly huge, which had already driven us through pitching seas and calm seas to this point. There were only 3,500 miles to go.

The *Socotra* floated there like a toy in a bathtub. White coral sand on the bottom of the bay bounced strong sunlight back and illuminated the underwater environment so brilliantly that swarms of fish of nearly every colour of the spectrum could be seen more easily than in any aquarium. Parrot fish, zebra fish, swordfish, jellyfish, sharks, and porpoises cruised about, startlingly perfect specimens on display in the transparent water. A lascar sailor walked by on deck with a pail of freshly caught fish, some red, others green or black. One needed only drop a hook and a line over the side with a little bait and the fish fought for the privilege of being caught.

A gorgeous turquoise lagoon filled the great half-circle made by the atoll's two outspreading coral arms. Poking up just above the sea, the narrow arms were topped by a mane of coconut palms that had somehow found a way to grow on the coral rock and sand. A bad turn of the sea would easily wash right over them. Two ancient pickup trucks waited at the tip of the arm nearest us, ready to haul to the centre of the island the goods the *Socotra* had brought. Dozens of deliriously happy, imported Gilbert Islanders had crammed themselves into two or three overloaded longboats, with two rafts in tow, rowing with heavy muscles that gleamed in the sun. We'd already had our welcome from the few white inhabitants of the island who had sped frantically around and around the ship in high-powered launches, triumphantly sounding screeching sirens and whistles. It was what is usually called a gala occasion. After all, their wives and children were arriving at the end of four years of wartime evacuation to Sydney.

The half-dozen civilians there manned the underwater cable station that carried communications between North America and Australia. (Coconut growing was the island's only other industry.) The wives of these operators had been evacuated in 1941, even though, except for submarines, the Japanese Imperial forces came no closer than about 1,500 miles. But in those early days of 1941–42 there was no telling how far they would eventually penetrate into the south Pacific.

Unlike the tars of Captain Cook's ship, none of the decadent Canadians, except for Lieutenant-Colonel Wethey and a couple of his officers, would be allowed to go ashore. Fanning Island, now known as Tabuaeran, lies about 1,100 miles due south of Honolulu, a distance considered almost next door in the vastness of the Pacific. About twenty Chinese and several dozen workers from the Gilberts — a thousand miles to the west — made up the main work force for the cable station and the plantation. After visiting the plantation house, Wethey told his diary of how the different members of the tiny group of whites had each taken him aside to tell him of the "impossible" eccentricities of the others. Four years of isolation on this exotic dot in the ocean apparently had strange effects.

Fanning was a marvellous relief to our voyage through limbo. Two weeks of tumultuous seas, grey mists, weather that fluctuated between cool and hot, boredom, and impatience, not to mention the ominous Captain West/Bligh, had worn down the Swiggers' endurance. The ultimate in temporal stagnation came on Tuesday, February 12, as we crossed back over the International Date Line and lived through the same day twice. We had at least regained the day we'd lost in 1945 on our westbound journey through the Gilberts. Sadly, though, this second Tuesday was a day without pay. As far as the paymaster was concerned, it didn't exist. Now back in the northern hemisphere, albeit by only four degrees of latitude, we were halfway between Palmyra Island and Christmas Island. It was progress, even at the *Socotra*'s snail-like pace.

All of the Swiggers were chafing to get ashore, but to do so one would have had to either swim the crystal clear, shark-filled waters, or steal a boat. Both were out of the question. Harry Wethey and his friends had taken the only boat not being used to offload the cargo for the island, and unauthorized white men would be easy for Captain West, guardian of our behaviour, to spot among the brown-skinned crewmen of the longboats. The urge subsided when word was passed around that there were no unspoken-for women on Fanning, and besides, there was probably far more booze aboard the *Socotra* than on the entire island.

The official visiting party went ashore in the small launch that also carried some of the women and children. In the same way that the colonel and his assistants had run up against Murphy's Law during their overland Outback trip in the staff car, encountering mishap after mishap, the brief voyage from *Socotra* to the island had its challenges. Escorted by a school of puffing porpoises, the launch first had engine trouble, then lost two anchors, and finally had to be towed by one of the longboats the rest of the way. Once on land, the group set off in an old truck for the main part of the island. The truck broke down partway to its destination, and had to be towed by an equally aged Ford roadster.

The 1CSWG officers and Captain West at last reached the heavily jungle-covered high ground where the "governor's mansion," a thatch-roofed palapa, sat. It seems that the big party began about then. Meanwhile, for their own amusement, the hundreds of wild men of the *Socotra* had to be content with staring at the giant necklace the atoll made on the bosom of the Pacific, marvelling at the fish and the turquoise lagoon waters, and tracing the flow of the blue-green water out of the gap in the coral into the deeper blue of the ocean.

A launch loaded down with islanders puttered up beside the ship, piloted by a bushy-haired, very brown, no-nonsense island boss with bloodshot eyes and tan shorts. He steered carefully but not too expertly to the shaky companionway that had been lowered for the officers. His passengers were half a dozen perfect Gilbert Islander specimens, four men and two women. The men's lurid lava-lavas — skirt-like costumes — covered them from waist to knee. They were bare from the waist up, revealing magnificently muscled, compact upper physiques. They were like bronze statues come alive. The women's equally colourful costumes came up a little higher. Their skin was a rich chocolate brown, their hair blacker than ebony, if possible, and there seemed to be no trace of any foreign dilution of their Polynesian stock. Their faces had high cheekbones and finely chiselled features, resembling some sort of stone idols painstakingly sculpted by an artist striving for perfection beyond the plausible. These were genuine South Sea primitives who could have come out of Gauguin's paintings, innocent of anything beyond the life they knew among these islands, as yet untouched by tourism.

The launch had barely bumped the companionway's lower step when this handsome half-dozen bounced up it almost effortlessly. In a twinkling they were over the taffrail and onto the deck. They turned out to be the household servants of the Australian families we'd brought home. They were all at once all over the ship, poking heads around doorways, forever grinning, squatting to hang headfirst over open hatches, and leaning so far down into the openings to see the mysteries below that they seemed suspended in midair.

Having inspected almost everything on the ship, they were soon up on the boat deck, the sanctuary of the families, quickly gathering up luggage. They carried some of it on their heads as they hustled on down to the launch. The families followed, waving back at the Canadians lined along the rail, the gleaming islanders flashing their brilliant teeth. The boat roared off in an explosion of foam and waves with the deadly serious, bushy-haired pilot giving his full attention to steering back to shore.

While all this was going on, dour Sergeant Jim Proctor from Montreal was outfitting himself for a fishing expedition on the other side of the ship. Laut and I were walking by just as Proctor was impaling a large chunk of bone and gristle, with some attractive chunks of red meat clinging to it, on a huge hook attached to several fathoms of one-inch rope. He was loaded for something big. Ever a man of few words, Proctor ignored us and dropped the big, baited hook, along with a few fathoms of rope, into the limpid depths. We leaned over the rail to watch for results.

They came soon. As if on cue, and perfectly visible in all its details in the light blue water, a shark about six feet long came swooping in a semicircle, darted in, and greedily struck the bait. Proctor yanked the line and set the big hook. He yelled. Laut and I grabbed the line, too, and some lascars came running. It took six of us to haul the spinning, thrashing, twisting shark up the side of the ship and onto the deck. There the sea beast thrashed about so wildly, drenching us with salt water, that we had to get out of its way to avoid its vicious flailing tail. Crowds rushed from starboard to portside to see the spectacle.

The lascars took over. All of them sat on the beast and they soon had a two-inch rope around its neck. They hauled it upright by running the rope over an overhead beam. The shark hung motionless. One of the lascars moved in with a knife to slit its belly, and it began thrashing about again in a wide circle. Its coarse, tough hide, ridged like rough whipcord, brushed the sailor on the arm and scraped off some skin. At last the shark hung still. Once it was declared dead, the lascars sliced off the best meat and took it away to the galley for a rare feast. Proctor hacked off the tail, tied his one-inch rope around it, and dropped it back into the water. Shoals of curious, violently-coloured fish swarmed around it, darting in now and then to snap up a bit of this bully of the deep that they would ordinarily flee from in terror.

Back on the starboard side, the "serious" work of unloading that portion of the *Socotra*'s cargo meant for Fanning was going on. Lighters and rafts were now being piled high with sawn lumber, boxes, and crates. Down below, about twenty happy, chattering, completely disorganized islanders were gesturing, grinning, and reaching up for the boxes being swung down on slings from the ship's gantries. The cargo itself suggested an interesting tale: two or three crates plainly marked "beds"; a grand piano in its distinctive box; a couple of dozen big crates of Australian beer; many cartons of canned food; and several unidentifiable boxes. Clearly, the return of the evacuated spouses had called for a major feast.

The workers seemed to be in no hurry. They stretched out on the rafts and passed around the single cigarette they had between them, all the while laughing and chatting — about what, we could never begin to guess. With great glee they would push one or another overboard despite those hungry hangers-on, the sharks, who could easily see thrashing legs in the clear water. But they were old hands at baffling the toothy monsters. They scrambled back onto the rafts, laughing and dodging about to get another puff of the cigarette.

Like viceroys of the British Raj, some Swig smokers tossed down whole packs of cigarettes to them. These were the days before cigarettes were known to be the lethal instruments they are, and they were regarded as a great prize, even among the troops. There was a monumental scramble, with more dunkings and a chorus of "Tonk you ver much, sors." Then the puzzle of getting through the packages' strange cellophane outer skins occupied them for several minutes. Despite the scrimmage, they carefully divided the cigarettes equally among all of them, and after a good smoke the islanders started work again.

Several hundred board feet of wooden planks hanging loosely in the gantry slings were lowered to them. Some of it actually did get piled carefully on a raft, but much of the rest slipped from the gantry's grip and dropped with a great splash into the water amid outbursts of laughter. Some tried to pull the planks within reach by gingerly stretching out their short legs and drawing them in with their toes. With the onset of evening, and the greater chance of a visit from the sharks now that the day's heat had passed, they were no longer so casual about being dunked.

Things changed suddenly with the return of the bushy-haired, bloodshot-eyed, no-nonsense foreman. He needed utter only a few short phrases and the collection of the spilled lumber became instantly organized. Darkness snapped on like an electric light snapping off. A shaded lamp was lowered over the side of the *Socotra*, recalling the moment when the pilot boat came alongside at the Sydney Heads. By its light, the last loaded raft was towed away to shore.

We thought we'd seen the last of the crew. But no — the dozen or more still in the lighters bounced up and over the rail and onto the deck, still full of laughter and chatter. With more agility than any 1CSWG member could ever have mustered, the islanders queued up in two rows along the rail and, without any audible cue and no visible leader, they began singing an island song in perfect harmony. We Canadians fell absolutely silent.

Cecil B. DeMille would have had his cameras rolling by then, although Hollywood could never have truly re-created the setting. The fantastically large tropic moon emerged from behind the clouds and spread blue-white light over the island, the lagoon, the ship, and the sea. Fanning Island's palm trees moved gracefully in the warm, light breeze, its lagoon lying like Conrad's black mirror of the sea in the bluish light. The enormous moon laid down a silver roadway on the placid ocean.

This was no tourist trap. Cruise-ship visits to these islands were still far off into the future. The islanders were doing what came naturally in gratitude for the cigarettes and this rare visit by a ship from across the water. They stood in silhouette against the moonlit island scene, all of a height, while the audience from the north stayed still and quiet, themselves hardly visible, only the red dots of their cigarette ends perforating the dark here and there.

The islanders finished their song. There was an instant of silence, then the Canadians went into wild, whistling applause that surely could be heard at the governor's house party. White teeth flashed in apprecia- tion among the figures along the rail. Another song began. More wild applause. An entire evening's concert of island songs followed. All had the flavour of missionary hymns, sprinkled with rhythms and sounds that evoked the sea and the islands. They went on and on. It seemed the islanders were there for the night.

A toot came from down on the water. The launch returning Lieutenant- Colonel Wethey, his officers, and good Captain West was nosing up to the companionway. The islanders kept on singing. It wasn't possible in the dark to identify the individuals who came over the taffrail and onto the deck. Some could plainly be heard trying to sing along with the choir and even belt out a boisterously off-key army ditty over it. Plainly, the governor's party had been a complete success. Amid the dark mass of bodies moving up to the officers' deck there was one long, bulky object being carted laboriously along by its members. The revellers vanished to their quarters, and we never learned whose unconscious body that was, but there seemed to be no sign of our well-known senior officer among them.

The islanders went on singing. They seemed to have no end of songs and it also seemed that they had the stamina to go on all night without stopping. Somebody got the clever idea of rewarding the singers for their impromptu concert. A couple of signalmen lugged a big cardboard box of chocolate bars up from the dry canteen to the deck. Stationing themselves at the head of the companionway, the two waved the singers toward them, and one by one the islanders moved past the box, still singing. They got the message; as each was given a chocolate bar and some cigarettes they went down to their lighters, giving out great cries of farewell. Soon, over the sound of the lighters' engines, the cries and songs faded as the boats vanished toward the blue-black lagoon.

Chapter 6

Welcome to Vancouver

Next to a muddy Ontario back road in early spring, there are few more miserable scenes than a view of the deck and superstructure of a tramp freighter in the drizzling rain, wallowing and heaving through a misty ocean, dully gleaming from the blowing wet. There was nothing romantic or dramatic about the *Socotra* as it bobbed over the mid-Pacific waves, far south of Hawaii. Fanning Island was 200 miles behind us and Vancouver still well over 3,000 miles to the northeast on Sunday, February 17 — Madeline's birthday — the day after we dropped in at the island. Now we wouldn't come within reach of land until we brushed past the big island of Oahu — by about 200 miles. The next sight of land would be Vancouver Island. The *Socotra* was now about 700 miles due east of the point where, thirty years later, the astronauts of Apollo 8 would make their returning splashdown. To us servicemen of the 1940s, of course, the idea of space travel was the stuff of the movies or the comic strips.

The surroundings were now dreary and depressing. The rain and slippery decks certainly didn't help the spirits of two Swigger miscreants who'd stolen a jeep back in Goulburn, Australia, to take their girlfriends home and ended up smashing it against a tree. Signalman Carl Sorenson, the driver, broke his leg and was left behind in a Sydney army hospital when we sailed. His fate in the military trial that was certain to follow was unknown. Artie deFranco and Tommy Randolph were unhurt, but as a consequence of the justice meted out by Lieutenant-Colonel Wethey they were now on permanent kitchen police on the *Socotra's* afterdeck, doing a transpacific pot-washing stretch.

Rain and shine they worked next to the latrines in soaked sneakers and coveralls, scraping and washing up after meals, lugging pails of hot water up from the galley. Seasick or not, they had to do the job. Sometimes, when the sun shone, the deck plates were too hot to walk on in anything but regulation boots. Somehow they persevered, even giving the odd grin, while we veterans of the galleys of the *Shawnee* looked on sympathetically.

The open ocean was rougher than we'd experienced even in the Tasman Sea, but our stomachs and our sea legs could now cope with the never-ending elevator ride. The *Socotra* was being pushed to its maximum speed of 16 knots, which tended to exaggerate the bounce and roll. Worse, the ship was unevenly trimmed because of the careless unloading of the cargo at Fanning. Our trucks and heavy equipment, untouched in the offloading, were stored more to port, and their weight caused that side of the ship to roll deeper into the water with each swell than did the starboard side. The *Socotra* was hobbling on its northeasterly course on a definite sideways slant.

This slanting world affected everything we tried to do. On deck you not only had to lean backward or forward to offset the ship's dives and rises but also to brace side to side by bending one knee a little and leaning to port or starboard to meet the off-centre roll. Sleeping was a challenge, as the tipsy yaw of the ship might flip you in your bunk from your side to your back or stomach every half-minute. No object, from ink bottles to plates of food, wanted to stay put on any flat surface. Walking along the deck, you would be climbing uphill in one instant and running downhill the next — without changing direction.

For a while, the rough seas tossed the *Socotra* up and down from stem to stern as it crossed each wave, heaving the bow out of the water, then letting the keel down with a jarring thud. The twin screws again were lifting entirely out of the water and spinning faster, sending a frightening shudder the length of the ship as they had done in the Tasman Sea. This cycle repeated itself every minute or so. The *Socotra* was like an enormous seesaw now, and we began to wonder if the plates would finally pop apart or if the keel would snap.

The most astounding performance was turned in by the lascar sailors with their progressive stripping of every square inch of paint on the *Socotra's* hull and superstructure. Clad in their blue pantaloons and red vests, they spent almost all the daylight hours tapping patiently with their square-headed hammers on the decks, along the rails, and, suspended in bosun's chairs, up on the mast and crossarms. The pitch, roll, and yaw didn't seem to bother them in the least. On days when the sea was calmer, they rode their bosun's chairs down the ship's sides close to the water, tapping the paint off the hull as the waves licked at their feet. Up and down they would go, on ropes slung over the superstructure, to reach their points of attack. A sailor might be sitting on deck with his legs crossed while he sewed a piece of sailcloth, the canvas gripped between two toes like fingers as he wielded the big needle. The lascars' feet were like an extra pair of hands. They would use them to grip ropes or the deck when needed.

About 210 miles due east of Hawaii and 2,000 miles west of Baja California, the air was getting distinctly chillier. We now wore shirts. Next came long pants and even sweaters. All this was needed in a latitude we'd thought of as so delightfully warm on our trip southwest from San Francisco in '45. It seemed that fourteen months in the tropics were enough to thin the blood to the point where even a 70-degree temperature made us cover up. There wasn't much sun, but at least the rains had stopped.

We could now hear *Command Performance* from the U.S. Armed Forces Radio Service at San Francisco over the ship's loudspeakers, and it triggered a culture shock in some of us. Before we were shipped overseas, we could instantly recognize every new hit record by the big bands; now, the numbers on the hit parade that came floating out to us were so new that the journey home seem more like a return from outer space. Unbeknownst to us, the demise of the big swing bands was a fait accompli. Oddly, there were new versions of really old tunes like "It's Only a Paper Moon," which only the old-timers over thirty could whistle.

The newscasts were also strange. Gone were the streams of reports on bombings in Germany or murderous battles near Japan which had been the meat of the news for so many years. Mostly the news was of European reconstruction, or about something called UNO — later shortened to the U.N., for the United Nations. Most interesting to us were stories about plans to test an atomic bomb in a Pacific location soon. Opponents of the idea warned that this would blast a hole in the bottom of the Pacific which would drain all the seawater down to the earth's molten centre, and the resulting steam would blow the world to pieces. Anxious talk began to circulate among some *Socotra* passengers that before we reached Vancouver, the ship might be rolled over in a tidal wave caused by the test — or worse, go down the drain. Most of us just laughed. Not too long after we reached port, the test was held. No hole was blasted in the ocean floor.

The effect of the lopsided loading became more obvious as the *Socotra* turned north gradually and paralleled the North American coast about a thousand miles off. Long, towering swells came in every minute from the west and rolled the ship even deeper on the port side than they had before. On that side we would be looking straight into a wall of water until the little *Socotra* slid sideways up its flank. On the far side it sashayed down into a trough, then slid up over the next mountain of water. This went on for days.

Temperatures continued to drop. We put on more and more clothing until we had no more to add. The sea became more and more shrouded in fog. Just a week before, we'd been basking in the equatorial sun; the heat in our quarters had even driven us to the outer decks to sleep directly under the Southern Cross. Now our quarters seemed like meat lockers. We were sleeping under long-unused blankets, with coveralls over our long underwear. Most pathetic were the lascars, still in their red and blue outfits and their bare feet. Some wore old oversized suit jackets as they did their usual tapping and painting. We had nothing extra to lend them.

Preparations were stirring for a landing at Vancouver. Big diesel generators we'd brought with us from Sydney to run freezer units were being shut down and re-crated. The frozen beef they'd contained was moved to the ship's refrigerators. The officers threw a party for Captain West and the remaining passengers, consisting of the added officers from other parts.

There were some fellow travellers whom we hadn't seen until we had left Sydney far behind. These included a half-dozen or so Canadian officers and sergeants of Japanese and Chinese extraction. Through casual conversations with the non-coms we learned that these were special forces people who'd operated behind Japanese lines in Borneo and Indo-China. They were among the 143 Asian-Canadians who had gone to Australia and India to be trained in guerrilla and wireless operations by the British

Special Operations Executive (SOE) in 1944–45. The first batch was sent to Australia a month or two before 1CSWG. They trained under some colourful Canadian officers from SOE and later worked behind the Japanese lines in a hazardous, obscure chapter of Canadian Army service in Southeast Asia. Their story is fully told in Roy MacLaren's 1981 book, *Canadians Behind Enemy Lines*.

Poker played a major part in helping us pass the time. And as home drew nearer, it occurred to some that it would be essential to have some extra cash at the ready to celebrate our arrival back on Canadian soil, so the card sharks turned things up a notch — games grew more intense, and lasting far into the night. Another pastime made use of the vast stock of empty beer bottles that had accumulated. Bettors would toss an empty bottle high into the air off the side of the ship and try to hit it with another one in mid-flight. It was something like skeet shooting. By the last couple of days at sea, these and other gambling innovations were refined to near-perfection.

The deep blue southern sea had given way to the olive-drab waters of the North Pacific by the time we were about 300 miles off San Francisco. The mountains of water still jerked the *Socotra* from side to side. The weather was getting more miserable each day, and the fog grew thicker the closer we came to Vancouver. In time, the swells lessened and the sea currents seemed to come from all directions, swishing about harmlessly. The water was coated with jelly-like blobs about two inches long, probably fish eggs, which were tossed high in the air when the water got choppier.

At mid-morning on February 26 we could see, faintly to starboard through heavy fog, a rocky cliff topped with tall Douglas firs. We knew we were almost home. During the night, it turned out, we had entered Canadian waters, passed Victoria, and were now nearing Vancouver. The fog thickened for a while, then thinned out again to reveal more ghostly, fir-covered cliffs almost a stone's throw away. The ship had slowed to 10 knots, and it seemed to be the only vessel abroad on this day.

All at once we were in Vancouver Harbour. The fog was dissipating rapidly. In the misty distance ahead we could see the unmistakable silhouette of the Lion's Gate Bridge. We'd finally completed a cycle of sorts, from the Golden Gate Bridge to the Sydney Harbour Bridge, and now back to the Lion's Gate, a stone's throw from where we'd started. The *Socotra*, still listing heavily to its port side, limped along, a pathetic little voyager dwarfed by the rising evergreens that — in those days — lined the banks surrounding Vancouver harbour.

An earsplitting din of whistles, sirens, and croaking foghorns suddenly erupted all around us, issuing forth from a welcoming fleet of tugboats, launches, and various small craft scattered both near and far around the harbour. The little *Socotra* limped slowly and heroically amid the shrieking and roaring. As she passed under the bridge, everyone on board lined the rails and occupied every level surface. Fireboats spouted up tall columns of water. A small launch pulled up beside the *Socotra* and a Signal Corps photographer was hauled aboard. Cheers came down from the bridge above us, where crowds with startlingly white faces waved arms and Red Ensign flags. Launches zipped around us, their horns blasting and sirens wailing, their crews waving wildly as they passed. The photographer got busy snapping pictures of us.

Royal Canadian Navy destroyers and other naval craft in the harbour sent up siren calls, and a huge passenger ship drowned out everything with a deep bass blast of its funnel horn. The hysteria went on and on as the *Socotra*, gamely pushing onward, edged majestically — as majestically as is possible for an 8,000-ton freighter — to the dock, its human cargo awestricken by this completely unexpected welcome. At last, it seemed, Number One Canadian Special Wireless Group was getting some appreciation from the people of Canada. Crowds massed around the whole dock area near the *Socotra*. The racket from the horns, whistles, and sirens was stunning, drowning out all human voices. Flags and bunting fluttered everywhere. Somewhere in the distance, the flat impact of a big naval gun shook the air in salute. Every soul aboard the *Socotra* stood with arms upraised in gratitude for the reception, shouting back inaudible words of thanks.

These Vancouverites had no idea of what 1CSWG or its mission were, but their welcome at last made the whole thing seem worthwhile. No Swigger would forget it — or the long trip home.

Long afterward, in November 1962, a news item noted that the British passenger ship *Socotra* had collided with the 8,200-ton Uruguayan freighter *Tacoma* at a dock in London. The *Socotra* put a hole in the latter vessel's hull, leaving the *Tacoma* listing and close to sinking. The *Socotra* sustained only superficial damage. Poor old *Socotra*, ancient in 1946 and still plying the seas seventeen years after bringing 1CSWG home! I wondered if

Captain West was still skipper. He would probably have clapped his helmsman in irons for the mistake.

The air at Camp Chilliwack, east of Vancouver, was crisp, cold, fresh, and dry. There was a clarity in the atmosphere that let you see clearly the ring of snowcapped mountains surrounding the camp in the distance. Just being there was a tonic to the Swiggers who were thankful to tread upon Canadian earth once again. We could take a step in our brown boots without have to swivel at the knee to walk a capricious deck. Chilliwack was, of course, just another army camp full of wooden barracks and mess hall lineups, but it was *Canadian* and full of Canadians. Even though we Swiggers stood out from the crowd with our deep tans and brown boots, we felt we were back where we belonged.

The feeling of being home and in a livable climate helped offset the memory of a brief ugly scene at the landing at Vancouver. Some hothead in a Canadian uniform yelled out that we were "a bunch of zombies," and he was plainly ready to start a fistfight until some mates of his held him back. Where he got that idea from we didn't know. But I can guess. Fancying himself as a combat hero — and perhaps he was — he'd probably asked one of the first members of our party to land what we'd been doing in the Pacific. Of course, we were forbidden to disclose 1CSWG's real work, so it wouldn't be hard to picture some lighthearted Swigger, caught up in the moment, telling him without thinking that we'd just had a party in Australia. That would have been enough to set the hothead off, if he were an NRMA hater, and by provoking a fight, he might gain a measure of revenge. Luckily, we were being hustled along to the waiting trucks or else there might have been a bloody battle right there on the dock. It stung to be so arbitrarily misconstrued after having twice volunteered for unknown duty overseas that could have taken us into any battle zone in the world, something this would-be avenger might not have done himself.

We were entitled to a month's disembarkation leave, but first we had to stay around for the final breakup of the unit. Only one thought was on our minds: getting *all the way* home. Our unit's members came from everywhere from Vancouver to Halifax. Some still faced a journey of several thousand more miles before they were truly home.

While he still had command of 1CSWG, Lieutenant-Colonel Wethey called an assembly in a mess hall for a final speech. We'd all performed marvelously, he told us, and everyone laughed. He hoped we'd all settle into new careers quickly and successfully. However, he had one important thing to say: not one word about Number One Canadian Special Wireless Group was to be uttered to anyone for the next thirty years under the Official Secrets Act. Thirty years? To a young signalman of 1CSWG who was only twenty, that may as well have meant forever.

Well, who wanted to talk about it anyway? Who cared about a crew of soldiers, mostly teenaged, who'd blindly violated the basic rule of the O.R. — "Never volunteer" — and had shipped off to the other side of the world to work our butts off listening to endless beeps through a set of earphones? To a Canadian public accustomed to stories of savage, bloody ground combat in Europe, the adventures of a bunch of signal operators in a war in which Canadian involvement was virtually unheard-of would probably be a letdown.

Decades would pass before the story of the decisive work of the various Allied units of Magic in the Pacific and Ultra in Europe and North Africa would be told in book after book. Their key role in helping the Allies outmanoeuvre the enemy gradually became known. Canadians might have been proud to know that 336 of their troops had been part of those Pacific Allied operations that thwarted Japanese plans to invade western North America and then played an important part in the later campaigns in the South West Pacific theatre. But the lid of secrecy lid placed on 1CSWG for decades dampened any attempt to tell of Canada's part in this remarkable victory. At the very least, had we been able to tell our story, it would have silenced those hotheads on the Vancouver dock.

After Lieutenant-Colonel Wethey declared Number One Canadian Special Wireless Group de-commissioned, we gave him a big hand and most of those assembled headed off for the wet canteen. Departure for eastern points was to take place in a few days. It hardly occurred to us that this would be one of the last times the unit would be together in its entirety. We were too elated by the fact that we would no longer be under the thumbs of the officers and non-coms who'd dominated our youthful lives to fully comprehend the inevitable. With a few exceptions — for there were some fellows we wouldn't miss, of course — it would be a strangely heart-wrenching experience to face the fact that, after almost two years of sharing our lives, our paths might never cross again. It only really hit home on the cross-country train ride, as one ex-Swigger after another was dropped of at the stations along the way, in British Columbia, Alberta, Saskatchewan, Manitoba, Ontario, and beyond.

The Canadian government at last made a magnanimous gesture of a kind we would have appreciated a few months earlier in Sydney. Instead of slotting us willy-nilly into milk train schedules a few at a time, or packing us into boxcars, they actually rented an entire Canadian Pacific Railway train to return us to our homes. Compared with The Ghan from Alice Springs we'd be going in real luxury, in bunks with sheets and bright Hudson Bay blankets, not to mention day coaches where you could lounge or go for a walk and not be buttonholed for kitchen fatigue or night picquet duty. Washrooms! And full meals on board at *tables!* This was no troop train. There were no flies on the Canadian Army for this junket.

The Rockies, half-buried in snow, were the final highlight of our far-flung travels. One ex-Swigger muttered that when the next war came he'd be hiding out down there in some snow-filled valley. The mountains with their caps of snow indeed offered a wild contrast to the overheated deserts we'd known over the previous year. All along the way, the ranks of the now-defunct 1CSWG sadly thinned with every stop as members got off at Jasper, Edmonton, Regina, Winnipeg, Fort William, and more. There was a major drop in our numbers when the train was broken in two at Sudbury, one part destined for Toronto and the other for Ottawa, Montreal, and the Maritimes. That was where we said goodbye to Boombaw, DeMal, and the others from farther east who'd sometimes gotten us in trouble but otherwise added spice to our lives in the service.

By the time the Toronto-bound train reached Union Station, only a handful of ex-Swiggers was left. Don Laut caught a bus for Bracebridge, the Gunner vanished into Toronto, along with some others, and a few of us continued westbound along the north shore of Lake Ontario. At Brantford, only Bert Pusey — bound for Sarnia — and I were left. We shook hands in goodbye as the train stopped, and I hopped off with my packs. As the train pulled away, I waved at Bert, the sole ex-Swigger still on the train. For both of us, Number One Canadian Special Wireless Group was finally dead.

Waiting for me on the train platform were my mother and father, and, of all blessings, my fiancée, Madeline. We all headed for home.

Epilogue

The war was over, and the members of the last Canadian army unit to return intact from overseas were now back on Canadian soil. But for some of us junior bods it was not yet time to bid goodbye to the army. Toward the end of our disembarkation leave, when we expected we would be called to Toronto to be discharged, about half a dozen ex-Swiggers — including me — got a letter from Ottawa ordering us to report to Kingston's Vimy Barracks, headquarters of the Royal Canadian Signal Corps, for further duty.

According to the army, we hadn't served long enough to earn sufficient discharge "points." It came as a severe blow; I'd already visited one of my former places of work to get hired again after discharge.

We half-dozen put on our uniforms, including our brown Australian boots, and our full pack and boarded the train for Kingston. We were instantly put on permanent fatigue duty, there being nothing else for us to do. There was a hint we might be shipped over to Germany to the Occupation Army, but that didn't happen. Instead, we cleaned up the camp — which was inhabited mainly by officers and non-coms who apparently needed some O.R.'s to do the dirty work — over and over again.

One day a youthful lieutenant grew outraged at the sight of us six O.R.'s in our coveralls and brown boots. This worthy complained to the C.O. about the outrage. Only officers were entitled to wear brown boots! he fumed. The storm passed after he was told why we had them, and he was cut down to size by the quartermaster, who told him that to issue us brand-new black Canadian Army boots would be an unwise use of army funds now that peacetime was here. We were allowed to keep our brown boots.

The mind-numbing routines of garbage and kitchen duties were broken one day by an order to take a truck to the Kingston railway station to pick up some boxes. Off we went, and found the boxcar containing the designated cargo in a newly arrived train. When the big door was slid open, we immediately saw a green wooden box with the words *Lieutenant-Colonel H.D.W. Wethey, Number One Canadian Special Wireless Group, Darwin, Australia* stencilled on its end. We gaped at it, then stared at each other in disbelief. We hauled the box and a steamer trunk back to camp, where we found out that the new commanding officer of Vimy Barracks was to be one Lieutenant-Colonel H.D.W. Wethey. We were too stunned to react.

We immediately twigged to the reason why we had just been ordered to give a coat of white paint to innumerable "saluting markers" scattered around the camp's walkways. (These were foot-high wooden stakes placed periodically alongside the walkways, and, incredibly, O.R.'s were required to salute them whenever they passed, as though the wooden stakes were actually officers.) It couldn't be anything else but an advance order from Wethey. We were once again about to be subject to the Harry Wethey brand of spit-and-polish discipline!

He was to arrive in a week's time. Almost immediately after learning of his return, we sad six received a new order: we were to go to Toronto for discharge! The government of Canada had, in all its benificence, scrapped the service points system. We were free at last! We left Vimy Barracks on the first train out.

We never laid eyes on Lieutenant-Colonel H.D.W. Wethey again.

The story of Number One Canadian Special Wireless Group was not quite over. In July, 2001, the Canadian Armed Forces Signal Corps held a ceremony at Leitrim, near Ottawa, in which a plaque was unveiled to commemerate the role of 1CSWG in the Pacific conflict.

Leitrim was the wartime headquarters for Royal Canadian Signal Corps interception operations, and the original base for the men who in 1944 became the key leaders of 1CSWG. It is still the headquarters for Armed Forces signals operations.

Biographies of Officers, 1CSWG

Lieutenant-Colonel Harry D.W. Wethey

Harry Wethey was a natural choice to head up the newly formed Number One Canadian Special Wireless Group. A Winnipegger by birth, Wethey had been in the Canadian Army Permanent Force peacetime army since 1931, joining as a lieutenant in the Royal Canadian Corps of Signals after graduating from the University of Manitoba as an electrical engineer.

During the more than forty-one years he was to serve as a soldier, he was shuttled back and forth across the Atlantic on special signals duties. Less than a month

Officer Commanding 1CSWG, Lieutenant-Colonel H.D.W. Wethey was a strict disciplinarian — with good reason. Among the three hundred and thirty-six men under his command were some happy-go-lucky individuals difficult to handle and needing a firm hand to keep them in line.

after the outbreak of war in 1939, Captain Wethey was dispatched to the U.K. He split the early 1940s between Ottawa and England as a rising young officer involved in field signals operations, both as a commander of special sections and as a liaison. While in England in 1942–43, Wethey, by now a major, was sent to a Signals Senior Officers School attached to a joint Canadian Army–Royal Canadian Air Force unit, and then to Senior Officers School at Brasenose College, Oxford.

Through 1943 and 1944, Wethey was Liaison Signals Officer between the Canadian Army and the United States Signal Corps at the Pentagon in Washington, D.C. He was bumped up to lieutenant-colonel for this assignment. Given his acquaintance with the Special Wireless operations of the Canadian, British, and U.S. forces, he was a judicious choice as C.O. of the new, mismatched agglomeration of recruits that was to be forged in 1CSWG. In a sense, he would eventually become a kind of Canadian military ambassador to the Down Under continent.

With his already impressive background in military management and his career on upswing, Harry Wethey understandably set his sights on the target of making 1CSWG a success in spite of any obstacle that might get in the way. The unit would be not only a showpiece of Royal Canadian Signals operational talent, but it would also sparkle with the spit and polish of a headquarters close-order drill squad.

After the war, Wethey commanded the Royal Canadian Signal Corps headquarters at Vimy Barracks in Kingston, Ontario. In 1948 he was the Army's representative on the Canadian delegation to the Provisional Radio Frequency Board in Switzerland, and for five years thereafter he was Senior Lieutenant-Colonel in the Directorate of Signals at Army Headquarters, Ottawa, where he was involved in various phases of radio communications. Next came command of the army's Northwest Territories and Yukon Radio System, headquartered in Edmonton, which operated twenty-two wireless stations. One can only guess at what these stations may have been monitoring.

Wethey retired from the army in 1957 and joined the Canadian post office two years later as chief engineer. By 1965 he was director of engineering, touring Europe and the United States in pursuit of a task every bit as daunting as heading up Number One Special Wireless Group: automating the post office.

Major J. Ross Mackay

Number One Canadian Special Wireless Group was fortunate — by design, of course — to have among its Intelligence Corps personnel several men who had spent their childhood in Japan (their parents having been Canadian missionaries) and who therefore were fluent in reading, writing, and speaking Japanese. Ross Mackay was one of these. His parents had been missionaries in Japanese-occupied Formosa (now Taiwan).

In 1941, although he had been offered a commission, he enlisted in the Royal Canadian Artillery as a gunner. After Pearl Harbor was bombed, he was transferred to the fledgling Intelligence Corps at Ottawa. The corps was just being formally organized, and Ross Mackay was its first enlisted man, or O.R. The administrative officer was Colonel Drake, formerly with Northern Electric. The chief cryptanalyst was Colonel F.J.M. Stratton, who had previously been a professor of astrophysics at Cambridge University. Mackay, one of only four who made up the original I Corps, eventually was commissioned and became Officer Commanding Number One Discrimination Unit at Ottawa and then O.C. of 1CSWG's Intelligence unit.

Sources

Documents

Wethey, H.D.W. Diary, 1944–46.

Murray, Gilbert S. Diaries, 1944–46.

Directorate of History, National Defence Headquarters. Summary of Number One Canadian Special Wireless Group's Founding.

Douglas, W.A.B. Correspondence with author, 1980–82.

Clark, S.R.I. Correspondence with author, 1981.

Mackay, J. Ross. Correspondence with author, 1982–2000.

Simpson, C.H. Letter to Lt.-Col. H.D.W. Wethey, February 2, 1946.

Ball, Desmond. *Reference Paper No. 27*. Canberra: Strategic and Defence Studies Centre, Research School of Pacific Studies, Australian National University, 1978.

Horner, D.M. *Reference Paper No. 28*. Canberra: Strategic and Defence Studies Centre, Research School of Pacific Studies, Australian National University, 1980.

U.S. Congress. Joint Committee on the Investigation of the Pearl Harbor Attack. *Pearl Harbor Attack: Hearings*, 79th Cong., 1st [-2nd] sess., pursuant to S. Con. Res. 27, January–February 1946.

Wethey, H.D.W. Correspondence with author, 1980–86.

Williams, James. Correspondence with author, 1980.

Morton, Fred. "Spitfires over Darwin," *Air Classics* September 1980.

Canadian Press. News item, 1962.

Wethey, H.D.W. Curriculum vitae, 1981.

Books:

Argyle, C.J. *Japan at War, 1937–45*. London: Arthur Barker, 1976.

Bateson, Charles. *The War With Japan: A Concise History*. East Lansing, Mich.: Michigan State University Press, 1968.

Collier, Basil. *The War in the Far East, 1941–1945: A Military History*. London: Heinemann, 1969.

Costello, John. *The Pacific War*. New York: Rawson, Wade, 1981.

Douglas, W.A.B., and Brereton Greenhouse. *Out of the Shadows: Canada in the Second World War*. Toronto: Dundurn Press, Toronto, 1995 (Revised Edition).

Elliot, S.R. *Scarlet to Green*. London: Hunter & Rose, London, 1981.

Hashimoto, Mochitsura. *Sunk: The Story of the Japanese Submarine Fleet, 1942–45*. Translated by E.H.M. Colegrave. London: Cassell and Company, 1954.

Johnston, George H. *Pacific Partner*. New York: World Book Company, 1944.

Kahn, David. *The Codebreakers: The Story of Secret Writing*. New York: Macmillan, 1967.

Kato, Masuo. *The Lost War: A Japanese Reporter's Inside Story*. New York: A.A. Knopf, 1946.

Lewin, Ronald. *The American Magic: Codes, Ciphers, and the Defeat of Japan*. New York: Farrar Straus Giroux, 1982.

Lewin, Ronald. *Ultra Goes to War*. London: Hutchinson, 1978.

Lockwood, Douglas. *Australia's Pearl Harbor: Darwin, 1942*. Melbourne: Cassell Australia, 1966.

MacArthur, Douglas. *Reminiscences*. New York: McGraw-Hill, 1965.

Macintyre, Donald. *The Battle for the Pacific*. London: Batsford, 1978.

MacLaren, Roy. *Canadians Behind Enemy Lines*. Vancouver: University of British Columbia Press, 1981.

Moorehead, Alan. *Rum Jungle*. New York: Charles Scribner's Sons, 1954.

Royal Institute of International Affairs. *Japan in Defeat: A Report by a Chatham House Study Group. Issued Under the Auspices of the Royal Institute of International Affairs*. Oxford: Oxford University Press, 1945.

Stevenson, William. *A Man Called Intrepid.* New York: Harcourt Brace Jovanovich, 1976.

Thomas, David A. *Japan's War at Sea.* London: Andre Deutsch, 1978.

Winterbotham, F.W. *The Ultra Secret.* New York: Harper and Row, 1975.

Winton, John. *War in the Pacific: Pearl Harbor to Tokyo Bay.* London: Sidgwick and Jackson, 1978.

Wolfe, James Raymond. *Secret Writing: The Craft of the Cryptographer.* New York: McGraw-Hill, 1970.